MW00874521

THE
Remarkable Plans
FOR
Captain Travis O. Evans

Transcribed and edited by

LOUISE CARROLL GEORGE

outskirts
press

The Remarkable Plans
for Captain Travis O. Evans
All Rights Reserved.
Copyright © 2021 Louise Carroll George
v5.0

The opinions expressed in this manuscript are solely the opinions of the author and do not represent the opinions or thoughts of the publisher. The author has represented and warranted full ownership and/or legal right to publish all the materials in this book.

This book may not be reproduced, transmitted, or stored in whole or in part by any means, including graphic, electronic, or mechanical without the express written consent of the publisher except in the case of brief quotations embodied in critical articles and reviews.

Outskirts Press, Inc.
http://www.outskirtspress.com

ISBN: 978-1-9772-4497-0

Cover & Interior Photos © 2021 The Evans Family, Michael Scott Herrera, Travis O. Evans, Kerry A. Nechodom. All rights reserved - used with permission.

Outskirts Press and the "OP" logo are trademarks belonging to Outskirts Press, Inc.

PRINTED IN THE UNITED STATES OF AMERICA

DEDICATED TO
CAPTAIN TRAVIS O. EVANS
and
EILEEN HERRERA

Table of Contents

Acknowledgments

There are some special people I need to thank for helping me put this book together. It goes without saying that Captain Travis is number one on the list. I cannot thank him enough for sharing the many hours we spent in interviews, his never ending patience in doing so, but most of all for the lasting friendship that began years ago out my back porch. Knowing him and hearing his stories and his testimony has been a significant part of my story.

Second in line is Travis' daughter, Eileen. She facilitated our interviews in every way possible. She traveled with Travis, and while we were interviewing, cooked, cleaned, ran errands, and more importantly, reminded him of stories and furnished some necessary details. She also edited the manuscript and provided pictures. It couldn't have happened without her.

I also need to thank Travis' daughter, Kerry, who went right to work when I told her I was looking for more pictures. She came up with a number of interesting ones you'll find scattered through our book. As for Susie and Jan, all I had to do was ask. Whether it was information or pictures, they were on it. Thank you all.

Jonell Williams and Jean and Bill Beaty read the manuscript and helped catch the typos, repetitions, and other errors. Gayla Martin also edited for me, ran errands and helped in other ways to allow me to stay at work. Many thanks to you all.

For all of the above mentioned people in my life, I won't ever find the right words to tell you how much your love, support and encouragement along the way has meant.

Thanks also to Tex Pueschel for the cover photo and to Sara Popp for allowing me to use her photo in the book.

Preface

Do Captain Travis O. Evans and I, Louise Carroll George, promise to tell the truth, the whole truth, and nothing but the truth? No, we don't. We do, however, promise to come as close as we can. Memories, some nearly a hundred years old, are the source for this book, and memories are often imperfect. As Captain Travis expressed it, "Remember, at ninety-seven some of the little details are hard to nail down in my thick saltwater filled head."

What a journey the captain's memories reveal! He was born in 1922 in the small town of Ada, Oklahoma to poor and uneducated parents who separated when he was eight. In describing the circumstances that followed, he referred to himself as, "a little orphan-like boy." Later, his father, Willie, remarried and like so many others, in the midst of the Great Depression, he loaded up his wife and four boys and left the dire poverty in Oklahoma, and headed for California in a half-ton pickup. Willie took a job on a farm and set up a tent for his family to live in. Helping his father provide for the family, Travis learned all about hard work on that farm. At age nineteen, he began his life on the ocean and became a successful commercial fisherman, a trusted ship's captain, a respected representative of the fishing fleet and a faithful disciple of Jesus Christ. How did all of that come about? Travis believes it was God's plan for his life.

Do I, Louise Carroll George, promise that this manuscript is a word for word version of our recorded interviews? No, I don't. It would be a challenge to read it if it were. Besides, removing the numerous "ands" and "buts," which made for extremely long sentences, I deleted repetitions, arranged stories into a logical order, and added a phrase here and there to set a scene or to close one. Some names have been omitted or changed in order to avoid any possibility of offending or embarrassing anyone. In making those changes to the captain's remarks, every effort was made to protect intent and accuracy. For the most part, Travis' grammar was left intact, so, it will read just as he would speak if you were sitting on the front porch sipping iced tea and listening to his stories.

Captain Travis is an excellent story teller and a pretty fair writer himself. He might have done a better job than I of writing his story, but he was far too busy, trimming his daughter's trees, or weed-whacking on some property he owns, or helping his grandson sand and paint the fishing boat called the Lucy L, or accomplishing some other totally unexpected and seemingly unrealistic task for a man of his age.

Some of the captain's poems, stories and excerpts from letters are included in this text. To identify his work, it will be italicized. This excerpt from a letter is an example:

Sometimes after writing a poem, I don't know whether

the thoughts or words are really mine, so I search my mind as to where they may have originated. Oftimes, I want so badly to use a thought or a phrase, but I will jot it down and begin to look in familiar places, such as a concordance or Bartlett's Famous Quotations. Quite often I will find references or exact wording in the Scriptures, in one version or the other. Once, after being at sea for months, I wrote a poem, and years later came across very similar wording in a literature text book for seventh grade school children.

Some time ago, on my early morning walk, the crows were in the tree tops making loud caws while other birds were singing sweetly and, I think, trying to attract mates, and this thought came to me, and it may be part of someone's lyrics or poem: "Not all birdsong is sweet and beautiful to our human ears, but to the creator of that bird or crow, it must be a glorious sound - sweet, sweet music." I thought I might end up putting those thoughts to rhyme one of these days. I believe that no one person owns those thoughts. They don't belong to me exclusively; nothing does. I just hope my thoughts give honor and praise to my Creator.

And I, Louise, hope my work on Captain Travis' story gives honor and praise to my Creator.

I know the plans I have for you, plans to prosper you and not harm you, plans to give you hope, and a future.
Jeremiah 29:11

I think my life has proven that scripture.
Captain Travis O. Evans

PART I
WHERE I CAME FROM
1922-1936

The Place

I, Travis Olando Evans, was born in Ada, Oklahoma, and that's where I lived the first thirteen years of my life. Ada was the county seat and a real nice little town. It was the first in that area to have an airport and it was the first to have a radio station, KADA. The people who owned the station would not allow any tobacco or alcohol advertising on the station. When I went back years and years later, I think that was in 1957, whoever bought the station, or inherited it or whatever, had a television station, KTEN, and they still would not allow it. If you watched a baseball game on that station, when the beer commercial was supposed to come on, some local people would come on instead. There was no alcohol or cigarette advertising on the radio or television in that town. Isn't that something?

That town was really a blue law town. You could not find a store open on Sunday anywhere, any time. You couldn't buy a loaf of sliced bread in that town. That makes me think; the first time I saw a loaf of sliced bread I couldn't believe it. My mother made bread, and oh, Grandma made the best bread, yeast bread, not sliced and I was used to that, but that sliced bread was something.

When I was a kid, most of the streets were paved and there were many brick buildings, even dwellings. There was much raw material in the area to make cement and bricks. Portland Cement Company was a very prominent employer. For a while we lived where we could see the plant with its tall exhaust stacks and buildings and its smoke and dust.

I remember the concrete sidewalk in front of our house. It had iron slugs, about a half inch around and two inches or so long, all through it. My dad, who worked at the plant for a short time, said they had started out as large iron balls to pulverize the raw product that made cement. When I took my family back there many years later, I told them about the iron slugs. We stopped by the place I lived, and there they were, still embedded in the sidewalk, except where I and other kids had pried some out to make ammunition for our slingshots.

The two largest buildings in town were the Hotel Aldridge on South Broadway and the Pontotoc County Courthouse. The courthouse had four stories with a fifth floor that had just a wall with no top. Prisoners ing around on that floor; I don't know where they slept. The Hotel Aldridge had five floors, and I remember their smelly back alley as I would cut through it going back to the newspaper office where I went to get the papers I sold on the street.

There was a dry cleaning and laundry shop, but I never knew anyone who used that service. Of course, we were the poorest of the poor, but in the twenties and thirties there were a lot of poor people. The only family I knew who had a phone was an aunt and uncle who lived in the country. It was a wall-hanging-hand cranked phone that served a small party line.

There were not many cars in Ada except on Saturday when people came to town to shop and maybe go to the movies. Only the wealthy could afford cars, but there was a whole block square used for a wagon yard where the farmers parked their wagons, and right behind the biggest grocery store, Piggly Wiggly, was a livery barn for their horses.

Ada had a movie theater, but I never ever saw a movie there. There was a circus every year, but I don't remember going to see it. I do remember all us kids turning out for the animal parade the circus always put on. There was a swimming pool that was heavily used in the summer. In the winter it was used as an ice skating rink.

The Folks

I was born in the hospital, right between Eleventh and Twelfth Streets in Ada, on October the thirtieth, 1922; I think the doctor was Dr. Briko. My full name is Travis Olando Evans. My father was Willie Floyd Evans and my mother was Mattie Gattis Evans.

My grandmother on my mother's side also had the name Mattie Gattis. My grandfather was Franklin Gattis. I really don't know a lot about my mother's background, but I do know that both of her parents, my grandparents, passed away in the Old Soldiers' home at Norman, Oklahoma. Franklin was a Confederate veteran, so that's why he and his wife were in that home.

My grandfather and his uncle, A.J. McFarlin, were partners and they built a hotel in Ada. I knew that, but some cousins in Ravia told me how that hotel came about. They said when my grandfather got out of service, he mustered out with some money, maybe a thousand dollars, and in those days you were wealthy if you had a thousand dollars. He didn't settle in Ada right away after he got out of the army, but he heard of some cheap land down in Texas and went down there, just across the border, and settled. He nearly went broke when they had a drought year. He had a few cattle, but he couldn't raise enough feed to feed them, so he sold out. He was able to save a little of that money, and he used it to help build that hotel. It was called the Stockton Hotel, and it stood for years right on the corner of Stockton and Eleventh Street. The Katy railroad station was right across the street from it and that building is still there, but it's now the Chamber of Commerce.

My mother had a sister named Cora. She lived in Ravia and was the post mistress. Her husband was the district railroad foreman for one of the railroads. The post office was in one end of the railroad station and in the other end was the Western Union Telegraph office. Will Rogers came through one time, and he got off the train to go to the restroom and whatever. The telegraph operator was sitting right there singing and picking the guitar. Will Rogers heard that and he said, "Man, you ought to be on Broadway."

Gene Autry was the telegraph operator. At that time Rogers was in the Ziegfeld Follies in New York, and he enticed Autry to get involved in that. Of course, he became famous, but up until then, his only audience was my Aunt Cora, the post mistress in the other end of the station.

I met my mother's sister-in-law, Aunt Stella, one time. She lived up in Pauls Valley. Now, how we got there, I don't remember, but our family went up there because they had a tornado, and my dad wanted to see the damage. I remember being on Aunt Stella's side of the street, and trees were standing and the sidewalk was okay. Across the street though, the trees were down and the sidewalk was buckled. Dad and Aunt Stella's husband went around town to see the damage. Dad said the wind had turned box cars over, and it was strong enough to blow a straw through a railroad track. It was an awful storm.

That's the only time I remember seeing any of my mother's family.

My grandpa on my father's side was Isaac Hamilton Evans. My grandma's name was Hulda Allen Evans. They both grew up in Tennessee. Her family was a big family, a bunch of kids, ten of them. She was one of the older ones, and she had to care for the younger kids a lot. If things didn't go just right with them, her dad became angry with her and sometimes abusive towards her. Grandpa went by her house on his way home from work every day and observed what was happening. One day he said, "Let's get you out of this mess. Let's just go get married."

The marriage license said Grandma was fifteen when they married, but they fibbed about it; she was really only fourteen. Grandpa was twelve years older than she was.

I have to tell you a story that Grandma told me after I was grown and married and had children. She said when they first married they lived out on a piece of land that Grandpa had cleared. He used the trees to build a log house, a one room log cabin. They had a wire across the center of the cabin where they hung a quilt to sort of divide the room. Grandma cooked on a fireplace with a Dutch oven and did the dishes in one side of the room, and their bed was on the other side of the quilt.

At that time, Grandma used snuff. She'd take a little willow branch and chew it till it was frayed and dip it in that snuff and put a little in her mouth. Grandpa didn't like tobacco; he didn't use it in any form. At night when they'd get through eating, Grandpa would put on a log to keep the cabin warm all night and go to bed. She'd hear Grandpa after he went around behind the quilt; he'd kneel down and start to pray. He'd thank the Lord that he had a job and for all the other things. Then he'd pray, "Lord, save that girl, get through to her heart, and break her from that baccy habit." Baccy was his word for tobacco. "Break her from that habit," he'd say.

She told me that every night she'd get so mad, she'd just steam. Sometimes she'd stay up purposefully, not even go to bed because she was so mad at him. It just riled her something awful. Finally she got so mad one day she told Grandpa, "I guess you think I'm going to go back home if you keep praying for me and making me so mad. Do you think I'll get mad enough to go back home to that house full of kids? Well, I ain't going nowhere."

There he was in there on his knees every night praying for her and making her mad, but as mad as she got, she wasn't about to leave and go back to her folks.

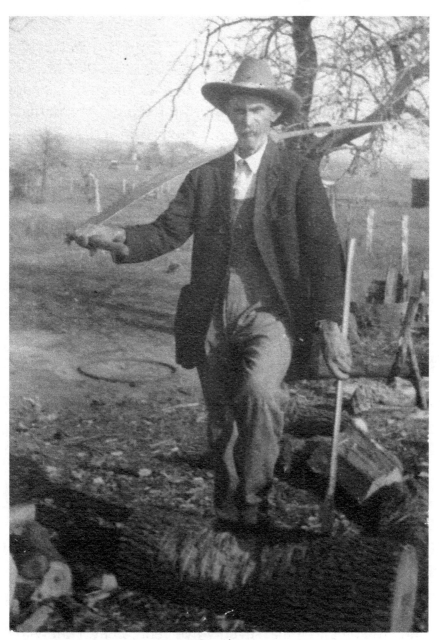

Grandpa

All Grandpa knew was what you see in this picture of him with a saw and an ax. At one time he was making barrel staves. He came home one night, now this was before they had kids, and he told Grandma he had quit his job. She said, "You quit? You'd better go back and apologize tomorrow and tell him you want your job back. You're making fifty cents a day. You can't quit!" She just raved and ranted.

He said, "The Lord will provide, Huldie. Don't you worry about it. The Lord will provide."

Every day he'd go out looking for work, and he'd take his saw and ax and shotgun. He'd bring back a squirrel or a possum or a rabbit or maybe a bird, and he had put in a little garden that provided a little food. This went on for some time, and she was on him every night. "You ought to go down on your knees and beg for that job back," she'd say.

"I wouldn't ever go and make barrel staves for those people again no matter what price they offered me."

Come to find out, the oak barrel staves that he was making were going to the Jack Daniels distillery for whiskey. Grandpa wasn't going to have any part of making whiskey, but Grandma wasn't a Christian yet, so it didn't matter to her.

For three or four months, every morning he'd go out and come back with his head hanging. But, he kept saying, "The Lord will provide. We just need to wait on the Lord."

One night he came home and said, "I got a job today and I'm going to make seventy-five cents a day. I knew the Lord would provide."

The job was making crossties for the railroad. He did so well at it, that pretty soon they raised him to a dollar a day, twice what he was paid when he was making barrel staves. The company Grandpa worked for wanted to put in a side by side railroad through that part of Tennessee and were expanding the rails coming west. Remember this was in the late 1800s. They paid the guys that were making a certain number of crossties more, and Grandpa made as much as $1.75 a day. About then, he and Grandma decided to go to Oklahoma for the land rush and settled in Ada.

Grandma and Grandpa had five children, Willie Floyd, my dad, and my aunts, Essie, Mae, Lorena, we called her Rene, and Alta. Two of my aunts, Rene and Alta, were pretty young when I came along, and were still at home. By then, Aunt Essie had married Elmer McDonald. They lived in a community about fifteen miles out of Ada. Uncle Elmer farmed and had livestock. They had seven children, six sons and one daughter. Aunt Mae married Joseph Alonzo George, everyone called him Lonnie, and they had three children, two sons and one daughter. They farmed some land about six or eight miles from Ada.

My father, Willie Floyd Evans, was born on April 16, 1895 in Moore County, Tennessee. He was a World War I veteran who served in France during that war. Dad told me just a little bit about his time in the service. He joined as a cavalryman in the horse detail, but when he got over to France, they didn't use the horses moving the guns and that sort of thing, so they gave him the job of delivering mail to the front line. He drove a motorcycle with a side car to carry the mail.

11

Willie

He told me about one time when he was off a day or two, he got to go into some town, and I can't recall the name of it just now, but he said he was taken aback by the sewer system. They didn't have any piped sewers. They had gutters, and all the dish water and wash water and everything else ran down those gutters. When you went to a public bathroom, they charged you. It wasn't a charge to use the bathroom, but you had to buy the toilet paper. I remember him talking about having to pay two cents for toilet paper.

One of the times that he was up on the front delivering the mail, the front line was gassed. The results of that was Dad only had one lung when he came home. He said there was a lot of mud in the field; the trenches were full of mud and water when the ambulance, which was an old government truck, picked him up. He didn't say what hospital or town he was in or how long he was there, but he sailed home out of Marseille.

One other thing he told me: in the early part of the war he was close to San Antonio, Texas at Camp Travis. That's how I got my name.

After Dad came home from the war he went to work on the Turkey Track ranch over in Texas. After he worked there for a while, they sent him over to the Circle Dot Ranch owned by the same people, some big bankers out of New York. The Circle Dot was down close to Ardmore, Oklahoma. That may have been where Dad met my mother; I think her family was from somewhere around there. I don't know how long he worked at the Circle Dot, but when he left there, he and my mother went to Ada where all his folks lived. We were always close to his side of the family.

My mother and dad moved to Ada sometime before I was born in '22. I was the oldest of three boys. After me, there was Floyd Lenard Rudolph, called Rudy, who was born in '25 and then William Junior Evans, called Bill, who was born in '27. Bill was born premature and only weighed a pound and fifteen ounces. When he was born the doctors said, "Don't plan to take him home because he's too little; he won't live."

Grandma said, "Now, that's up to the Lord."

And Bill made it. I don't think he would have lived if it hadn't been for Grandma. He slept on the door of the oven all winter long in a shoe box. I remember it well, for he was so tiny.

Mama was sick quite a while after Bill was born. She was always tall and thin and frail. Looking back, I would say she had anemia. When he was two, Bill had polio, or what they called infantile paralysis. Then Mama had a sick little boy to care for. Grandma lived close enough that she could walk over and help her, and Aunt Alta and Rene would also go over and help, even take the laundry home to do on the rub board. Still, the care she got was not too good, I'm sure.

Mama took care of us boys the best she could. I remember that she dressed me so carefully – always trying to get the best clothes for me. I also remember that she was always very loving - very loving.

Being A Kid

When my parents first came to Ada, my Dad went to work at the cement plant where they crushed rock to make cement. Since he only had one lung, he wasn't able to hold that job. He couldn't tolerate the powder that crushing those rocks left in the air. He worked for a while as a driver for a moving company. I don't know where else he might have worked, but I know, after I was big enough to remember, he was a drover hauling equipment to the oil field.

Sometimes Mama rode with him. When that happened, we went to Grandma and Grandpa's. They lived not too far from us, and anytime it was needed, us boys were dropped over there. If Bill was too sick to leave the house, Mama had to stay with him. Sometimes I would be the only one to go to Grandma's.

Aunt Essie's oldest son, Homer was just a little older than me, and Aunt Mae's son, J.A. was just a little younger. My dad had an old Model A for a while, and every now and then we'd all pile in that old car and go for a visit with Aunt Mae and Uncle Lonnie and their kids out on the farm. Aunt Essie and her family might be there too. Us boys had a lot of fun doing what boys with a little freedom can do out on the farm.

Homer stayed with Grandma and Grandpa some too, so we got to spend quite a bit of time together when we were little kids. Grandpa loved his grandchildren. Homer and I could do no wrong. I think we were special to him because we were his first grandchildren. Really, I think we were his favorites.

Grandma did a lot of sewing; she sewed for a lot of people around town, so she had quite a few of those wooden spools that thread came on. Homer and I made good use of the empty ones. Grandpa helped us, and we took a little stick of some kind and ran through the spools and used them for wheels. We used one of those flat sardine cans and fastened the "wheels" on the bottom and made a wagon. Then we'd catch us a horny toad and make a string harness and hitch him up. We dug little roads around under the tree stumps and put that horny toad to pulling the wagon on them.

Grandma was great. She just loved us to pieces, but she was pretty strict. When we got a little older, we had marbles, but Grandma wouldn't go for us playing marbles. If she wasn't around or we were together at our own homes, we'd play marbles. You'd just draw a ring in the dirt, put your marbles in the center and take turns using your thumb to shoot your marble to try to hit the other guy's marble out of the ring; if you did, then it was your marble. Grandma didn't like it; she called it gambling.

We had a stick we used to hit a little wheel to make it turn, and we'd run around with that, and we had a tin can that we'd knock around with a stick, kind of like hockey. We built kites too. Grandpa taught me how to take strips of wood and build them. Homer lived out in the country, and he was a lot more mechanically oriented than I was. He built a box kite, and instead of the little old cotton string I had to use on my kite, he brought some bailing twine, that jute, from the farm to build it. Man, we'd put that box kite way up there.

I was sort of sickly when it was time for me to go to school, so they held me back a year. I had a heart murmur and I still have it, but it's not so bad now. I stayed with Grandma and Grandpa during that school year. At that time they lived out on the King Ranch, east of Ada. Grandpa planted gardens, took care of the livestock and did general farm work. Grandma cooked for the King family, and helped take care of Mrs. King who was quite ill. I don't know that I ever saw her.

I wasn't big enough to go cut wood with Grandpa when I stayed with them. He cut trees for firewood in and around Ada. He also cleared some swampland on the King Ranch. He was very methodical about his work, and he never got paid what he was worth. Furthermore, he never spent what he earned. He gave every penny of it to Grandma and the girls who did the shopping.

Grandpa called me his helper, and really I probably wasn't much help, probably in his way more than anything, but I thought I was a little man because I was his little man. The main thing I could do to help was when he sharpened his axes. He had to sharpen them a lot. He had a big grinding wheel that had a cultivator seat and pedals like a bicycle. He'd put me up on that, and I'd pedal and pedal while he stood there and ground his ax.

The buggy wheels, in those days, were wooden, and he made iron rims to go around them. Where those rims had been forged together, he'd get the metal real hot and then hammer the two together, and that needed to be ground to smooth it off. So he'd hold it on the grinding wheel, and I'd pedal. We'd do that right by the creek, so he could dump the iron rim in the creek, in that cold water, to harden.

Grandpa used to tease me. They would send me out to the woodshed to bring in a load of firewood. They cooked with it on the fireplace. I'd go out and bring in just a few sticks at a time, and Grandpa would say, "Grandma, look at that lazy kid. He doesn't even carry a full load of wood."

Then the next time I'd bring in so much wood I couldn't even see over the top of it. I'd be struggling up the steps and kicking on the door for someone to open it, and he'd say, "Grandma, look at that lazy boy carrying that much wood, so he won't have to make any more trips."

I got in trouble with Grandpa one time. He gave me a spanking. Someone had put a new roof on an old farm building on the King Ranch where Grandpa was working. There was a big shingle pile, and he told me "Now, I don't want you playing in that shingle pile because there's still nails in there."

It was summertime and everybody, even our teacher, went barefoot in the summer. I was running around playing with no shoes on and ran across that shingle pile and sure enough, I stepped on a nail that went clear through my foot. Grandpa came and picked me up and patted my little behind, his spanking was kind of like love pats, and said, "Didn't I tell you not to get in that shingle pile? Now, you come with me."

We went out to the smoke shed where he smoked bacon when he killed the hogs. There was a little can of kerosene; he put a little of it on a rag and wiped my foot off good, then he opened that hole up and pored kerosene through it. Boy, that hurt. I cried through the whole thing. It took a while to heal up.

Anyway, on that ranch there was a hilly area that ran down to a gully and stream. Grandpa made Homer and me a little sled to go down that hill. He copied it off of a sled that he hauled his plow and farming equipment on, only he made it smaller so Homer and I could handle it. There was dried grass in the summertime. We'd go around behind the barn pulling that sled and get on at the top of the hill and slide clear down to the bottom. It was like being on snow. I was young, and the slide going down toward that gully and creek seemed like it might be a mile long. Of course it wasn't, but going down that hill was real exciting.

I helped Grandpa when he was shelling corn. I wasn't very good at it, but he showed me how. He put his corn crop in a big old tank, a metal tank that would probably hold five hundred or maybe even a thousand gallons of water. It had a leak in it, and instead of water they used it for storing grain. It had a sheet metal door at the bottom, and you could lift it up and get grain by the bucket for the hogs or cattle.

One of my jobs was to catch baby possums. They're not hard to catch. It's finding them that's hard. Once you find them, you just throw a stick and hit them, and they just stop and play dead; then you grab them by the tail. When we caught some, we'd put them inside that tank and Grandpa lowered a bucket of water in there for them. When they got big enough, Grandma baked possum and yams.

One day Homer and I were out playing on the sled when

he saw a snake. He went and found a forked stick and stuck it over the head of that snake; then he picked it up by the tail and bashed it against a fence post. Another time, we were in a little thicket down on the ravine, and we came upon a snake swallowing another snake. Homer killed it with a rock. I got out of the way. He was much braver than I.

Uncle Elmer, Homer's dad, raised cotton and he had a cotton gin; he raised sorghum, so he had a molasses mill; he had cows and hogs and did wood shredding and other things. He always had plenty of work for his boys, so Homer had more opportunity to learn about things like that than I did, and he was a lot more aggressive. I learned a lot from him.

There on the King place is where I learned to read. I learned from Aunt Rene, who was a senior in high school, and Aunt Alta, who was a freshman. Every night they lowered the quilting frames down from the ceiling, and Grandma and the girls sat there and quilted. They had a fire place over in the corner that Grandma cooked on, and of course, it was the only source of heat. Grandpa put a log on the fire and sat there and corded cotton. There were two or three kerosene lamps, and they had me reading the Bible to them. Aunt Rene or Aunt Alta had taught me the alphabet and a few words, and if I didn't know a word, or didn't say it right, one of them corrected me and told me what it meant; usually not Grandma because she wasn't as educated as her daughters. One of them said, "This is the way it's pronounced. Now, spell it for me." That's the way I learned to read. I actually read through the whole Bible before I started to school.

Just a Kid

I remember very well my first day of school. I was back home with my parents by then, but we lived real close to Grandma and Grandpa. Aunt Rene walked me to school. I think she filled out the papers because Mama was sick and also had my very sickly little brother at home.

One reason I remember that day so well is - right across the street from the school there was a tiny little grocery store. I don't think it was any bigger than our living room, and that's not very big. The store sold Cracker Jacks, and Aunt Rene bought me a box. When I opened the box, and I think the teacher made me wait till recess, there was a little red cellophane fish in there. In those days, we didn't have the plastics like we do now; they had cellophane. If you took a piece of that cellophane and put it in your hand, the warmth of your hand would start it to moving. When I held that little fish in my hand, it started flopping. Oh, that was really something.

When I started to school, my spelling was good. Every Friday they used to have a spelling bee. In the first grade,

I'd be able to spell down third, fourth, fifth or sixth grade kids. At Christmastime, they put me in the second grade and at the end of the term, I was put in the third grade, and that was only my first year of school. But remember, I was a year older because I had missed that year. By the end of the second year, I had finished the fourth grade, and they wanted to promote me on up again, but my mother said no; she said they were going too fast. They wanted to put me up because by then, I was spelling down the eighth graders, and I knew how to pronounce words they didn't, and I knew the meaning of words they didn't. That was all because of my two aunts. They were very persistent in teaching me.

We had Christmas every year. Mama strung popcorn and that sort of thing. On Christmas morning we would get an orange or an apple, or maybe both. We didn't get toys like kids do now, but one time I did get a toy. It was one of those little wooden jumping jacks that you pull the string and it climbs up and down the string; that was the only toy I got. I let my little brother, Billy, who wasn't very old, play with it, and you know how babies are, he threw it in the oven, and the string burned up. I lost the only toy I had three or four days after Christmas.

When I was eight or nine, Aunt Rene gave me a toothbrush for Christmas. That was the first toothbrush I ever had, and I used it till I got married. As I said, in those days they didn't have plastics like they have now. They used celluloid to make a little handle and at the head of the handle was a little baby elephant's head. I'll never forget that little toothbrush.

Where we lived everybody had an outhouse on the alley, and just across the alley was an outhouse for the neighbor. There was an old man, Mr. Coffee, who had a couple of mules, and they went all over town cleaning toilets. You couldn't hear it when he came around, but you knew he was working next door by the smell. After he finished the job he'd sprinkle a little lime to keep down the smell some. Mr. Coffee was a round faced guy with a bald head, and he wore a little bowler hat. Us boys would go out and holler, "Mr. Coffee, make your hat wiggle." He'd just look at us, and that little bowler would start going up and down. He was a very jolly fellow, and kids all over town asked to see that trick. We all liked him.

We had a cow pen out in the back and a little barn we put hay in. We had some chickens to keep us in eggs, and when some of them came up missing, Dad just knew somebody was stealing them. We didn't have any air conditioning or fans, anything like that, and one very hot night, we were all sleeping in the doorway of a screened in porch so we might get a little cool air. Sometime during the middle of the night, maybe one or two o'clock in the morning, somebody was out there prowling around. Dad got his gun and shot right through the screen to scare them away. Another thing I remember about that house was we had problems with mice. Dad put a wash tub filled with water right in front of the screen door. Sure enough, the next morning there were a couple of mice in that tub.

Most everybody that lived out there had a cow. The neighbors that lived catty-cornered from us had a little cow pen out behind for a mother cow and her young calf, probably a hundred and fifty to two hundred pounds, not very old. The calf was tethered so that the mother cow could go into the barn to eat straw.

There was a tornado that came through there one time. When it hit, Mama and Dad and all us boys were in the storm cellar where we kept canned vegetables. There was a kerosene lantern and some quilts and things to sleep on.

If it did any damage to our house I don't recall it. But the neighbors across from us had a stove out on their screened-in back porch. When it was hot in the summertime, they cooked out there; a lot of people did that back then. When that tornado hit, it took the stove from the porch, along with the calf from the barn with a rope and part of a stall still around its neck, and put both of them up in the loft of our hay barn, a distance of probably two hundred feet. I don't have any idea how they got that stove and the calf down out of the loft.

My dad worked as a drover for some time for J.T. Adair Drayage and Storage of Ada. An oil company had found oil out at Fittstown in about 1929, and Adair moved boilers and heavy equipment and those big wooden derricks for that company. Dad might have six, eight, ten, maybe twelve horses in a team. When he took a derrick out to the site, there was a wagon up front and a wagon at the back. When they got to the site, they had to stand the derrick up. They used a block and tackle, and one end of the derrick was anchored. Dad had trained those animals. They were big heavy draft animals, and the lead horses were hardly more than ponies. Dad placed the team where the big ones were backed up right at the doubletrees, and when he cracked that whip, those horses started to pull. They'd get down to where their bellies would almost touch the ground. Then Dad would pick up a handful of dirt and scatter it around over the whole team and say "Scat!" Boy, that team stacked that derrick up. I remember it so well. I was real young, but it impressed me.

At night he'd bring the team and wagon home and put the team in the cow barn and the wagon on a vacant lot next to us. He'd bring the harness in and let us boys help to saddle soap it. On the hames, Dad had little copper or brass bells so that when the horses stepped they would tinkle, tinkle, tinkle. He took pieces of old manila rope and tied a bundle of them about so long and frayed the ends of them out. Then Mama dipped them in Rit Dye boiling on the back of the stove and made different colored tassels. Dad put them on the hames of the collars, so when the horses went through town, they just looked beautiful. Dad was so proud of them when they were dressed up, and those horses seemed to know they looked good too; they would really strut.

When I got up seven or eight years old, I got to ride with Dad a lot of the time when he was working for Adair. I remember one time, Dad had a pretty good load of something to deliver, I forget just what it was, but it was something for the oil patch, and I got to go with him that day. Along the way, we had to cross the Canadian River. We came to the river and the horses balked. They just didn't want to go; they kept backing up, so Dad put the leather to them, but again, they got to the water so deep and balked. A drover always carried a little corn and grain for the animals to be

25

fed, and finally, Dad reached around behind his seat and took a corn cob that was dry and had the husks off, and he lit it. Then he reached for that horse's tail and stuck that corn cob up his rump and yelled at me "Hang on!" And I mean we crossed that river! Actually, what Dad did didn't hurt the horse; the flame was out before it reached the target, and it really didn't hurt the horse, but it was warm enough to make them go. And boy – we did go!

I guess I was eight or nine when my mother and dad divorced. I didn't know it then, that they weren't getting along very good, but they had stayed together for about a year before they divorced. I couldn't imagine why they were separating, because I remember that earlier they seemed happy when they were together.

In my reasoning and thinking back about that situation now, I don't think Mama left so voluntarily. The closest one of her family lived at Pauls Valley, and they never came around, so she didn't get the kind of support a family gives. But Grandma, Aunt Rene and Aunt Alta were around us continually, and I'm sure Mama got plenty of nagging. I don't think she was much of a housekeeper, but with three little boys it would be hard to keep an orderly house, and I'm sure she was nagged about that. Grandma was very domineering, and I don't imagine that Alta and Rene were always kind to her. I was young, but I didn't much like Grandma being at our house all the time; I remember it well, and it seemed like she was interfering. I know now that she was only trying to help, but I wonder if my mother took what she had to say personally. She may have felt she was being run out of the family. She may have just given up.

I just have one picture of my mother. It was when I was a baby; she was holding me in her arms. You know everybody was so dirt poor they didn't make many pictures. There were those little Brownie cameras people had, but the cost of film was thirty cents a roll, and you had to take the film in some place to get them developed, and that was a nickel a piece, so people just didn't make many pictures – not unless they were better off than we were.

Anyway, when my mother left the family, us boys went to Grandma and Grandpa's house, and we stayed with them a good while, maybe fourteen months - over a year anyway.

Where Grandma and Grandpa lived after they moved back to town from the King Ranch, it was kind of like being out on a farm. There would be a house, then a vacant lot, a house and another vacant lot. The house we lived in had electricity, I remember, but we never had a radio. We sure enjoyed the lights though; they were a lot better than a coal oil lamp. We had water at the back door, but not in the house. Some of the neighbors had a fence around their place. We didn't, but we did have a cow lot and a little barn.

There was a pond not far from the house, not a very big one, but it had catfish in it. Grandpa would get a chicken that died and cut it up and use it for bait to catch catfish. Grandma didn't like catfish, but she cooked them anyway; meat was scarce. Up the road from the house, there was Floyd's Hatchery, and across from that was the country club and golf course. From there down to Grandma's house was a steep hill.

During that time Dad came to see us when he could. I remember only seeing him once in a while; Dad smoked cigarettes, and my Grandma didn't approve of that. Anyway, he had to come down that steep hill when he came. I remember the truck he drove; it was a Model A, and that model didn't have a fuel pump. At the dash level on the outside was a tank for the gasoline, and it gravitated down to the carburetor. The only way you could go up a hill was to back up. So when Dad left, we all watched him back up the hill.

The hatchery had two or three dogs that came out and barked at the wheels, even when Dad came down the hill at a pretty good clip. So, one time he wired some gunny sacks on the wheels, and when he started backing up the hill those dogs came out and grabbed ahold of those gunny sacks and their teeth got caught in them and they were going flop, flop, flop up that hill. They weren't hurt, but they didn't want to chase a car again. Dad broke them from that.

The house where we lived was kind of elevated, and there was always water under it. Grandma raised ducks and geese under there. She always kept a lot of ducks. When she was going to make feather pillows or a mattress, I got to help pick the down feathers from around the neck. She told me how to hold the duck; you put their head under your leg. They're okay if you just pull the down, but if you pull a feather, it hurts and they will bite you. I learned that the hard way. I got bit many a time.

I learned another lesson about a goose. There was a bunch of bushes in the back that had sort of what looked like a blue flower on them, but they weren't flowers – they were thistles, and they would stick. The older they got, the thornier that sticker was. One of Grandma's mother geese had a nest out there. Grandma said to me one morning, "Don't go out by that old goose's nest because she'll flog you." Well, when you tell a kid not to do something.... Anyway, I went out there and that old goose hissed at me. And, I hissed right back at her. Boy, she came and gave me a flogging. I went right into those thistles trying to get away. I came out of there bawling and squalling, but Grandma gave me what for anyway. "You'll learn to mind," she said.

Grandpa had an old mare named Maude, and he and Maude and I plowed the vacant lots all over town. One thing I liked about that was Grandpa helped me catch the little baby cottontails that were turned up with the plow, and we took them home and made a cage for them. They were my pets for a while.

Grandpa planted different vegetables, mostly onions and potatoes and peas and beans. Then when he harvested them, he'd give half of them to the people who owned the lots. On one lot he'd plant black-eyed peas, and the one across the way might have Kentucky Wonder beans and so on. When the beans got dried out Rudy and I would stomp on them to get the shells off, then we'd get a tin can and pour the beans down into another container for the wind to blow the hulls away. Winnowing is what they called that back then.

When Grandpa dug potatoes, I was going along behind him with a bucket to put them in. And in the summer when we harvested the onions, I got to help tie them together. We tied a half dozen of them together with this old manila jute twine; then we'd tie on another half dozen or so turned the other way. Grandpa threw them over the rafters in the barn to dry. Then when we wanted onions, we'd just go to the barn.

Grandpa always had a ditch full of straw on the north side of a building packed tight where he stored potatoes and vegetables. We always had dried beans and peas, and Grandma canned many, many quarts of beans, peas, tomatoes, and so on. Uncle Elmer made molasses, and he'd bring gallons to us. Actually, Grandma and Grandpa didn't buy very much.

All the time I was growing up my brothers and I got along fine. Bill was quite a bit younger than me, and the polio left him not real capable in his hands and feet, so he was kind of handicapped and always sickly. Rudy and I got along alright, but we were brothers. Homer and I were pals, and that's different than a brother. Rudy was just a kid, and besides that, I had a slingshot and he didn't.

Homer was my pal alright, but he got me in trouble with Grandma a few times. One time I cut my hand pretty bad while I was peeling an apple to feed a goat. I wasn't supposed to have a knife, but I did. It was Homer's. Another time, he was at our house visiting and he said to me, "Come on. I'm going to show you how to smoke."

They were grapes on four or five bushes out behind the barn, so we went out there, and he cut a piece of grape vine, and we lit it and puffed on it. Oh boy! It burned my tongue.

Pretty soon Grandma called us to dinner. We went in and she said, "You boys go wash up now."

When we went in to the table to eat, she said, "What have you boys been up to?"

"Oh, nothing. Just playin'."

"You boys have been smoking grape vines, haven't you? Now, don't you lie to me or you'll get two whippins."

We were out behind the barn, and I know nobody saw us. We must have acted guilty, or maybe she smelled the smoke on us. Anyway, she knew, and she gave us what for.

We really got along pretty good when we were living at Grandma's and Grandpa's, but we knew who was boss, and it wasn't Grandpa. Grandma ruled the roost. She would sort of fly off the handle every once in a while and get all over him - for nothing. He never retorted; he was just a sweet and gentle man. He was really sort of henpecked. Even Aunt Rene and Aunt Alta would sass and talk back to him. He was so meek and gentle though, that he never fussed with them.

Grandma, Aunt Rene and Aunt Alta all attended the Nazarene Church and of course, we all went to church when we were staying with them. Well, sometimes Grandpa didn't go with us. Grandma had become so legalistic that it kind of soured Grandpa. He wasn't liberal, I don't mean to say that; he lived a Christian life. But, Grandma was harping on him for some little thing she thought was wrong all the time. It got to where Grandpa wouldn't even go to church with her.

It was a pretty good sized church we went to, and I think well structured. It was built with a basement, and that's where the Sunday School rooms were located. Every room had a window for light and ventilation. Aunt Alta and Aunt

Rene had talked with me about Jesus and prayed with me. My Sunday School teacher's name was Mrs. McCutchan, and she was such a good teacher, a sweet teacher. One day when I was about nine, after she explained so well who Jesus was and what He could do in our lives, I knelt in the class room, along with several other children, and accepted Jesus as my Savior.

I wish I could tell you I walked the straight line, but as a teenager I slipped over and changed just like most of us did. But, I went back and repented just like most of us did, more than once, on one occasion after I was an adult with several children.

When Aunt Rene was in high school, she was friends with a girl named Ruth; everyone in our family called her Ruthie. I remember when those two girls, they were probably twenty-two years old, were fresh out of Eastern Oklahoma Teachers College and were getting ready to go to God's Bible School in Cincinnati, Ohio. They both wanted to become missionaries and were planning to go that school together. I remember them sitting around at night making their clothes to go to school. Times were tough, and buying the clothes they needed was kind of out of the question. Back then, everybody bought flour and sugar in hundred pound bags. They'd take those sacks and wash and bleach them to make their underwear, and they'd dye some to make blouses and stuff. They both worked some, mostly housekeeping, and the Nazarene church took up a collection, and Grandma and Grandpa gave what they could, probably around twenty dollars, and they raised enough for the fare and the tuition. And, off they went on the train to Cincinnati.

There's a story about when Aunt Rene and Ruthie came home for Christmas that year. At that time, Grandma had a stove that had a big mantle over it and a water reservoir on one end, and when you built a fire it heated that water. Grandma kept a crock on the mantle. It was just an old cracked crock bowl, about so big, that Grandpa had made a wooden lid for. Grandma kept a potato in there to make yeast, let it ferment. That old crock had a crack down one side of it, and it was always oozing dough. It looked kind of ugly sitting there, but it served the purpose. She'd take it down and take out so much to make her bread, and oh, that bread was so good.

Anyhow, when the girls came home for Christmas, they brought Grandma a new crock to keep her yeast in. It was a nice flowered crock. Grandma seemed just so pleased with that new one and put her dough in it right away. She never wasted anything – nothing – not anything, so she had Grandpa make a flower pot out of her old crock.

Aunt Rene and Ruthie were home for close to a month. They went around and spoke at different churches to get money to go back to school again. I remember my dad giving Aunt Rene a dollar and a half, or something like that. He was proud of his sister; she was the only one that ever went to college. Anyhow, after they left, Grandma had Grandpa take the dirt out of that old crock, and she cleaned it up and used it. That new one didn't make yeast like the old one. Well, it probably did, but she didn't think so.

I guess I was ten or eleven when Dad started peddling fruit, going over to Hope, Arkansas and buying apples and little baskets of Concord grapes and bananas. The banana boats came from the Caribbean clear up the Arkansas River to Hope. Dad had an old pink Packard convertible, a big old eight cylinder thing, with a four wheel trailer behind that he used to bring the fruit back after he met the banana boat.

While he was doing that, he met Rosella, because her step dad, whose name was E.G. Fears, everybody called him Pug, was also peddling fruit. I think he was sort of a lazy shyster who would do about anything to get a bottle of whiskey. He talked Dad into being sort of like a partner. Dad had rented a stand on the main street in downtown Ada, to sell his produce. Pug had a six-legged hog weighing about two hundred pounds. It had a couple of small legs sticking out behind the back legs. Pug came up with an idea and convinced Dad that he could put that hog in his stand and charge people a dime to see it. Well, you've got to feed and water the animal and clean up the mess, and it was really messy and stinky. Besides, not many people had a dime to spend. Now, how are you going to make money that way?

Anyway, that's how Dad met Rosella - through her step dad. She was a divorced widow with one little boy about eleven years old. His name was Nurney Cornelius Harper. I don't know just when Dad and Rosella married, but Dad came to Grandma's and got us, and we moved into that hotel that my great-grandfather helped build, the Stockton Hotel. Dad introduced Rosella as our new mother, and we accepted it. She was a good woman – a really good woman. She believed in God, but she didn't really practice Christianity. She never used any foul language or anything.

She was good to us boys, but we got just as stern a discipline as her son, and he got just as many whippings as I did. Dad was just as strict with him as she was with us.

For a while, and it was not long after Dad and Rosella married, I sold newspapers on the street there in Ada, the Ada Evening News. As I walked down the street I would kind of sing - calling out "Ada Evening News, three cents." We'd call out the headlines too, something like "Read all about Bill Murray's cucumber!" He was governor and supposedly had an interest in H.J. Heinz cucumber factory that hadn't been reported or something like that, so he was in the news for a while.

If I sold ten newspapers I had a dime, and I took that home faithfully because we needed it. A dime went a long way in those days. It would buy a pound of margarine, they called it oleo; you couldn't buy butter. The margarine was white; they weren't allowed to sell it colored; the dairy lobby would holler too much. It came with a little pellet of yellow coloring, and you'd get the margarine warm and mix that in to make it look like butter. Sometimes when Dad was selling fruit, we'd be down to pennies, and he needed money to buy the fruit. I usually made ten or fifteen cents a night and that helped.

Way down on the east end of Eleventh Street, there was sort of a lower class building, and I didn't normally go down that far, but one particular night I did. I went to that building and going up the steps I was calling out "Ada Evening News," as I usually did. A woman came to the door. She had on a thin kimono and was smoking a cigarette, and I looked and there was a half a dozen women behind her. One of them was my mother. She had a cigarette too. I had never seen her smoke. Seeing my mother like that just tore me up. She came and hugged me and was crying. I think, now I don't know for sure, but I think all of them were prostitutes. In those days, probably you could sleep all night with a woman for twenty-five cents.

I didn't sell many newspapers that night. I went on home. That was a big disappointment. I never told that to Rudy or Bill; Rudy was three years younger and Bill five, and my dad never knew as far as I know. I never did mention that to <u>anybody.</u> Well, I think I might have told Katherine after we got married.

That happened during starvation times. There were people dying from starvation in those days. You couldn't get a job for a nickel an hour. People were doing things they wouldn't ordinarily do, robbing banks and stealing from their neighbors, because of the things that were going on. So, if my mother was involved with that, it was something so she wouldn't starve. It probably was a matter of either that or starve.

That was along about '33, when I saw my mother; then I didn't see her again for a long time.

Grandpa died when I was thirteen. I wasn't allowed to go to the funeral because I didn't have decent clothes. I would have gone in my long handle underwear if they had let me. The bad part of it was when I went squalling to Grandma and Aunt Rene, they said, "Your dad said you weren't going 'cause you don't have any decent clothes." Even Aunt Rene stood up for him. There were three of us boys and there probably wasn't money for clothes for all of us. Still, I think Dad and Grandma made a mistake not letting me go. That really hurt.

The strange thing about that was, three years before that, an evangelist, our pastor and the song leader at our church were all killed in an automobile and train accident right near where we were living. We heard the crash, and we started to run over there, but the folks wouldn't let us. It drug that car about five hundred feet and killed all those men. We had been in church with them about an hour before that. When the funeral came I got to go to that one. And I had gone to other funerals before that. My grandpa had a brother by the name of Joe Evans and his son had a baby that died at birth. We all went to that one.

When I was in about the fourth grade one of my play mates at school lost her father. She was in the same Sunday School class as I was, so we were closely tied that way. I went to that graveside service. I'll never forget it. That girl stood there shivering and sobbing and crying during the whole service. They don't do it so much anymore, but back then at the service they lowered the coffin, and the family stood around and threw flowers down; then they'd start putting the dirt down. Anyway, when they started lowering that coffin, that girl jumped right on top of the coffin in the grave, screaming as loud as she could. They had to pull her out of there.

That so impressed me, and yet three years later when Grandpa died, I couldn't go. I didn't understand it. My school clothes weren't fancy, but they were clean. I might have had to wear tennis shoes, but so what? My grandpa was such a great guy, and I loved him so much, and to be denied that.... But then, when you're just a kid what can you do?

Over my lifetime I've thought of Grandpa many, many times and the good times we had working together when I was staying with them. For me, a little orphan-like boy, my grandpa was just the greatest. I never heard him get angry. I never heard him raise his voice. The cruelest word I ever heard him say was dagnabbit. He'd say to his horse, old Maude, "Dagnabbit Maude, I told you gee not haw." But that was the most he'd ever say.

Grandpa was one of the nicest men you'd ever want to meet. Everybody in town loved Grandpa – everybody. They all spoke well of him. I just wish my children could have known him, and I wish they had known my dad too.

Grandpa was my hero. Actually, he was closer to me than my dad was. He was the best grandpa ever. I put this tribute together when I was in high school.

Definition of I.H. Evans

He was a man that was clean both inside and outside.
He never looked up to the rich nor down to the poor.
He lost without squealing and won without boasting.
He was considerate to women, children and old people.
He was too brave to lie, too generous to cheat and
He took his share of the world and let others have theirs.

That's just what I thought of my Grandpa.

PART II
THE PROMISED LAND
1936-1940

An Adventure

Soon after Grandpa died, we moved to Henrietta, Oklahoma. Dad thought he would do better selling fruit up there. There wasn't much in that town, but just above it was a smelter. Dad rented a big old vacant store right off the road between Henrietta and Eufala. He sold his fruit out of the front of the store, and we lived in the back. We were there part of the winter, and I remember being cold a lot of the time. That building was a high-roofed thing and hard to heat.

I started the sixth grade there, but I didn't finish because after only about two months, we moved up to Eufala where Dad rented a long narrow building that at one time had been the newspaper office. The floors were all cement with deep cavities where they had mounted their presses. Rosella took wire and quilts to section off our living quarters in the back of the building. It had high ceilings too, and we thought the building in Henrietta was hard to heat, but that one was impossible. Nurney and I went down to the corner and across the railroad tracks where we could get corn cobs for free. We'd get gunny sacks full to try to heat the building, but we still shivered from cold.

The school year in Eufala was not a good one for me. None of us liked the principal. Us boys had a nickname we called him - behind his back, of course. Anyway, we'd be standing in the hall around the radiator when the bell rang, and he'd say in a gruff voice "Get in your stalls." Everyone would start to their rooms, and he'd say to the last one in, "Close the gate behind you." He never said please; he just demanded. If he'd been more courteous, we might have learned better. I don't think I learned a thing in that school.

It was less than a year after Grandpa died that we left for California. Things were getting worse and worse in Oklahoma. Some of the good farm land along the Canadian River, what they call bottom land that gets the silt and natural fertilizer from the river, went back to the bank or was sold for two dollars an acre. But, who had two dollars? Of course, that situation came along with the Dust Bowl. It was terrible. Sometimes when one of those storms came in, men could not see to go from their barn to the house. Some of them died trying to make it. It is good character building experience to go through something like that; a life of ease never built anything; it's the challenges you meet that builds character. Still, I hope our nation never gets back to that.

During that time many, many families went to California to try and find work. You've read the Grapes of Wrath, I'm sure. John Steinbeck made a story of it, and he told it pretty much like I remember it.

Dad came home from the war with only one lung after being gassed in France. As far as I know, the only compensation he ever got for his injury was about $1,000. It was a long time before he did, though. You remember that the war was over in 1918, and it was in late 1935 that he got that money. A few months after he got it, he got us boys all together and explained that with jobs so scarce and the Dust Bowl blowing everything away, we weren't making it there in Oklahoma. He said he heard there were lots of jobs in California and he said, "I'm gonna take this money and buy us some transportation to get out there."

Dad bought a '36 Chevrolet pickup, and we left Oklahoma in the early summer of that year. I was fourteen years old. We went down toward Mexico and over close to El Paso and Las Cruces. I really don't know why Dad chose that route. I think most of the highways were paved at that time, and there were other choices.

I didn't grieve much about leaving the family we had always been so close to - Grandma, my aunts, my pal Homer and my other cousins. We had already left Ada and moved up to Henrietta and Eufala, and I didn't get to see them that often anyway. I was old enough to understand that going to California seemed like a necessary thing. I never thought about who we were leaving behind. I was a kid, and it was going to be an adventure. Too, we were leaving hard times with great hopes. California was the promised land.

When Dad bought the pickup, he had a pipe rack built to fit the back so he could make a two-story shelf for us to sleep on. He and Mom and brother Billy slept in the bottom. They had to crawl in; there was barely enough room for them to turn over and not enough for them to sit up. Nurney, Rudy and I slept up on top. We had a canvas that we pulled over us. In those days I don't think sleeping bags had been discovered. We made our own bed rolls.

When we were on the road, us boys rode in the bottom where we had about three feet. We could sit up and look out or lay down on a pallet. We were traveling during the summer months and coming across the desert country, it got pretty hot down there.

Of course, we stopped all along the way to work and earn a little money to get further down the road. Dad worked and so did Nurney and I; we were old enough; Rudy and Bill were still pretty young. We stopped every night and built a fire out on the ground to cook on. We mostly cooked potatoes and once in a while, we got other vegetables from wherever we were working.

The pickup had six tires and wheels; there were wells in front of the doors on each side of the pickup where the spares were mounted. The tires were supposed to be a really good brand. I remember very well one day when we weren't far from San Antonio, I was sitting on that rack when one of those tires in the well blew out. We never knew what caused it to blow out, but if I had to say now, I would say it was the heat; it was absolutely unbearable. When we got into San Antonio Dad found a store that carried those tires and explained that the tire had never been on the ground. They replaced it, of course.

We weren't fifty miles from there going toward New Mexico when one of the tires that was on the ground started a bump-bump-bump. Dad pulled off on the side of the road and found it had formed a big air bubble and was rubbing on some of the structure. We weren't anywhere to get one replaced, so luckily we had that brand new tire. We got it mounted and were back on the road pretty soon. Anyhow, my Dad said, "I'll never buy that kind of tire again as long as I live."

We went across Arizona, and I remember we were down by that big river close to Yuma, I think it was the Gila River, and we went to work picking cotton. Dad looked at that field and he said, "We ought to get a lot of cotton picked out of that field." We had never seen cotton like that in Oklahoma. It was Egyptian cotton; it had a lot of bush and growth. We went to work with big expectations, but you had to push the bushes around to get to it, and boy, it was hard to pick. We just stayed long enough to make a little money for gas and food and then we moved on.

One time we had camped between a cotton field and a vegetable patch that had lettuce and stuff. Dad pointed something out to us. He said, "Don't you ever eat that celery because they fertilize it with human waste." I don't know that they did or didn't, because it sure smelled bad, but that was Dad's idea of it. I laugh every time I remember that.

The Promised Land???

It was August before we got to California, and when we did, we went to Buttonwillow right near Bakersfield to see one of Dad's relatives. We stayed there only two or three days while Dad looked for work. There's a little town about twenty miles further north named Shafter where they raise a lot of potatoes, so we picked potatoes for a couple of days to make gas money to get on up to Tulare County. There was a big farm corporation there that had hundreds of acres of peaches and nectarines and prunes and grapes. It was a big, big spread. There was even a railroad siding right on the farm for loading up the produce. It was owned by a bunch of bankers, I think, and they hired quite a lot of workers. Anybody that was in the Central Coast of California around that time will remember that ranch.

Workers didn't get paid in cash, but in tokens which

you could spend at the company store. So, the company was making money off of their workers that way too. They had small cabins that workers could rent. Nowadays, those cabins wouldn't be allowed. There was no sanitation whatsoever; they didn't even have running water.

When we first got there, we were promised one of those little cabins when they had one come empty. We worked there three weeks and stayed in our tent; the pickup held most of our things. When Dad saw the charges we had at the company store, he told them, "Don't bother to save a cabin for us. We're moving on."

That was about twenty miles from where we wound up on a farm working for Mr. Swearingen. His place was about three miles from Farmersville. At that time the town of Farmersville had one grocery store, a little Methodist church, a filling station with two pumps that you had to pump by hand, and a library that was in someone's home. Back then, they never kept a population count, but I'd guess there were six to eight hundred people there. There's probably ten thousand people there now, so it's grown up quite a bit.

Mr. Swearingen was kind enough to let us put a tent under a big oak tree alongside his creek. It was a sandy creek that we could bail water out of. We just dug a trench for a latrine; Dad and I dug it by hand. The tent had a dirt floor that Rosella, or Mom, as we were calling her by then, wet down every day and swept, sometimes two or three times a day during the summertime.

It was not an easy life, but you never heard a complaint out of Rosella. She cooked on a wood stove, and she was a good cook; she'd make anything into a meal. When other people came to eat with us there might not be enough, but she'd scrape around, add a little more milk to the gravy or something, and come up with enough for everyone.

It was tough – I mean tough times. Mom canned everything we didn't eat. She was so good about that. We had a little shack out back that was a store room for all the canned goods. She had quart jars of pickled beets, tomatoes, peaches, green beans and so on. We dried raisins and apricots and peaches.

We used to have what they called a prune orchard; they called them that, but they were actually a French plum. When you harvest the plums, what you do is: you have big canvases, about a twelve foot square, and you take two of them and put them around underneath the tree. Then you use a long hexagon shaped pole that has a hook on it to reach up and get the limbs and shake till there's no more plums left. They fall on the canvas, and then you roll the canvas up and dump the plums out into forty or fifty pound lugs. After the trees are all harvested, you might go back later and see some that weren't ripe enough and hadn't fallen. You'd go talk to the landowner, and he'd say, "Yeah, you can go clean those trees." So we cleaned them to get a few more plums that we could dry to make prunes. To make prunes you use a tray about six feet long and three feet wide. There's a paper that fits it and after you put it on the tray, you spread the plums out to let the sun dry them.

In the spring we thinned the peaches so the trees wouldn't be too burdened. After that job, you wanted to go jump in the stream and get all that fuzz off yourself. When

47

they ripened, we'd get peaches that we could dehydrate or Mom could can. We also picked cherries, shook olives and picked up walnuts - just something to eat on, whatever we could get. Everybody was hungry in those days.

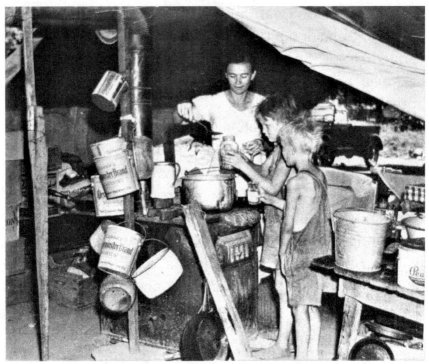

Rudy and Bill helping Mom in the tent

We had a fifteen acre pear orchard that got flooded every winter. It brought in burr clover that had little tiny burrs on it, and the pheasants just loved that. When ripe pears began falling, they liked that too, and here they'd come. I set traps to catch them, and then we kept them in the back yard. Any time we needed it, we'd just go wring the neck of a pheasant. I'd set traps out for cotton tail rabbits, and I carried a twenty-two with me all the time. When we were chopping or planting cotton or putting furrows in, and a cotton tail jumped up – boom. We had rabbit for dinner. And every now and then, we had wild pigeon.

Right about a mile from where we lived in that tent, a railroad went through. In those days the engines were all steam and put out little puffs of steam along the tracks where it was gravelly, and it was good clean gravel. Coming up along the tracks here and there was something green like spinach or collard greens. We'd pick those, and you might have to go a mile to get a mess of them, but it helped make a good meal. And maybe during that time a cotton tail would jump, and we'd have a big supper. Sometimes Mom got a pork jowl and made red eye gravy and blanched those greens in that. Boy, was it good.

Dad was sick a lot of the time. With only one lung, the dust, heat and fumes from the tractors made him sick, and he'd have to stay home, but Mom would be somewhere working. She was a hard worker. She went out in the field and worked just like my dad. She'd go and work wherever she could get a job in the era of WPA. The WPA had sewing rooms where women worked for maybe twenty cents an hour sewing for the government. I think they were making military uniforms, I really don't know. When she went into Visalia to work for them, she carpooled with other women who lived near us. Gas was ten cents a gallon, and they could save a little by carpooling. At one time Dad worked for the WPA, so Mom rode in with him. They didn't earn much, but they got commodities; they stood in line to get a few groceries. After she left WPA she got a job at a peach cannery cutting peaches, and later she worked at a liquor store there in Farmersville from five in the afternoon to eleven or something like that.

When us boys came home from school, we all had chores. We had to wash and dry the dishes at night, Bill might dry, but he never washed. Rudy and I took turns washing, and when Nurney was home, he did. Sometimes we'd get in an argument over that. One of us would say, "I washed last night." And the other would say, "No, I washed last night." Then Mom or Dad took over and decided.

We scrubbed the clothes in the back yard with a rub board, winter and summer. We took turnabout scrubbing, not only our own clothes, but the family's clothes. After I washed a shirt and started to rinse it, Mom would say "Let me see it," and she'd inspect the collar and cuffs to see they were clean. I ironed too. We had those flat irons that were heated on the stove; I ironed with those old things. When I ironed a shirt, Mom looked at it, and the first place she looked was between the buttons to be sure I got that part good. She taught us boys how to cook and clean and wash clothes; she taught us all those things. At the time we resented it; we thought that was women's work. But now, I'm glad she taught us. She was an excellent mother, and she was a good teacher. I can't say enough good about Mom.

From the time I was fifteen until I left home, I had to cook the breakfast meal. I got everything ready the night before; I put the wood in and got the paper to light it with. Every morning I got up at five o'clock, lit the stove and got it going, and had biscuits in the oven before I woke Mom and Dad up.

My brothers were sometimes pests. Rudy and I got along pretty good; he worked in the fields just like Nurney and I did. Bill, we had to do for him quite a lot. He wasn't very strong, and we always favored him. He became dependent on somebody else doing for him, and that happened all through his life even after he was married. He never did learn to drive a car. He could ride a bicycle for a few years, but I think by the time he was twenty-two, he wasn't able to do that anymore. He wasn't able to do a lot of things us older boys did, but he was just one of us in other ways; he got along with everybody. Most everyone called him Bug. I think Aunt Rene started calling him June Bug because his real name was William Junior Evans. He didn't talk real plain, but he went to school some, and it was really hard for him. I think the third grade is as far as he got and that took at least a year extra.

Nurney was a good, good fellow. He was like a brother to me. He was a year older than me, but small for his age. He wasn't very studious and not what I would call ambitiously bright. A lot of times I helped him with his homework. We had kerosene lights, and Dad set a certain time we had to turn the light out. Kerosene was a nickel a gallon.

We picked cotton the first fall we were there at Mr. Swearingen's, and when we went to work, a lot of times we started walking, and maybe we'd have to go two miles before somebody in a car came by and picked us up. Sometimes there would be five or six others in the car, and I would have to sit on somebody's lap. The driver got a nickel from each of the riders to help pay for his gas.

Dad and I worked together well. He had a lot of good work ethics, although he smoked and had to stop and roll a cigarette every once in a while. But, he worked and he expected us boys to work too. He said, "They are paying us for an hour's worth of work, and we're going to give them an hour's worth of work." He'd stay after dark or start before daylight just to get a job done, and he wouldn't even charge for it. Dad was a good fellow. He was a man of character. He barely could read, but he knew right from wrong, and he always did the right thing.

Pastor John Wylie held church in a tent; it didn't have a name, it was just Pastor Wylie's church. It was set up about three hundred feet south of the little Methodist church in Farmersville. The Methodist church had a wooden building with a steeple. It has been preserved, and I think they made some sort of a museum out of it. Most of us attended Pastor Wylie's church because the Methodist church only seated maybe forty or fifty people. The tent seated about a hundred people. In the summertime, they'd roll the flaps up on the outside so we could get a little air. Inside those flaps, there was mesh that was left down so the flies couldn't get in.

Ready for church

Brother Wylie worked in the fields too, chopping cotton or picking cotton, and he had a bunch of boys who also worked. But every night, five work nights, he preached. Saturday night he didn't, but on Sunday he preached twice. Then on Monday mornings, he was there to work right alongside the rest of us, and, by the way, his wife was there too.

They had three or four boys, a little bit older than Nurney and me, who worked with us, and then there were three younger boys. The youngest was Paul. His mother was picking right alongside Dad and me and Pastor John. Most of the men carried a twelve foot cotton sack so they wouldn't have to go to the scale so often, which meant they could stay picking longer and make a little more money. Us boys and the women pulled a nine foot sack. Mrs. Wylie did, and when little Paul was two or three years old he rode on that sack half the time. The Wylies had an old four door black sedan they kept at the end of the row, and the boys who weren't big enough to pull cotton were supposed to keep the baby there, but they'd get out of the car and get busy doing what little boys do, so Mrs. Wylie would go get the baby and pull him on the sack.

Pastor John had an old model A Ford pickup, and he'd drive up the Mineral King Highway toward Sequoia to a place called Kaweah, a part of the Kaweah River. There's tons of fish in there, but in the fall of the year, that river dried up. When the fish couldn't swim any further, they got into little pools. Pastor John would go up there and get a whole pickup load of fish, put them in gunny sacks and bring them to town. Then he'd spread them out in his front yard. People came and helped themselves to the fish. Of course, that endeared him to the community, and the church tent would be packed with people coming to hear him preach.

Dad worked for several farmers, and every time we needed to move, we'd fold the tent up, pack all our belongings in the pickup and go where the work was. Sometimes we had to make two trips because we couldn't load all our stuff in the pickup.

We worked seasonal for Roy Griswald for a couple of years. He was just about a mile from the Swearingen farm. He had two hundred acres where he had cattle and raised cotton. Of all the men Dad worked for, he was the one that had the most empathy and compassion for his workers. He was a real good boss.

Not long after we moved to the Griswald place, our mother came to see us boys. I don't know how she found us on the place we were living unless maybe Rosella was writing to her. I didn't know Mama was coming, but I was so pleased to see her. It had been about five years. She had married an oilman from up in Kansas. I remember being impressed with their new car and the way they were dressed. They had driven all the way out here just to see us boys. My Dad was out working, and Rosella was in the tent. My mama and I sat in the shade of a tree, and I guess we talked about an hour. Bill and Rudy were running around playing while we visited. They were pretty young and didn't have memories of our mother like I did. She asked if we were happy and if we needed anything. Before they left she gave each of us a quarter or something, I can't remember, but a coin. I never saw her again. I never even knew when my mother passed away.

In hindsight I wish that I had demanded that we spend more time together, learned more about her life in Kansas, and her husband, but you know, I was just a kid, and back then, at that age, you didn't speak out like that.

Mr. Griswald leased the Youngworth place from the family after Mr. Youngworth passed away. He and his wife were from Germany, and she couldn't even speak English. Their two boys wanted more than farming, so they left their aged mother there on the farm alone. I remember there was electricity to the pumps on that farm, but the old couple actually never wanted electricity in the house. My dad ran a line from the pump house to the house so Mrs. Youngworth could have a light in the kitchen. That was the only bulb in the house. She was a little bitty thing, so Dad hung a string for her to pull to turn the light on. At night she got up on a chair and then onto the table and unscrewed that light bulb. She didn't think the electricity went off just because you turned the bulb off.

They had forty acres on one place we worked, the Youngworth place, and there were big oak trees. In the fall, Dad looked for one that had a beehive in it. We'd cut it down, rob it of its honey and then cut it up for firewood. When I helped with that, it meant I was on the end of an eight foot crosscut saw. Dad pulled, then I pulled, till we were about out of breath - and if you do that for a while - you _will_ get out of breath. One time Dad said to me, "Son, I don't mind you riding that saw, but do you have to drag your feet?"

Roy Griswald was a great boss. I chopped a lot of cotton in those days, and when we worked for him, we were paid for the week's work on Saturday afternoons. He always had a big washtub full of Cokes, or R.C. Colas or other soft drinks, in bottles back then of course, all iced down. A lot of times there were fellows in the pay line other than his workers. Those guys were there just to get a cold drink and ask the boss for a job. Some of them were so desperate for a job, they offered to work for less.

One time, I remember it very well, this guy kept pestering Roy for a job, but first, I need to say that my dad kept a file in his back pocket to keep the hoe sharp, and he kept the water jug on each end of the row in the shade. Now that helped. I was pretty wiry and strong, and I could chop just as many rows of cotton as my dad, and he could chop as many acres of cotton in a day as anyone that ever walked in that field; ever – ever.

Anyhow, one day that guy said to Roy, "How much are you paying that kid? Does he chop as much cotton as a man? What are you giving him? Fifteen cents an hour? I got three kids at home that need to eat. I'll work for a dime an hour, and I'll chop just as much cotton as anybody."

He kept pestering Roy like that while he was busy trying to write out checks, and finally Roy looked up and said, "Mister, I'll make you a deal. I'll hire you and if you'll come Monday morning and work alongside…" that guy had called me a kid, but Roy said, "…if you'll work alongside of this man and chop as much cotton as cleanly as he does, then you're hired, and you'll get as much as any man here. But, I'm the boss and I'm the inspector, and if your cotton is not spaced the eleven inches apart like I want, and if there's any grass around any of them, they're not as clean as his, then you're working that day for nothing."

That guy said, "Oh, that's a deal."

Some of the men in the line said, "Mister, you think you're going to chop as much cotton as that boy? Well, you're going to be working for nothing. We can't keep up with him." They talked him out of trying. He didn't even come back.

When the farm workers all got paid, they'd go to town and head for Nickel Pay Less, a grocery store that had everything else; actually, it was more of a general store. People came in to cash their last checks and pay their grocery bill. And, when you paid your bill up, you got a nickel candy bar for free. Everybody looked forward to Saturday.

One time while we were working for Roy, we had a horse, Old Fred. I really don't know how that came about, he might have been on the place when we got there. Most all the time I was growing up we had a dog, and it wasn't necessarily our dog, it might just wander onto our place. Dad was an animal man, and he would take it in. His dog always had a place to sleep outside, and he always had chores too.

We had one dog that was half chow and half collie. He had a black tongue like a chow, but his features were more like a collie, so we called him Collie. He was very obedient, and he just loved my dad. Dad would put him in the saddle on Old Fred and send him down to the back side of two hundred acres, and he'd bring all the cattle up – him and Old Fred. That was a good thing because in some places the Johnson grass grew higher than a horse's head, and the seeds got down your neck and into your shoes and into your pockets, and you had to wear leather chaps because the leaves of that grass would cut your pants.

Collie rode in the saddle down there, and if one of the cattle wouldn't come up, or if one of them strayed off some, that dog jumped off the saddle and went and bit his ears or feet. Collie and Fred drove them up the lane, and it was a narrow lane, around the corner, and up to the corral without a person having to go. They never missed a cow or a calf. Dad had trained them to do that. He was good at training animals.

One time Roy's friend, a man by the name of Lopez, pastured a little buckskin horse out on the place. Mr. Lopez was Portuguese, and he lived in Visalia and was a lawyer. The horse, her name was Nancy, had been ridden, but it hadn't been trained much. Dad taught that buckskin mare the difference between a steer and a heifer. You could stand that little mare by the gate without anyone on her, and as the cattle came through, she'd make sure the heifers went in one pen and the steers in the other. The thing about Nancy was, she wouldn't do that if she didn't have a bridle and saddle on. If she didn't, she'd just stand there, but when you put that bridle and saddle on, she thought she was in charge, and she separated the boys from the girls.

Another thing, a lot of people couldn't get a horse to take medicine if they had colic or something. But my Dad could. He'd get a bottle of something he'd mixed up, paregoric and something, and he'd get that horse by the nose, lift his head up and put that quart bottle in his mouth, and that horse gulped it down. Anybody else try that, and the horse jerked their head away at the first taste of that sour stuff, and they wouldn't take anymore. The way Dad did it, they took their medicine.

Later on, he took some of the animals he trained to the county fairs around there. You know how big a Clydesdale or Percheron is. They have hooves that are thick and big around. Dad took a regular apple box, and to reinforce the corners of it, he put a 1 by 1 inch board in each one. The way he did that, the box wasn't any bigger, and of course, the crowd never knew it was reinforced. He'd hold up the box to show them the size of it, and then he'd hold up the hoof of one of the horses to show the size of it. He had trained those big, big horses to get up on that box. They put one front hoof in a far corner, then the other, then put their other feet up and stood on that box. Their hooves would be overlapped along the edge of the box.

Dad trained one of those big brahma bulls to perform at rodeos. The bull was white with just a little bit of black in the tufts of his hair. Dad fed him a little bit of cotton seed cake, and it made his coat so shiny. Dad groomed him and polished his horns and on top of them he put little caps of brass that he could polish too. So, that bull was a show case himself.

At that time there was a beer company out of San Diego called Aztec Brewing, and they had a big white Cadillac convertible with their signs on the sides of it. Dad trained that bull to jump over that Cadillac convertible. A man drove it down one side of the arena real slow, and that big old bull, now he must have weighed a ton, jumped over it. Dad and the bull ran across the arena, and when that car came by, he jumped over it again. That act would bring a real crowd.

Dad was kind to his animals. One time we were at a rodeo in Visalia watching a calf roping event. This one rider's horse made a mistake and missed the time and was disqualified. The man took the rope and started beating the horse across the head. Dad was handling the gate and when he saw that, it made him so mad, he grabbed a coil of rope and went out and knocked that man's hat off with it. "You don't treat your horse like that," he yelled and walked away. After the guy picked his hat up, he stomped across the arena ready for a fist fight. Dad just popped him in the face with the rope one time. The fist fight didn't happen.

Anyway, back to the farm. Mr. Griswald had twenty-three acres across the creek, Cameron Creek, which cut through his two hundred acres on an angle. That land across the creek got flooded every year, and it brought Johnson grass and its seed with it. One year, Mr. Griswald said, "We're not getting anything on that twenty-three acres back there. Why don't we get some hogs and turn them in on those back acres?"

So, he added a few hogs, and Dad learned how to get rid of the Johnson grass by having them. He learned if you dig deep enough you find that Johnson grass has long succulent roots, and they get big, as big around as a man's thumb, and they have joints in them. Hogs like those roots. Dad had a plow that went deep, so he plowed down, I'd guess about three feet, and turned those roots up. We let the hogs in, and they ate them all. The Johnson grass was gone, and the next year we planted a crop.

I think I was fifteen when I took Old Fred and helped drive cattle from Visalia to a forty thousand acre ranch in Arroyo Valley. It was, I guess, thirty or thirty-five miles up there. Oscar Warren had a herd of cattle that he wanted taken up there for the summer. That is a higher altitude up there, and that means better grazing in the summertime.

When you're driving a herd of cattle like that, you better keep up your side of it because, every driveway, they're gonna want to get in it, and maybe tear up a flower garden or something on the way. At every intersection they have three ways to go, but they'll go this way or that way, but not the right way. That makes it a tricky job. We drove them that thirty-five miles or so in one day. I was pretty tired by the time we got through.

I was left up there with those cattle. They were fenced in, but on forty thousand acres? I had been given Old Fred, some sacks of dry oats that had been poisoned, a shovel, a hammer, and a bunch of staples. I had an old boot that was cut off and had a wooden bottom so I could hang it on my saddle to carry staples to repair fences.

I'd get up in the morning and go around looking for ground squirrel holes and put out those poison oats; if a cow or a horse steps in one of those holes, they can break a leg. After that, I'd start working the fence line. At the end of the day there would be a little cabin or some sort of shelter where there was food, and if it wasn't near a creek, there was usually a barrel of water. Sometimes the shelter was nothing more than a rocky outcrop that I could put my bedroll under. I'd put a hobble on Old Fred and go to bed.

I was up there probably a month, maybe six weeks, but it seemed like two years. The only person I saw was a cowboy riding through. We talked some, but mostly about those squirrel holes; I asked him how much poisoned oats I ought to use. But, you know, I don't remember being particularly lonesome. There wasn't that much going on at home; there wasn't any entertainment of any kind, and we didn't do a lot of visiting between us. While I was up there, I could talk to Old Fred anytime. I don't remember ever talking to my dad about what went on up there.

I never got paid a dime for doing that. All the pay went to my dad, whether I was chopping cotton or picking cotton or irrigating or anything else, almost all the money went to the family. That's the way it was back then. It was so hard for families to get by, us kids had to help.

School Days

When we came to California I had just finished the sixth grade. Dad worked for Mr. Swearingen during the winter months that first year while Rudy and Bill and I went to Union School, a two room school about two miles away. Mr. and Mrs. Swearingen had three boys. The oldest one was Eldon, the next one they named Weldon and the next one was Aldon, who was about the same age as Bill. Those boys joined us, and there we'd be, all six of us walking to school, some of us talking about our school assignments, and some of us throwing rocks or chasing rabbits or something.

I finished the seventh grade there while we were on the Swearingen farm, but it didn't do me any good. I really should have been in the eighth grade. I was at the top of the class, not because I was so smart, but Oklahoma had a higher standard of teaching than California at that time. That was because of the sudden increase in population. Besides, I think it was because Aunt Rene and Aunt Alta had taught me so well that I was ahead of the other kids in my grade. Some of the older kids thought I was teacher's pet because she always called on me to go to the blackboard and explain things.

Later on I wasn't a good student. In fact, I was a very poor student, especially in English. I don't mean to say I was a bad student because I was mischievous or in trouble, but really, I wasn't a disciplined learner and, too, there was always work. Dad wanted us to go to school, but sometimes work <u>had</u> to come first. We <u>had</u> to earn money. I remember that in my freshman year, I sometimes irrigated cotton or crop all night long and went to school all day long. So I wasn't very alert. If school wasn't going, Dad worked where us boys could work fulltime. Working like that was necessary for us to eat and get by. You know, a man picking cotton only made about $3 a day, so Dad needed our help.

There was a lady who lived not an eighth of a mile from us, and she cut my hair. She only charged twenty-five cents. If you went to Farmersville it was seventy-five cents. I rode my bike up to her house, and when I got there, if she was cutting someone's hair, she'd say, "Travis, while you're waiting, would you go out and water my tomatoes?" She had a little hand pump out beside her house, and so I'd do that or some other little chore she might have.

The only shoes I had to wear to school were tennis shoes, and one day she told me that I shouldn't be wearing those shoes. "They'll ruin your feet" she said. Dad had bought me a pair of oxfords, but he insisted I have a cowboy heel put on them because I rode the horse a lot. He didn't want one of my feet getting through that stirrup and maybe wind up getting drug. I couldn't wear those shoes to school; the kids would have made fun of me. That lady sort of got attached to me and bought me a pair of oxfords. My folks thought I only had tennis shoes, so I had to go by her house every morning on my way to school to get my shoes. She'd set them out on the porch, and I'd go by and change. I've never forgotten that. She was a real kind lady.

The next school year Dad got a job picking cotton at a big farm up at Chowchilla, so we moved up there. All the farm workers lived in tents; there were probably ten or twelve tents right close to the farmhouse and barn. It might be cold and overcast in the Central Valley, and all the buildings might have icicles hanging on them, but when it warmed up just a little, the men were out there pulling bolls.

On one edge of the farm they had a two room school. I can't remember the name of it, but it was a little tiny school with about ten children in the lower grades and probably ten in the seventh and eighth. I was in the eighth. From the tents where we lived, we just walked across the farm, over a blacktop road and we were at school.

Our teacher for the sixth, seventh and eighth grades got

sick with pneumonia, and another teacher came in for a week or two, and then she left. There was nobody to teach those grades. There was a Mexican girl my age, Lupe, and they had the two of us teaching the upper grades. They lost the teacher for the younger children a little later, and most of them were of Mexican descent and didn't know any English, so Lupe went over to teach them. We did that for about a month.

Lupe and I were like sweethearts. We'd walk together arm in arm, close to a half mile, back to the tents. Her mother always had her big old cast iron stove burning wood. On the way home in the wintertime when it was cold and there was frost in the fields, I knew I could stop there, warm up, and get a hot tortilla and some beans off the back of the stove.

I didn't even finish the school year there at Chowchilla. Dad got a job back in Tulare County, so we moved, and Rudy and I went to school in Farmersville. There wasn't a high school there, but there was a good grammar school. First grade had a room, second had a room; third and fourth were together, fifth and sixth were, and the seventh and eighth. The seventh grade was such a snap that I didn't learn much, but when I got into the eighth grade, I kind of had to work at it some.

George Snowden was principal, and he also taught seventh and eighth grades. He was an absolute perfect teacher. He was dedicated. I'll tell you just how dedicated he was. The school district couldn't pay his salary for two years, but he taught school, was the janitor, cut the firewood for the steam radiators in the winter, kept the grass mowed and the fences around the school yard repaired. He got up of a morning and delivered the Fresno Bee and the Visalia Times Delta newspapers all around the countryside and got to school in time to get the radiators hot in the wintertime. And he didn't get a penny from the school for two years.

Now, I don't mean he didn't get some benefits. Clyde Karr, who was a world champion cowboy, had what I would call a mansion in those days, a big yellow house not too far from where our tent was. Mr. Snowden's wife took care of Clyde's aged mother, and they got to live with her for nothing. Right next door on the east side, on about eighty acres was Marshall's Dairy, so the Snowdens got all their milk and cream and butter free, and other farmers chipped in with food. But those few pennies he made delivering newspapers was all the salary he got for two years.

The next year I started high school in Exeter, a nice little town only four miles from Farmersville. Some of the kids from Farmersville rode the same school bus, and they told me that Mr. Snowden was getting paid at that time. I don't know if they ever caught up for those two years, but I was glad to hear they were at least paying him a salary. All of us who graduated that school loved and respected him. At a school reunion years later, we all said we graduated from the "George Snowden University." He was a wonderful man.

When they built a new elementary school in Farmersville, they named it after him.

I took wood shop the year I started school in Exeter, because I didn't know anything about it, and I was interested in it. I learned to use a carpenter's square, a T square, a hand saw and a wood saw. I had a great teacher, and I wish I could remember his name. Oh, he was such a generous wonderful man. Some of us boys really appreciated his wife, too. She was our study hall teacher. She knew which ones of us were up irrigating all night, so she sat us at the back of the classroom where we could lay our heads on the desks and sleep for a few minutes. She understood and was kind enough to let us rest a bit.

We had to build a piece of furniture in wood shop during our freshman year. My teacher had a drawing for a bedside nightstand that was the cheapest, smallest thing I could build and pass the class. I didn't have all the money I needed to buy the lumber and sandpaper and other things we had to have; I only had four dollars, and the cost for the project was going to be seven dollars. When I told the teacher, he said, "We can buy this piece of mahogany and these mahogany planks, and there will be plenty of sandpaper left over, so we won't charge you for that, and that boy has more varnish than he's going to need...." and so on. That's the way he helped me build that night stand for only four dollars. I put seven coats of varnish on it. It finished out so good that I got an A. It sat in a tent for six years, and it's been hauled to lots of other places over the years. My daughter has it in her home right now. It's still in good condition and that's because I had such a good teacher.

That shop teacher taught me enough so that we put a floor in the tent for Mom the next summer. It was a big tent, forty by forty, that was our living room, dining room, kitchen and bedroom for Mom and Dad, and there was a smaller tent out back for us three older boys.

My dad and I gathered enough apple and prune boxes for the lumber to build the floor. We didn't have any tools but a saw and hammer and a square, and we did it all by hand. We raised the floor up on the edges. Where we lived in the valley, in the wintertime, icicles will hang for weeks, and you won't see the sun for weeks, and there will be thick old fog and cold. Raising the edges a little kept some of the cold out.

At first, Mom didn't like that wooden floor. She could keep that dirt floor just like cement. She'd wet it down a couple of times a day, and all the dust just went right on out. But with that floor we built, all the dust went down through the cracks. Made out of apple crates and boxes, it wasn't tight. She complained a little about it, but when wintertime came with frost and cold and the ground got frozen, and she didn't have to walk on it, boy, she changed. She praised that floor then.

We put it in during the summer before I started my sophomore year. I think that was when Dad went to work for Hathaway Nursery where they grew trees. He worked for them two or three years. When we moved to that place, I was eligible to go to high school in Visalia, Redwood High, the only high school there at the time.

A friend, Bobby Elam, rode the same bus into Visalia. He was a sophomore too, and we were both farm kids. His family lived about a quarter of a mile from us. They had a dairy farm with beautiful Jersey cattle, and I mean beautiful. They had a grade A barn that was much better than the tent we lived in. Bob and I sat together on the bus, and we both were going into agriculture, we took shop together, we had the same P.E. period, he played handball well, and I did too. So with all that we had in common, we paired off and became good friends.

Mrs. Mitchell was our American Literature teacher, and she was a good one. I was not at all interested in poetry before Mrs. Mitchell's class. Bob was inspired to try to write poetry, and so was I. We got interested because of the poem *The Cremation of Sam Magee*. We really studied that poem, and I think we memorized parts of it. One line I've remembered and tried to live by all my years is: A promise made is a debt unpaid.

Art Timothy was a young athletics teacher and was also my public speaking teacher and my sports coach, the different sports. He was probably thirty years old when I was in my junior year. I was very reluctant to talk in front of a class, but Mr. Timothy encouraged me, and I got better at it. I never excelled in athletics, so I wasn't on any team. During P.E. he would challenge us to a game of handball. Since I was thin and quick, it was really hard for him to beat me at handball. When he was busy, Bob and I played.

Another one of my friends was Lee Hicks. Neither one of us was very good at sports, especially at offense, so Coach Holiday had us sitting on the bench a lot. The boys P.E. class was near the girls P.E. class, and sometimes girls came over and talked to us while Lee and I were sitting on the bench. One girl came over one day and said, "Would you boys like to meet me after second period tomorrow?

I'm going to run away from home, and I'd like you to walk me out to Mineral King Highway."

I said, "We'll get in trouble if we do that. I'm supposed to be in history class at that time."

Lee said, "I'll go."

I didn't think much of the plan, but when Lee said what he did, I agreed to go along. The next morning when she got off the bus, she didn't go to class. She went off on the road going toward Mineral King Highway and put a gunny sack full of her clothes into a dry irrigation ditch. After second period, we knew we weren't going to be playing, so we took her up to the Mineral King road. While we were walking up there, I don't know how the conversation began, but she said she was being mistreated at home. Her mother had remarried, and her step-father was mistreating her.

During the conversation as we were walking along, she talked about her and one of the other boys in our school. She said they slipped out to the barn sometimes, and she told us stuff I had never heard of before. None of us guys talked like that, and when she did, it was a surprise. We walked her out to the highway like she asked, and I never knew what happened to her after that.

Rosella was my confidant. After that girl told us what had been going on in her life, and Lee and I helped her, I just couldn't share that with my dad. I shared it with Rosella. I said, "What do you do about it anyway? What causes it, and why would a girl want to reveal it?" Rosella had to explain all that to me. She had always been our confidant, Nurney and me and Rudy. We'd get in a fight with a neighbor kid or be out with some girl, and she'd say, "Now, don't let your dad know about this." I knew I could trust her.

That year I was also buddies with Bill and Jack Phipps who had gone to the Farmersville School like me. Bill and I became friends when we were in the eighth grade. When I moved to Visalia, we were sophomores, and Jack was a couple of grades higher, a senior I think. We became really good friends.

They were interested in electronics. In fact, after World War II, Jack started a radio and television shop in Farmersville; he was that good. Anyhow, they taught me how to make a crystal set radio. We took a Quakers Oats box and wound it with copper wire, got a little germanium crystal with a cat whisker, and an earphone and we made a radio. I think I spent something like two and a half dollars for the whole thing. There was no electricity required; we got sound out of the radio waves in the air.

It didn't have audio, only a single earphone. When you were listening, the rest of the family couldn't hear. I'd give it to Dad, and he'd listen for a while, and then somebody else, and Mom would listen during the day. Usually, we only got two stations. At night, we could get the Fresno station, forty miles away, and KFI in Los Angeles, 640 on the dial, and the strongest station on the west coast. KFI had, I forget what it was, something like a thousand watts, but enough so we got it at night. That's when you got better reception, especially if it was damp. I strung a big copper wire from a prune tree over to another tree and back to the house in an L shape, so we could get a station from both directions. Every once in a while on a damp night, we'd get another station, XERB which was Rosarito Beach down in Mexico. They had a real strong station. The biggest part of the music they played was American music, mostly Western. Their audience was mainly Americans because very few people in Mexico had radios. The owners of that station, I found out later, were Americans. They couldn't get a station license in our area for one as strong, that had as many kilowatts as KFI, but if you went over the border, just below Tijuana, you could get a license for any amount of power you wanted. It was strong, but still, we couldn't get that station all the time, just on a damp night.

There wasn't much in Farmersville for young folks to do, but they had a little boxing ring, and on Friday nights, they'd get two kids of the same size and let them box till one of them gave out or was knocked out. If you won, you might get a coke or candy bar or something like that. I wasn't very forceful, but I was quick and sinewy and strong, so I could hold my own pretty good. A few Friday nights I got my nose bleeding though.

I belonged to a Boy Scout Troup when I was in high school, and I wish I could remember that scoutmaster's name, he was just the nicest guy. A big tall man, he was a farmer and lived just east of town. In 1939 he took us to the World Fair Exposition at Treasure Island in San Francisco Bay. Those of us who earned enough credits got to go on that trip, and that was a strong initiative to earn the next merit badge.

There was probably ten of us boys that went. The trip up there was quite an experience because our transportation was the scoutmaster's farm truck. He and his assistant were in the cab, with all of us boys in the back. It was a stake bed, just wooden stakes and slats. We just piled our bed rolls in the back, and then we all squeezed in. We camped in the Charles Lee Sheldon Regional Park up in the hills back of Berkeley. We went down in the daytime to see the fair; went over the San Francisco Bay Bridge to Treasure Island. That island was made from the spoils of dredging the bay and now has water deep enough for big ships to go in.

The scoutmaster found little chores we could do to make a dollar or maybe fifty cents. Because I had a little training, he got me a job taking care of the Royal Mounted Police horses. They had a portable stable, kind of like a barn, where I fed the horses and cleaned up after them. I could make twenty-five cents doing that. It was a pretty good job for me because after I got my chores done, I was free to wander around and see the sights.

They had pictures of the dancing girls all over, pretty risqué for a kid like me, but I really wanted to go see the show called Folies Bergere. It cost a dime, and I had a dime, but when I went up to pay my way, the lady said I had to be accompanied by a grown up. I went back to the stable and was sitting there in the shade sulking when a member of the Royal Mounted Police came up to me and said, "What are you doing here? Why aren't you enjoying the fair?"

"Well, I wanted to go see the Folies Bergere, but the lady wouldn't let me in."

He started reaching into his pocket and said, "Didn't you have the money?"

"Yeah, but she said I had to have an adult with me."

"Come on," he said. And he took me to the show and paid for his ticket and mine too, and we went in to see the show together. That's how I got to see the dancing girls. But, really, there wasn't that much to see.

Years and years later, my wife, Katherine, and I discovered that we were both at the fair on the same day. We didn't meet then; it was some time before that happened. She had come down with a neighbor girl and her family. They didn't stay overnight; they just came down for the day. Katherine told me she had a dime when she got to the fair. I told her when I got to the fair, I had a dime too.

PART III
ALL GROWN UP
1940-1943

A Good Job

My step-brother Nurney, had moved up to Watsonville, gotten married and gone to work at a slaughterhouse owned by Ed Peterson. Because of Nurney, I got an offer of a good job. For one thing, it wasn't on the farm and for another thing, it was twice the wages I'd be making on the farm. So, I left high school a short time before I graduated and went to Watsonville to go to work in a slaughterhouse.

The reason Nurney wanted me to come to work there was because he had done so well. Peterson had about sixty employees, but he had taken Nurney, who wasn't going to finish high school, and put him in this position and that position and worked him through the line until he was able to pass the test for Amalgamated Meat Cutters and Butcher Workers of North America Union. That meant he was eligible to get into the union and make forty dollars a week. That was a lot of money in those days.

The only way I had to get there was hitchhiking. I started out at Visalia and the trip to Watsonville was close to two hundred miles. When I left I had a dime in my pocket; ten cents is all I had. I picked some oranges and some grapes along the road, so I was surviving. One night I decided to sleep under a big billboard. I didn't sleep much, but as soon as it was light I got out and got my thumb up. I made it to Madera, and while I was at a service station, I got a ride with a cattle truck. I met the driver in the station, and we were talking; I told him I was going to Watsonville, that I had a job offered to me over there.

"What doing?" he asked.

"It's in a slaughterhouse."

"Ed Peterson? That's where I'm going and I'd like some company. Climb in."

He was driving a big truck, a Fageol truck. Those trucks were made in Oakland, California starting in about 1910. They were famous because they had gas engines. The back wheels, on the truck we were in, were driven by chains. It was a double decker and was loaded with sheep and calves. As we were coming down the Pacheco Grade, the brakes failed. We were going too fast, and that makes it difficult to make a curve - and we didn't. The sheep were on the top deck, and out they went. We scattered sheep all along the highway. We finally got down to a place where there were some small willow trees, and the driver got the truck stopped by running over some of them. It wrecked the radiator on the truck, but we were okay.

There was a fire station about a quarter mile away, and some of the men came down and towed us up to the station. The truck was repaired later that day, and we went on to Watsonville that evening.

Later, I got to know the driver pretty well because he not only drove trucks for Peterson, he repaired fence around the slaughterhouse. The company had cattle lots, with calves in one lot, bulls in another, steers in another and pigs in another. So, that truck driver could keep busy just repairing and keeping the fences up. I saw him every now and then in the cafeteria.

I had the job when I stepped off the bus; Nurney had arranged it for me with Ed Peterson. Nurney and his wife also let me stay with them.

The first job I had was in the killing chute, knocking

calves in the head, then the big cows and bulls. Then I went out on the killing floor where you hang the sheep by their back feet and cut their throats; then I cut pigs' throats and ran them through scalding water. From there I went to the gut room, took the guts from the animal, turned them inside out and cleaned the ones that were used to make the casings for sausage. It was a stinky job. I worked for a couple of weeks with a Mr. Gutierrez who had been doing that for a long time, and he taught me that job. He was held in almost reverence in that whole building because no one else would have that stinky job.

Another thing about Mr. Gutierrez – he was the first to invent the turn signal, but he never got around to getting a patent on it. His turn signal was an arm with an attached bicycle reflector that hung outside the car. Inside was a metal disc that indicated the positions the driver might want. There was a pulley and a lever with a small cable that ran through a hole in the door frame and activated the arm. You pulled it up to the first notch if you were going to stop, to the second notch if you were going to turn left and the last notch if you were going to turn right. The Peterson Company had five or six sausage trucks that delivered to all the markets in three or four counties and a couple of big trucks that hauled in livestock to be butchered. Every one of them had Mr. Gutierrez' homemade turn signals.

Anyway, I worked right on up through the sausage picking room, through the hide cellar and then into the sausage kitchen for two or three months where I made lard and cracklins, sausage links, wieners and bologna. Then I went onto the cutting floor where the beef halves were cut into the different meat cuts. I went right through those jobs, thanks to some good mentors along the way, especially two older German fellows who took an interest in a young man.

From the cutting floor, I went into the office and did the billing for everything that went out on the delivery trucks to the different meat markets.

The owner of the slaughterhouse also owned a meat market, M&M Market there in Watsonville, and one over in Carmel, Kip's Meat Market. He sent us trainees into one of those stores. He offered me a job in the M&M Market cutting their steaks, pork chops, loins, and so on, and I went to work there. I didn't make much money during the time I was training at the slaughterhouse. I started out at twelve dollars a week and got up to fifteen, and when I worked at meeting the public in the meat market I was making eighteen dollars a week. I only worked at M&M for a month before I decided to go back home and finish school.

I think it was about Christmastime when I went back. I learned quite a bit while I was away, but I regretted not finishing school. Too, I was living with Nurney and his wife, and I wasn't very comfortable there. I started back to school for my final semester in January, 1940 and graduated in May.

After I finished school, I went back to Watsonville and went to work for Pio Codiga. He and his wife owned a little corner grocery store with a meat market and one gas pump. That was in the days when you pumped the gas up by hand, and there was a little cylinder with marks on it that showed the gallons. Nobody ever bought more than three or four gallons because gasoline was eleven or twelve cents a gallon.

The Codigas treated me like I was their child. They had two little boys; one was about a year and a half old and the other about six; Richard was the baby, and the other boy was Billy. On Saturday night the Codigas would want to go to a dance or bowling or to a movie or something, and I would baby-sit. And every Saturday night I had dinner with them before they left. They were Swiss-Italian, and Ann cooked that type of food, like polenta and big salads, and she was a good cook. So, I looked forward to a real good meal every Saturday night. Pio, like all his people from the old country, kept a gallon of wine sitting by the table, and they had a little bit of wine with their meal. He treated me just like I was his peer; he'd pour me a little bit of wine too.

When I turned eighteen, Codiga said, "We're going to celebrate your birthday. We're going to go bowling and we're going to..." He said we were going to do this and that; I can't remember all he said we were going to do. He took me in their 1936 Pontiac four-door Sedan. Boy, that Pontiac was something. On the way to the bowling alley, he took a beer, and he gave me one. By the end of the evening I had smoked a package of cigarettes and drank enough beer that I didn't know my head from my...well.... The next morning when I woke up, oh, I was feeling so bad. I didn't live far from the market, so I didn't even start the car; I just walked over to try and clear my head a little. I was usually at the store at seven o'clock.

Anyhow, that morning after we celebrated my birthday, when I got to work, Pio said, "Son, you are late."

"Yes sir," I said, "I walked to work. I was too sick to drive. Boss, why did you do that to me?"

He said, "Do you think you'd like the taste of beer this morning, or do you want a cigarette?"

"I can't even stand the thought of the smell of them."

"That's why I did that. I've been hooked on cigarettes all my life, and I didn't want you hooked on them or beer."

It worked. It took. I never smoked, and I never drank again - ever.

After Work

After I moved back to Watsonville, I met Mary Kostares, a beautiful girl, and I asked her to go skating with me, and she agreed. We went skating several times. One time she told me that her family went to the Nazarene church. That was the church my family and I always went to, so I started going there. That's where I met my future wife, Mary's sister, Katherine. It was a good while before we started dating, because she was only fourteen at that time.

Katherine's folks had a little rooming house; she called it a hotel. Her parents were Christos Kostaras and Mabel Harms Kostaras. Besides their own living quarters, they had probably eight rooms they rented out. When I rented a room there, I got to know the rest of the family. There were four children, Frederick was a senior in high school, Mary a junior, Angie, a sophomore, and Katherine a freshman. Now, I think that's the way it went.

As I said, it was some time before Katherine and I dated. I had a couple of girlfriends before her, but there was nobody I was serious about at all; she was my first real girlfriend. Even after I took her skating a few times, and to church, riding on the back of my bike, I dated a girl who was named Miss California at the Golden Gate International World's Fair. She was a Slavonian girl and a beauty. She was probably a year older than me.

A much younger me

I learned to drive and drove a car on the farm, but I didn't get a license until I was in Watsonville. I don't remember exactly when that was, but it was there that I bought my first car. It was a pretty car, an eight cylinder Ford New York Roadster. It was a convertible with a white top and beautiful imitation leather upholstery. It had a rumble seat in the back that folded up.

I taught that beauty queen to drive. And pretty soon, she thought she fell in love with me; oh, she was infatuated. But, I wasn't serious about any girl at that time.

Whoever I could have the most fun with, was the one I dated. I never did learn to dance, but I would go to the dances. A girl would come with their boyfriend, and he might get to dancing with some other girl too many times or do something else the girl didn't like, and she'd come to me and say, "Will you take me home?" Of course, I did, and that happened more than once. Sometimes I made a date out of it. I took Miss California home a lot. She was very cuddly

Katherine had a really close girlfriend, whose family were Basque Spaniards. I knew her father; I had worked with him at the slaughterhouse. One time, after Katherine and I started going together, the girlfriend missed the bus; she lived about five miles out in Green Valley. I had gotten off work and gone back to my room, and the girls were doing their lessons or whatever in her family's living quarters. It wasn't long till Katherine came and asked me, "Would you take my friend home? She didn't get there in time to catch the bus." I agreed.

At that time, the stations used to give out little stickers when you bought gasoline, and I had stickers all over my little roadster. Everybody knew whose car that was. If they saw that car, they knew it belonged to Bud Evans. Back then everybody called me Bud because Travis wasn't a very popular name. In fact, I never knew of another Travis before; it was a long, long time till I heard of anyone else with that name.

Anyhow, I was taking Katherine's friend home, and she snuggled up, and I asked her if it was okay to park for a while. We were sitting there talking when another car came by. It stopped just down the road and then backed up. Those stickers gave me away. One of the passengers rolled down the window and hollered, "Bud, it's awful late and I don't want you parking out here with my sister." So, I started the car and took her on home.

The next day I found out that when her brother got home later, he bawled that girl out just something terrible. He said if he ever caught her parking again, he was telling their parents. And, when I saw Katherine, the next day she bawled me out something terrible too and wouldn't hardly speak to me for a while. So, I didn't get away with anything.

But we got past that, and before long it was just Katherine. I'd take her to church and to the movies. There was a movie theater right across the street from the boarding house, but the best one was down about a block and a half. Mostly we went to the movies so we could neck, I think, but now, she wouldn't want to admit that. There was a little plaza where a band played on Saturday nights. If I didn't have fifty cents for the movies, we'd go and listen to the music. Sometimes we'd go down there and sit around in the park for a while. On the way home, we might stop by a hamburger stand and get a ten cent hamburger and a five cent coke and split them. I began writing silly little poems when Katherine and I were dating, and I've been writing poems ever since.

My boss, Pio, and I were good buddies all this time; we'd get up in the morning and go duck or pheasant hunting. His wife, Ann, would open the store at seven on those mornings, and we'd get back about eight or so.

Then it got to where he'd go duck hunting one day, and I'd open the store, then the next day, he'd open the store, and I'd go. Katherine would get up before daylight to go with me. It was still dark when we got there. She was in school, and I had to get her back in time for school. We opened the store at seven in the morning, and school started at eight-thirty, so that was no problem. She rowed my little skiff while I shot the ducks. It took some talking, but I finally got permission for her to go fishing with me in the evening after her school and household chores. We'd go out and try to catch a fish, but it was mostly to be together.

Hank

All the time I worked in Watsonville and lived at the boarding house, when I was off, I went down to Santa Cruz, which is only seventeen miles, and visit with a friend. I first met him in June of '40. His full name was Henry Hugo Haquist, but everyone called him Hank. He was an old Norwegian gentleman. He only had one leg; the other one was shot off in World War I. He built himself a crutch that fit just under that stump and went up to his arm pit. Hank was very innovative and the most conservative person I ever knew. He was also a very kindly man, and I liked talking to him.

Hank had a little fishing boat, and he'd sit on the dock and bait hooks. He used about three hundred pounds of bait, which had to be cut to the right size to bait five thousand hooks. Well, anybody can bait a hook, so I'd sit there with him and bait hooks, and we'd talk about fishing, and navigations and so on. He knew a lot about fishing and was very patient and a good, good teacher. He taught me to read a compass and a chart and so on.

It wasn't too long until Hank said, "Come and go fishing with me when you're off this weekend."

I went fishing some with Mom and Dad and caught fresh fish out of a creek somewhere out of Ada; but I didn't, and I don't, have much patience catching fish one at a time. The first ocean fishing I did was with Hank on his little twenty-eight foot boat called the Fred, an old boat built in 1904.

When I took that first fishing trip with Hank on the Fred, I had learned enough that I wasn't anxious or afraid. I put the gear in the water and pulled fish, with Hank there to instruct me how to do every little thing. We used anchovies and sardines for bait. He showed me how to make the bait swim so that it looked like a live fish; how even the speed of the boat could help make the bait swim naturally, and that made your production better. There's a lot of science goes into fishing.

I went with Hank several times and learned more every trip. There were several patient, friendly helpful men, mostly Italian, there on the dock, who also helped me learn about ocean fishing. It was quite a task for a dumb farm teenager to mix and try to learn something as foreign as commercial fishing from a bunch of mostly uneducated Italian and Portuguese fishermen who barely spoke English. But, those Genovese Italians were patient, generous, kind and willing to help anyone; they taught me mostly by example; I just watched them. The dock master, Dad Lyons, taught me a lot too. Everybody loved and depended on him. I made lifetime friends while I was learning from those men.

Back then we didn't have a lot to fish with. We had a wicker basket with a little twine cord in it, and at five fathom we had a string tied around the cord, and at ten fathom another and so on, clear up to a hundred and fifty fathoms; at six feet to the fathom that was nine hundred feet of line. We'd have as much as a fifteen pound lead on the end. That lead was concave, and the bottom end was bell shaped, and we put a little bees' wax in the cavity. When we dropped the line to the ocean floor, and heaved it back, you knew how deep you'd been because of those marks on the line, and when you turned that lead over you could tell whether it dropped in black mud, sand, shale, green mud or whatever. All the deep canyons and so forth are green mud, and the sides of a canyon are sand or rocks, and then maybe at the top of it, it would be shale. The green mud was between the sand and the shale; that's how it is deposited by the currents. So, those tools helped to give you an idea of where you were, as well as the depth. Now, there are electronic devices called fathometers, or sounders, that show depth, ocean contours and even fish.

Our running lights and mast lights on the boat were kerosene. We didn't have a storage battery on the boat; the engine was hand cranked, it didn't have a starter and there was no spark plug. There were two pieces of iron with a mechanism that moved on a cam, and when it came up it made a spark. One side of the iron was grounded, the other was fired by a magneto, just like the ones on the old hand cranked telephones we had on the wall, and when those two pieces of iron made that spark, I'd gas it a little bit and here we'd go.

It was a very crude method of sailing, but later after I went to work for Hank, we went from Santa Cruz to San Diego and on into Mexico in that little boat with only a four inch compass and a coastal chart.

Sometime on those first fishing trips with Hank, I began to wonder whether I'd ever be able to make a living like that.

When Hank offered me a job a little later, I said, "I'd really like to try it on my own."

He said "Well, I've got a little boat and I'll sell it to you cheap."

"How much is cheap?" I asked.

"Oh, fifty dollars. Do you want to go look at it?"

So, we walked out to the end of the pier where there was a big warehouse, and there it was. Actually, at one time it had an outboard engine, but it had been converted into an inboard. It had a propeller shaft and a clutch so you could take it out of gear, but it had no reverse. It had a little sail and a pair of oars. That boat was called the Kitty.

"Hank," I said, "I've only got thirty dollars to my name. Will you trust me for the rest of it?"

He agreed, but about that time my brother Rudy came by to see me and he said, "I'll go in partners with you." He fished with me for a couple of weeks, and when he left, he left with me owing him twenty dollars. I don't think I ever did pay him back that twenty, but I took him enough crabs and fish through the years that he was more than paid back.

The motor the Kitty had was like one you'd have on a lawn mower. Once it got hot, and you turned it off to do your fishing, you couldn't get it started again. It had Reed valves, and if I had known enough about mechanics, I probably could have replaced those valves, or possibly just cleaned them and got it started. I wouldn't have had near the trouble I did if I had known more. When it wouldn't start, I had to put the sail up and take the oars and row. Actually, we didn't call them oars; we called them sweeps. They were about the same length as my height. So you stood up and pushed against them to row. The Kitty also had a removable mast and a sail that I used often to sail back to port in the afternoons.

When you are miles offshore, and a heavy wind comes up, and you've got to row against it, you get pretty tired. Rowing against that northwest wind in Monterey Bay, sometimes I wouldn't get back to the dock till dark. There were times when I would be completely exhausted by the time I got back.

Sometime that year I went back to work for Pio Codiga, and I guess I worked six or eight months before the war started.

World War II

Katherine's dad, Chris, and I became good friends. We both liked to hunt and fish. We did some ocean fishing, but only onshore because he got seasick. We also fished near-by lakes. We hunted ducks, geese, mud hens and pheasants, all with twelve gauge shotguns. Chris had given me an old double barrel shotgun.

Sometimes four or five of us would go hunting together. One time when a bunch of us were pigeon hunting up in the Santa Cruz Mountains above the little town of Aptos, Chris and I got to talking, and he asked me if Katherine and I had talked of marriage. I told him that we had, but we thought we'd wait till after she graduated. He said, "Whenever you are ready, you have my permission and also my blessing." I knew, by him saying that, how much he thought of me. And too, he told me things about his life that were confidential. I've never told anyone – not even Katherine.

That was a day I'll never forget. My future father-in-law more or less proposed to me, and that was the day the Japanese bombed Pearl Harbor. December 7, 1941.

Everyone in the bunch I was hunting with that day had a rifle and a pistol. If anyone needed help, he fired the pistol. One of the guys went back to the van for something, turned the radio on and heard the news. He fired his pistol, and we all went to see about it. That's when we heard about Pearl Harbor.

That day, we reacted like everyone else in the country did. We were shocked and saddened and angry, all up in arms about it; the whole area was. We had been living just a normal peaceful life when, all of a sudden, the Japanese farmers living near us were our enemies. There were a lot of different nationalities in our area including, Filipinos,

Portuguese, Slovakians, Italians, and so on. After war was declared, people became fearful of their neighbors - no matter their nationality.

Soon, Japanese families were being taken from their homes and put in what they called internment camps. I'm sure most of them were good people, but they were treated like criminals. The Japanese were hated and feared by most everybody. One of Katherine's teachers even told her class that all Japanese should be sent back to Japan.

Not only were we apprehensive about our neighbors, but being right on the coast, we were afraid of an attack. We were all on edge. Later in December of 1941, the Japanese sank an oil tanker, and I'm not sure when, but they also fired on a refinery just up the coast from Santa Barbara. After that we were more apprehensive than ever; it seemed like we were for a very long time.

Precautions were put into effect. Street lights weren't turned on, and window shades in your home had to be drawn. Cars weren't supposed to have their lights on. They had their headlights taped up except for a tiny slit. All a driver could see was a very little light so he could miss another driver coming down the street. All the coastal towns had rules like that.

The government started rationing some products including sugar, coffee, tires and gasoline. Why, you couldn't get a piece of meat without stamps; it was rationed too.

Nurney was already in the service when the war started. When conscription came along in 1939, I think, if a man wanted to sign up, he had a choice of which branch he wanted to go into. Nurney volunteered in the Navy.

It wasn't long after the war started that my brother Rudy was drafted into the army. Homer worked in the Civilian Conservation Corps before the war, so he went into a special Marine unit called the Seabees. It seemed like all my school buddies volunteered. It must have been January of '42 when I signed up with the Coast Guard. I took the original Coast Guard exam, and they put me down as a candidate for Officer Candidate School. I thought they would call me right away. I was so sure, I began to get things in order. I left the job with Pio Codiga so that he could hire another butcher to take my place, and I decided to give the Kitty and the trailer to my dad. I got ready to go.

One day, while I was waiting for the Coast Guard to call me, I went to see Pio. He said, "I've got a deal for you, Travis. The owner of the store in Aromas is getting old and he wants to retire." Aromas is a little town about fifteen miles east of Watsonville. Pio went on, "I could buy that store and meat market, and you could run it, but what I'd rather do is loan you the money to buy it, and you pay me out of the profits. We could set you up in business."

I said, "Pio, I've enlisted in the Coast Guard, and I can't be sure when they might call me."

"But this is an opportunity of a lifetime. I can buy that store and the inventory for three thousand dollars."

Of course, three thousand dollars sounded like three million to me. I didn't have ten dollars in my pocket. I told him I didn't think that would be fair. I said, "I have promised the U.S. government that I will go to war, and then

I'm going to promise you I'll pay off that debt? I don't think that's kosher."

So, I didn't do it, and that might have been a mistake, but looking back on the way things worked out, my career as a fisherman has meant so much more to me than being a merchant would have.

I knew the owner of another meat market and grocery store. He drove a bread truck too, and serviced all the stores around there, including the meat market that the Codigas owned. One day I saw him, and we talked some and he said, "I need someone to run my butcher shop up in Boulder Creek." I told him that I had signed up for the Coast Guard, and they could call me up at any time, but I'd work till they did. He agreed, and I went to work there. That didn't work out well at all, and it didn't last but a couple of months.

After I quit the job at the meat market in Boulder Creek, I went back to Watsonville where I got a job with a creamery as a soda jerk. The store I worked in was about two blocks from the high school, so practically all our customers were high school kids. I'd only been there about three weeks when the manager was drafted. The owner made me manager. There I was, just a little bit over high school age myself, and I was manager. That was interesting, but I only stayed a short while.

I was friends with a Japanese boy Katherine had gone to school with. His name was Tommy, and he was the sports editor for the Pajaronian, a local newspaper. He had just graduated high school. The owners of the bus station were looking for someone to operate the little Greyhound Bus café which was called the Heidelburg Café. They sold us the franchise. We bought it together, but it wasn't much, five or six hundred dollars apiece. The buses that came through there were going to Santa Cruz and further north, or south to Salinas. When the bus stopped at the station, all the passengers piled off to get coffee and sandwiches and stuff.

Tommy was working for the newspaper, but he'd come in in the evening when I closed up and help clean up the dishes and scrub the floors and get everything ready for the next morning. He also made out orders for fresh eggs and lettuce and whatever; he took care of that in the morning while I opened up. He didn't actually work behind the counter or anything like that. That was all up to me. I did the cooking and waiting and everything. It only had about three booths and maybe ten stools along the counter.

Since Tommy could speak Japanese and English fluently, and could write well, they took him in the Army as an interpreter. We'd only been in business a short time when Tommy was drafted into the service. That left me running the whole thing by myself.

Three months later Tommy was killed on some island in the Pacific.

There were two bakeries just down the street that traded with me a lot. By the time I opened up early in the morning, they were already making bread and getting ready to send their trucks out to deliver. They brought me fresh donuts for the café and had breakfast with me. One of them said he would be willing to take over the store, so we made a deal, and I went back to the farm to help Dad and wait for the Coast Guard to call.

When I went home, I still owed twenty-five dollars on my car. I bought it from one of Katherine's teachers. I paid eighty dollars for it, twenty dollars down and ten dollars a month or something like that. It was a six cylinder four door Chrysler with suicide doors, the ones that opened from the back side, and oh my, it was in beautiful shape. My dad loved that car, so he said he would pay it off if I would trade it for his Model A Ford. So we did that.

Dad thought he could preserve the paint on it, so he washed it and took a rag soaked with kerosene and wiped it down to make it shine. All it did though, was to attract the dust. Living out on a farm in a tent with no garage for it, that poor old Chrysler got pretty dirty. Of course, they had no running water, so Mom would go down to a service station and use their hose and clean it. The next morning it would be dirty again. That was a lesson in futility.

The Two of Us

Katherine and I wrote back and forth after I went home, and she always told me how much she missed me. One day my mom, Rosella, got a letter from Katherine's mother and she said, "Is it all right if we come and visit you? My daughter is just wasting away."

We were in love, and I'll admit it – we were really in love. But, I couldn't afford to take a day off work to go see her. She had finished her sophomore year and was out of school for the summer, so they came over.

There was a partition across the tent, and Mom and Dad slept up in the front. On one side of their bed was the "living room." There was no bedroom for Katherine and her mother to sleep in, so they had to sleep in the back part of the tent where the kitchen and dining area were. Of course, there was no electricity, no inside plumbing and no running water in the tent.

Even with those conditions, Katherine and I were thrilled to be with one another. By that time, we had known one another, maybe two and a half years. One day I said to her, "If the Coast Guard doesn't call me pretty quick, we ought to get married." She thought that was a good idea.

I had a job then; I was working with a cousin on my biological mother's side, N.V. He and I were chopping hay. After the hay was cut, winnowed and dried, we took a big buck rake and bucked it up to the site where an engine driven chopper chopped it and blew it up into a silo.

Anyhow, when I asked for the day off to get married, the boss, he was a brute of a guy, he said, "No. You can't get a day off to get married."

I said, "Well, we can't get married on Sunday. All the law offices are closed and everything. We've already gone and gotten our blood tests; so I'm going to quit."

"No!" he said, "I want to get that hay in the silo."

"Then you'll have to let me take the day off."

"Well, I'll tell you what. If you guys will chop a day's worth of hay, you can have the rest of the day off."

Normally, in a ten or twelve hour day we could chop about eighty tons, and that would fill one silo, and that guy had several of them. He didn't tell us what time we had to start. Actually, you're not supposed to start until that hay is a little bit dry, but we went out early and got to chopping before daylight, and we chopped eighty tons of hay before twelve o'clock noon.

We were both drenched with sweat, of course, when we finished and went home. There was a creek that ran back of the tent, so I had a bath out there. Then I went in, and we loaded up, her mother, my mother, and Katherine and I, and we drove over to Hanford, eighteen miles away, and got married. There were four people at our wedding. There might have been five, but Dad was working. That was on June 16, 1942.

Afterwards, we came back home and had dinner together. The front room only had a little settee and a couple of chairs. One of them was an old cane bottom chair that - well, when you sat down, your bottom went through the hole. That's all there was in there except the battery powered radio and the coal oil lamps. After dinner, the rest of them all went to the living room and visited.

While they were still visiting, I was so tired from bucking that hay that I went on to bed and went to sleep. I didn't even know when Katherine came to bed. The next morning, I woke up about five o'clock and started thinking about getting up and going to work, but then I realized that my bride had been in bed with me all night, and I didn't even know it.

Bill, Rudy, Mom, me and Katherine

On the following Monday, I borrowed twenty dollars from my dad so we could rent a house, and on Tuesday morning Katherine found a house about three quarters of a mile from my folk's house, and we had our first home. Right away, I began teaching Katherine how to cook. I knew how to cook a lot better than she did, thanks to Rosella, my stepmom.

My cousin N.V, and I quit the job chopping hay and went to Exeter and got a job unloading fertilizer. It came in fifty or a hundred pound bags on railroad cars. All day long we unloaded those bags from the railroad cars onto trucks. Then they were hauled to the farms to be used for fertilizer in the orchards and vineyards.

They call that fertilizer guano, and it comes from Peru. There are huge schools of anchovies in the ocean there, so the cormorants that feed on them are just thick. There are some rocky islands that they have roosted on for decades.

The hills are just white from the bird droppings. When the Peruvians finally learned that those droppings were good fertilizer, they began to harvest it. They took a pick ax to dig and shoveled it into bags. They didn't wear masks, and a lot of the men died, not right away, but years later, from lung problems because of breathing the dust from that stuff. Finally, they realized the problem and made all the workers wear protective gear.

Anyway, N.V. and I didn't work there very long before we found a job with a farmer by the name of Andy Anderson. Andy was a really good boss. He had grapes and two different kinds of oranges. He also sold property and managed a lot of properties out of town. He did tractor work too; plowing, disking and that sort of thing. He had a foreman named Lawrence Girardi; four or five of us worked under him. If we weren't pruning, picking or hauling to the sheds at the wineries, we were plowing or disking. There was always plenty of work to do. We worked there all winter.

My dad, Willie, was an auctioneer. I don't know how he learned that, but he could speak very rapidly and he had really good eye sight. If a person barely nodded his head, Dad would respond. He didn't make much doing that; they paid him just a percentage of the day's sales, maybe two percent or something like that. He got a little more if he was selling farm equipment, but on Wednesdays he was down in Hanford at the auction selling livestock. Katherine and I were down there one time, and before the auction started, my dad, who was a horse lover and trainer, said, "Son, if you want a good young horse, you'll probably get that palomino if you bid on it."

Katherine and I hadn't been married very long, and I don't remember if she asked for a horse, but I knew she liked them. I bought that one. It was a small palomino with black mane and tail, so he wasn't going be a show horse like some palominos with flaxen tail and mane; that's what is desired. That horse I bought wasn't that attractive, but he was a nice little horse.

At that time, we lived real close to Mom and Dad. On the place they lived, there were five or six acres that bordered on a creek, and a horse could pasture that whole area and get water from the creek and not require much attention. From Hanford to Dad's place was eighteen miles. I didn't have a trailer or truck to haul the horse in; we only had an old four cylinder Dodge. Of course, we didn't go very fast, but on the way back Katherine held on to the halter, and that horse ran all the way home. Not once did she have to tug on the line.

We named the horse Prince. He was broken so that the average person could ride him, but Katherine had never been on a horse before. So, we led the horse, with her on it, until we thought they were comfortable. But one day, Katherine was there on the horse while my brother Bill and I were stacking some tires that we used for smudging the prune orchards and oranges. We were rolling the tires over to the stack when one of them skidded and scared the horse. Dad was right beside Katherine and Prince, but he couldn't hold the horse, and off she went.

I think that's why we lost our first little baby; she had a miscarriage. I sort of blamed myself for it. Bill and I shouldn't have been rolling those tires around the horse, but I never thought about him being that skittish. We had just learned that we were going to have a baby, and we were very excited about it. That was our first big disappointment and a pretty tragic one.

The winters in that area around Exeter were very cold, and the summers were very hot. Katherine didn't like that at all. She had been raised on the coast where the weather was not so extreme. We went back to the coast in the spring of '43. We went back to Watsonville where I was pretty sure I could get a job.

PART IV
MAKING A LIVING
1943-1948

Finding Work

When I worked at Codiga's market, one of the customers was Joe Crosetti; he was a big name in lettuce and tomatoes around Watsonville. He had a huge packing shed and owned several places with a hundred or so acres each. He offered me a job, and I took it as sort of a temporary thing. He hired me to run a crew of Mexicans to plant tomatoes for forty cents an hour – the same amount he paid the workers.

I didn't work too long for Crosetti, and then I worked for a butcher shop temporarily. After that I took a job driving a bulldozer building a new little airport in Freedom, about four miles from Watsonville. I made sixty cents an hour if I worked day hours; if I worked night I made sixty-seven and a half cents an hour, so I worked nights for a while. The airport was built for the government to train pilots and bombers for the TBF Avenger. The TBF was a two man torpedo bomber. The government built several of those training airports at little coastal towns in California.

One day I went to visit Hank, and he asked me, "Why don't you fish for kingfish off the pier here at night?"

So, Katherine and I decided to try that. We drove seventeen miles over to the Santa Cruz Municipal Pier in an old Dodge. We had a little red wagon, one of those Radio Flyer wagons, and we put a fish box that would hold two hundred pounds of fish in that wagon. We'd tie six or seven hooks on a line, bait them and throw the line out. We'd go up another fifty feet on the pier and throw out another six or seven hooks. We'd do that all the way to the end of the pier. Then, we'd come back to the first line, take off the fish, bait that line up and throw it out again. Maybe we'd catch a hundred pounds of fish. At seven cents a pound that was seven dollars. I found I could make more fishing than I could bulldozing or working hard all day long in the fields.

Katherine and I fished like that for almost two weeks. One night the watchman came by, he knew me, and he said "Bud, you're going to have to keep that lantern down because the Coast Guard says we're not to have any lights." Everybody had to comply with those rules, so we had to quit fishing that way.

I had been waiting all that time, over a year, for the Coast Guard to call me, and they finally did. By then I knew quite a bit about the ocean. Hank had taught me a lot during the time I was fishing with him. Not only about fishing, but about boats and how to keep them in good operating condition and how to start and stop them. I knew how to box a compass, and I knew tides and winds. When I signed up, the recruiting people at the Coast Guard thought I was just the right candidate for OCS. But, when I went up for the physical exam, they found I had that heart murmur and I couldn't hear out of one ear. They sent me home. I never understood that. As an officer I could have been useful training men or working in an office or something.

When I knew I wasn't going to go into service, a doctor and I went in as partners on a little boat called the North America. That lasted only a short while. It just didn't work out. Then, for the second time Hank offered me a job, and I very gladly accepted. He said, "I can teach you a lot because I've been fishing a long, long time, and I have a pretty good boat. If you'll fish with me, I'll give you a third, I'll take a third and the boat will take a third; that way we share expenses." If we had good fishing, I'd make five or ten dollars a day. That wasn't much, but it paid the rent.

The war was still going on when I went to work for Hank, and fishermen had some strict regulations. We had to check in with the Coast Guard every morning when we got ready to go out. We had to tell them how many people were aboard, and list their names, how much gasoline we carried, and about where we were going to be fishing. We had to check in with them every evening when we came in. We weren't allowed any fishing lights at night, so we had to come in before dark.

Hank and I did that for three or four months while we fished for salmon. Once we broke down off Point Sur, and we couldn't repair the boat. Hank being so experienced knew what to do. We improvised and used our quilts and blankets to make sails. We sailed and drifted two days and nights before we made port at San Simeon. There was a short pier there that William Randolph Hearst had built to unload materials for the Hearst Castle. After anchoring and securing there, we ground the valves, and were back fishing in a day or two.

Late in September, one of the local boats found some albacore up off of Davenport, offshore about twelve miles. Hank said, "Tomorrow we're going to go tuna fishing."

I asked, "Is that anything like salmon fishing?"

Hank only said, "You'll see. It's a lot easier."

The federal government's Office of Price Administration, OPA, set the price on everything. They had set the price of salmon at 18¾ cents. But they set the price of albacore, in relation, quite a bit better. We were getting $375 a ton. Like Hank said, it was a lot easier to catch a ton of albacore than a ton of salmon. By the way, salmon is now bringing $8 a pound, or more.

The first day we fished albacore we didn't get a lot, maybe a thousand pounds or so, a couple of hundred dollars. The next day we followed the fleet, but we were the slowest boat in the fleet because we had that old boat with an eight-horse one cylinder gasoline engine that was made in somebody's garage up in Seattle. We might be three or four miles, or maybe as many as eight miles, inside of where the other boats were looking, but we'd follow the streak of water right where the blue and the green meet. Where the two colors change is called the thermocline. The difference in the color of the water has to do with the currents and temperature of the water. There may be only one degree difference in the temperature of the blue and the green, but in the colder water you'll find little strings of kelp and grass and stuff floating. Then out in the warmer water you'll find little fish called needle fish. They have a sharp pointed nose and little yellow eyes, and they come right up to that thermocline. The tuna feed on those needle fish, and that's where those big old fish would latch on to our hooks.

One day, we were about fifty miles out when we found a good school of fish right on the edge of the thermocline. We stayed right there, and that day we caught 113 fish that weighed 3,600 pounds. At $375 a ton that was pretty good. That was the last day we fished together that season.

That night Hank said, "Tomorrow I've got to go to the

VA. This stump is bothering me, and they're going to cut some more off. You take the boat and go ahead fishing."

We had only fished tuna about a week, so I said, "Hank, I don't know enough about it to take the boat and go."

"Oh, you know enough about it. You start that engine, steer the compass course, put the lines in and pull fish as good as anybody. Don't you worry about it, you go."

The next day when I came in, I had exactly the same number of fish that Hank and I caught the day before. All by myself. Boy, I felt so proud. But, when I unloaded and had the fish weighed, I only had 2,900 pounds. That didn't make sense. I caught those fish out of the same school of fish that we caught the others.

I knew the kid that weighed the fish, and I said, "There's something wrong here. I had more than 2,900 pounds."

"No," he said, "That's the weight."

I swore at him, "You're a damn liar. Where are my fish?" I said

"Oh, they're all in the holding room there."

"Well, run them out here. We're going to weigh them again."

So he did, and the first cart weighed what he had written down, and the second one did, but about the third one, I got to looking around and saw that he had a pair of wet gloves laying on that balance scale.

I was so angry, I grabbed him by the collar and said, "You blankety-blank-blank." I used some pretty foul language. "You've tried to cheat me; that's what you've done."

I pointed at those wet gloves and said, "Whose are those?"

"Oh, I didn't know those were on there. I guess they're mine, but I didn't realize...."

"Come on; who do you think you're kidding? Listen, if you want to buy my fish you're going to weigh them all again."

So, he did, and I had nearly the same number of pounds that we had the day before, lacking about four or five pounds. What he did made a difference in actual weight, and that meant some money.

When one of the guys that worked in that market got his own boat, he hired me to work with him. We used that boat to lampara fish. That's where you wrap the net around a school of fish, and you only do that with wetfish[1] like sardines, mackerel, anchovies and squid. They are sold daily to the cannery. You do lampara fishing in the bay, maybe in water only fifty or sixty feet instead of five hundred fathoms, or three thousand feet, like in other places we fished. With the lampara we ran along the beach, and it might take three hours before we set the net because we had to find a school of fish.

Fishing in the bay on the lampara boats, we also got some market fish, like kingfish which was only seven cents a pound, but if you got a thousand pounds mixed up with your other stuff, it added up. We would get some pompano, too. That's a little shiny fish about three or four inches long, almost as round as they are long and sort of flat like a perch. When we got those we would get fifty cents a pound. The OPA ceiling on them was eighty-five cents, but the price

---

1   Footnote for landlubbers
     Captain Travis - Wetfish: fresh fish that you don't freeze.

was set every day. Sometimes, if they were nice big ones, and we got in before they set the price in the morning, we'd get that eighty-five cents. Most of the time we got sixty cents, but if you had a hundred or two of them, like the kingfish, it added up. We only got forty-two or forty-three dollars a ton for the wet fish. I'd get a percentage of that, which wasn't much, but it kept the rent paid.

I fished on that lampara boat for a while, and when another man built a bigger boat, I took a job with him. I worked on both those boats as a deck hand that winter. It was good experience for me because I learned a lot about net mending and how to find schools of fish.

Mending a net

I could have fished with Hank year round, but in the winter when you went for black cod, you had to go quite a ways offshore, and the weather sometimes can be pretty rough for a little twenty-eight foot boat. Sometimes, when I wasn't lampara fishing and the weather was good, I would fish for Hank. I'd bait up the line and go out and set for black cod and rock cod. Cod was good for the government, because you could salt it down, and it would keep for months. It was good for feeding the troops.

Come that next spring, when we were rigging up for salmon Hank said, "Travis, I saw a little clipper boat over in Monterey, and we could buy it pretty cheap."

"Hank," I said, "I don't have any money. I have a new baby about four months old. I can't do it."

Hank made me an offer I couldn't refuse. "I'll buy the boat," he said, "and you can pay me for your half of it out of the catch. You'll be the captain and you can hire the deck hands you want." So, that's what we did.

The clipper boat was called the San Giuseppe, and it was a good little boat. It was a twenty-nine foot Monterey type boat with a clipper bow like the old sailing ships. It was built in San Francisco by a man named Bachichi. He only had one eye, but he could look at a plank and see where it had to fit, take a plane and file it down till it did. That guy would be building two or three of those little boats at a time.

When we first got the San Giuseppe, it only had a single cylinder Hicks gasoline engine, but it was a better engine than the Fred had, and parts were easier to find. Like the Fred, you had to hand crank it. It had a big fly wheel about eight or nine inches wide and maybe three feet across. You had to get down on your knees and put a little gasoline in the pipe cup that held about a thimble full of gas. Then, you had to get that fly wheel moving pretty fast, and when it hit another piece of metal and made a spark, you pushed the exhaust valve open and you got apum, apum, apum, apum and off you went. When it sparks, if there is a vapor of gasoline, it's gonna fire.

After we got the San Giuseppe, Katherine and I rented a little house in Santa Cruz, and we moved there in 1946, I think. A Portuguese fellow and his family lived right in front of us. His name was Dominga Cordoza, and he didn't speak much English. After they came to the states, he had been a feeder in a chicken farm where they raised chickens for eggs. He was out of work, so I offered him a job. At one time, he had been a fisherman over in the Azores Islands, fishing with a hook and line. They fished deep water with hand lines. It was nothing on a large scale like we did.

When we fished for black cod, we had a mechanical puller to pull our lines, and we fished five thousand hooks a day. That meant we had to bait five thousand hooks daily.

We coiled the line in a basket in rotation so that one baited hook would go out after the other. We couldn't have any tangles in the lines coming out of that basket because we set the gear at eight or ten miles an hour, and one of us stood and turned the basket with the hooks, and they'd go flying off the stern. When you came to the end of one line, your helper stuck the next basket up to you and took the old basket out of the way; you made a quick tie and started turning the basket again. We'd just keep going till the line was all out. It was six miles long. It would take us an hour to set the gear.

Dominga worked for me through one winter until salmon season opened, and I didn't need him any longer. When you fish salmon and albacore you really don't need help.

When salmon season opened in the spring, I was ready to go. I fished salmon until the Fourth of July when we heard they were catching albacore down off of Mexico. A helper and I went all the way to Mexico in that little old single cylinder powered boat. We delivered our catch to "pick up boats" which were anchored at islands that furnished fuel, groceries, ice and gear at discounted prices because the canneries on the island wanted our fish. We followed the tuna up the coast. Tuna is a migratory fish, or what they call pelagic, and we might be fishing off the northern coast of Mexico in July and off the Central Coast of California in September. Because of their migration, we were like gypsies following them.

A Boat of My Own

In August of 1945, my helper, Ben Rollerson, and I were fishing albacore outside of San Clemente Island in southern California. We had gone into Cherry Cove for the night. Ashore there was a battalion of military that had two or three boats with antiaircraft on them. In the middle of the night while we were sleeping, all of a sudden guns started going off. I hollered at someone on one of those ships and asked what was going on. He answered "The war is over!"

Ben and I talked a minute about how great it was that it was finally over. Then we went back to bed; we were going fishing early the next morning.

After Hank bought the San Giuseppe, he wanted me as a fifty-fifty partner, so I began to pay out my share of the cost of the boat. The total cost of the boat was only three thousand dollars, so I owed fifteen hundred. That seemed like a million at the time. Anyway, I would pay my third of the expenses, and a little bit out of my share to pay him for the boat.

I had a surplus radio and a surplus direction finder[2] on the San Giuseppe, and I knew a young kid in a neighboring town, Tony, and he wanted to get his ham operator license and was interested in our marine frequency. He brought some of his text books for us to study, and we went to the library and studied about electronics. We got together and developed a method of matching the wave length. Well, that's sort of technical. All ships have an antenna to transmit from their radios, and a ship is big enough that they can take the full wave length of the antenna and run it from mast to mast and down to the radio to match wave lengths. We can't do that on a little fishing boat; we don't have that distance. When we went to the library we found that you can devise wave lengths in various sizes. We determined that we could do that by wrapping wire that would send radio frequency on a cane pole. So, we used that method and made it work. We also made a direction finder. It was helpful with navigation, and if someone within the fleet had a problem, you could find out where they were.

After the war, I got to be pretty popular with the fleet because I understood electronics. A lot of surplus electronics

---

2   Footnote for Landlubbers
    Captain Travis - Direction finder: a radio device that you use to get a cross reference from two radio signals to determine your location.

from the Navy ships and airplanes were becoming available about then. I had converted some of those radios and radio direction finders from the military frequencies to our frequencies for marine use, so I was able to help a lot of guys get those things installed on their boats.

Altogether, I worked for Hank about five years, and all that time his leg got worse and worse. They kept amputating till they got plumb up to his hip. One day he said, "Travis, I just can't get around anymore, so I want to sell you my half of the boat." It wasn't much, but it took any excess money I might have had that season.

By the time Hank retired and sold the San Giuseppe to me, we had put in a brand new six cylinder gasoline engine, an automatic pilot, new fuel tanks, electric lights and a water tank, and we had re-nailed it, that is put in new nails where the old ones had rusted. Because we had improved the boat so much, I probably owed Hank another two thousand dollars. I'd been paying him all along, and I'm not sure what I did owe him when he retired, but eventually, I paid him back. I had a boat of my own, and it was a good one.

I learned pretty early that persistence and being prepared were essential to being a good fisherman. If you're a good producer you're called a high liner. It didn't take me too long to gain that title, and some of them began to call me the "boy with the golden arm." All of that was because Hank taught me so well, and too, I think it was because I was persistent. I'd be the first on the grounds and the last. Now, I might not catch as many fish as fast as some of the other guys in the fleet, but at the end of the day, I had as many fish as anybody, and sometimes more. Really, persistence paid off.

The boy with the golden arm

I also learned to carry a lot of redundancy - like spare filters, fuel pumps, belts and other parts, so if anything happened, I'd be ready. The tuna season is only about a hundred days long, and I didn't want to go on a trip and have it broken. Once you're on the fishing grounds, you want to stay there as long as you can, because sometimes it takes a week to get into town, and then you wait to get unloaded, and you have to clean the boat, and get fuel and groceries. By the time you go in and get back to the fishing grounds, you've probably lost track of where the fish are. The fish move, and you've got to move with them. If you can stay on the grounds, even if you have a day or two of slack fishing, you've got a lot better chance. If you've got good buddies, and they're catching fish, they'll give you a direction finder bearing, and you can get there in a straight line. Otherwise you lose time which is valuable.

By the Way

During the war, my dad got a job in a shipyard up in Stockton, I think it was late '43 when they moved. Rosella's step-brother, Lawrence Green, lived up there, and I think that's how Dad got on. The shipyard was building wooden mine sweepers and wooden ships for the government. It was a pretty good job compared to what Dad had been doing on the farm. He was probably making ten or twelve dollars a day, maybe more. My brother Bill was still with my parents; he stayed with them till after war. They stayed at Stockton about a year before they went back to Farmersville, and Dad went to work on a farm.

When the war was over, there was some land just south of Union School, the little school us boys went to, where tract homes were being built. Dad bought three lots there. He and his next door neighbor built a house. They built it without any studs to speak of. The law requires a stud every sixteen inches, but they used 1-by-10 inch and 1-by-12 inch planks and just put enough horizontal studs to nail them together. Then they used that old roofing tar paper to put on the sides of the house. On the inside Mom made a paste of flour and water and put layers of newspapers on the walls. That was the insulation to keep the wind from coming through, and it was the wallpaper till we tore the house down.

Rosella was thrilled to have a house with running water, even if it was only plumbed to the bathroom. She had to go the bathroom to get water for the kitchen. The dishwater went to the chicken or hog pen. She was so happy to be out of the tent and into a warm house.

Aunt Essie and Uncle Elmer and their family moved to California after the war started; I don't know just when. There was a big need for help in the ship yards, aircraft factories and other industry related to the war. Uncle Elmer wanted to farm, but Aunt Essie took a job over in the Alameda shipyard as a "Rosie the Riveter" type thing helping build ships. Some of the boys got jobs in the shipyard too. Uncle Elmer went to work for Henry Kaiser who built the Willys Jeep for the government.

My cousin and old pal, Homer, had worked for the CCC, and had quite a bit of background in building, so he joined the Navy Seabees soon after the war started. He was stationed at Port Hueneme down in southern California. He really made an effort to come see us; he rode a Greyhound bus about three hundred miles to Santa Cruz. It was a great reunion for the two of us. Homer had never met Katherine, and he just fell in love with her. That was when we were expecting our precious Eileen.

You remember that Katherine and I lost our first little baby, and that was a big heartache, but we were overjoyed at the birth of a healthy baby girl a year and a half later. Eileen was born December 27, 1943. In the spring of '44, Grandma Hulda rode a Greyhound bus from Ada,

Oklahoma to Santa Cruz to see our baby. That was the first time I had seen Grandma since we left Oklahoma.

After Eileen was born, our family grew quickly. Fred was our first son, then Tom, then Phil and then Richard, the last boy, was born in 1950. Our first five children were all born in Santa Cruz, all delivered by the same doctor. Our doctor was named Norman Gael; that's why Phil is named Philip Norman. When our last boy was born, we named him Richard Gael. We thought an awful lot of that doctor.

I was there when all of our babies were born except Richard. I was at sea when he came. And there's a story about that. Katherine and the children were living in Santa Cruz, and I was fishing outside of San Luis Obispo when we were expecting him.

Tony, the boy who helped me rig the antenna for our boat radios, could get on our marine frequency with his ham radio. We had an agreement that if Katherine called him and said it was time, he would relay the message to the fleet, and they would get it to me. Well, she called Tony, and that day there happened to be a lot of radio traffic. He tried and tried, and when he finally got on, he said, "Mayday! Mayday! Get this message to Travis Evans on the Giuseppe - his wife is being taken to the hospital right now."

Boy, that message came down to me in a hurry. Nobody knew it was a pregnancy. I could hear them as they were relaying it down, and the message got more and more serious as it went along. By the time I got the message first-hand, from a boat that was forty or fifty miles from me, it was a dire emergency. The men in the fish market heard it on shore, and one of the guys, Sid Peterson, had an airplane, a little Piper Cub, waiting for me. As soon as I got to the dock, he met me and said, "I've got an airplane for you. You get on it, and I'll get you to your wife."

I told him I didn't think it was that serious. I got on the phone and talked to Katherine's sister. She said that Katherine was in the hospital, and congratulated me on having a healthy baby boy. I got there as soon as I could to meet my new son.

I missed a lot of things with the family like when Richard was born, but that happened right during tuna season, and actually, I needed to be at sea.

It was about Thanksgiving one time when I left my boat in San Diego and went home on a Greyhound bus. I stopped at Montgomery Ward in Salinas looking for something to bring Katherine. I was thinking of Christmas, so I bought her a gift. When I got home I put it up in the rafters in the garage. I told Katherine, "Now don't let the kids get up there in the garage because I've hidden something. It's going to be part of our Christmas."

"What is it?" she asked.

"I don't want you to know."

"Well, give me a clue."

So I thought a bit and said, "It has fifty-two movable parts."

And that was all I'd tell her. She didn't catch one word. She thought I said moving parts, but I said movable parts. There's a big difference. It was a new set of dishes. After a few days I went back to San Diego to move the boat home. When I came back, the kids kept asking me what it was. "We won't tell Mama," they said.

But I wouldn't tell them anything except, "Well, maybe there is something for you too."

It was a big surprise for all of them, and we used those dishes for years and years. The fact that I could be home made it a good Christmas, and that surprise made it one to remember.

An earlier Christmas was not so good. It was in 1947, the year Tom, our third child, was born, the same year Hank retired, and the first year I was on my own. It was a rough year financially. I was hardly able to pay our house rent. Well, actually we got behind some during the winter months. Sometime later, I wrote a story about that Christmas.

THE PERFECT GIFT

For you to understand this true story, you need to know that I have been a commercial fisherman for most of my adult life. This story happened the Christmas of '47. My wife, Katherine and I had two little toddlers and a baby boy still in the crib.

The government had cancelled all of the fish orders for the troops, and meat no longer required ration stamps. Everyone, except the good Catholics on Friday, were enjoying beef and pork. Of course, traditionally people turn to turkey, goose or ham for the holidays. Chicken farmers were going broke, and the fishing industry was really hurting. The Office of Price Administration had lifted the price freeze, and fish prices to the boats had plummeted.

We were behind several months in our rent and boat payments. There was no money for our children's gifts, and food was scarce on our table. I won't say we missed many meals, but we sure postponed a few. The relatives would have to supply the children's gifts. I hadn't learned to depend on the Lord yet, but I was trying hard in my own strength, and finally managed to trade some of my fresh fish for a few hundred pounds of sweet potatoes. I sold a few of those around town, and that helped, but things still looked very bleak. As Christmas drew near, we remembered another fishing family with three small boys. The Bergens were in a similar situation, except Lloyd's boat was smaller, and he produced even less fish than I. So, we carefully chose and cleaned a gunny sack of sweet potatoes and tied them with a makeshift ribbon. We planned to surprise that needy family with a gift of food. Sweet potatoes! That was all we had to offer.

When we arrived at the Bergens, we got a surprise. Lloyd had traded some of his fish catch for a sack of pinto beans, and they had bagged and ribboned about fifty pounds of beans for the needy Evans family. What a joy to know that each family, in their dire need, was thinking of ways they could help others. We had a big laugh, and decided we would have Christmas dinner together. Sweet potatoes, pinto beans and fish.

I like to think that God had the biggest laugh, for on Christmas Eve, when I went to the wharf to check on my boat, our fish buyer called me over. He asked if I would be seeing Lloyd. I replied that we would be having Christmas dinner together. He had a twenty pound turkey for each boat that had delivered regularly to him that year.

Our families had a feast and both Lloyd and I could say as Jacob did in the 29th chapter of Genesis, "Surely, God has had His hand in my life and I knew it not." What a lesson for us. Down through these many years, we have found that when we choose Him and His way, there is no limit to what God can do with the inherent potential in each of us.

And that, friend, is the Perfect Gift.

PART V
BUSY, BUSY YEARS
1949 - 1957

A Dream Come True

The San Giuseppe was a good little boat, but after I had been fishing a few years, I saw the need for a larger vessel. We were spending so much time running in to the fish market, unloading, getting fuel and groceries and so on, and missing a lot of fishing time. So, I really wanted to and was making plans to build a boat.

The fish market I sold to was called the San Luis Fish Company. It was run by Dick Kirby. He often heard the guys in the fleet calling me on the radio to tell me where the fish schools were and inviting me to come and join them. I was doing well with the San Giuseppe at that time, and Dick saw that there were more fish in my boat than any other boat that size. One day he said to me, "Hey, you're the biggest producer I have, and I wonder when are you going to get yourself a bigger boat?"

"I'm saving money toward it. I have two friends, the Makela brothers, just back from the service, who said they'd help me build a boat. They know boat building; they've built several. Before they went off to war they promised they'd help me when they got home. As soon as I get the money, we're going to start my boat."

Dick said, "How much will it take?"

"I don't know, but maybe five or ten thousand dollars."

"Would you like a partner? I need a boat to fish for me year round for the market. If you'd like to have a partner, I'll furnish half of the money."

It was going to cost five thousand dollars just to buy the lumber. You buy the lumber first and air dry it for close to a year. Anyway, he put up that money.

In the winter of 1948, I went to see the guys who were going to help me. One of them said "Yeah, you're next." The brothers and I went to Fort Bragg to the Union Lumber Company and handpicked all vertical grain lumber needed for building a wooden boat. We hauled it out to their father's house and stacked it and covered it over with canvas so it would be air dried by the time we got ready to build.

So I went back to fishing, and sometime in there, I injured my hand pretty badly. I was working to bring my boat, the San Giuseppe, onto the pier, and it was very cold and stormy. I didn't feel it but, I looked down and saw blood. Then I looked at my hand and realized the tips of three fingers on my right hand had been cut off in the winch. I ran to the car where Katherine was waiting for me. The man who was working with me found the fingertips, picked them up, wrapped them in a handkerchief, and followed us to the hospital.

A surgeon, who had done a lot of plastic surgery during his time in the Korean War just happened to be there, and he sewed the tips back on my fingers. While he was doing that I asked him a question.

I said, "Doc, after this heals up will I be able to play the piano?"

"Sure you will," he answered.

"Well, that's just great! I never could before."

He got a laugh out of that.

It took a long time for my fingers to heal and it was very painful. I wore a bandage for four months and slept with my hand taped to a cup to avoid reinjuring them. I wasn't able to work for a while, so I sold the San Giuseppe. I got six thousand for it, and half of that I took to build the boat, and the other half I put back for my family to live on while I built it. We started to work on it in October.

I knew for a while that I was going to go fishing for tuna when the boat was finished. In a small boat, most of your fishing is day fishing, so you deliver every night, especially salmon and cod. But when we'd go to Mexico to fish albacore, I'd fill the fishhold with ice. The first day's catch we'd keep on deck all day and cover it with wet burlap bags. Then at night just before we went to bed, we'd open the hatch, take out ice for the next day, shovel it out of the way, even out onto the deck, then put the fish down in the hold and cover them with ice. An ice boat should be well insulated, the decks especially, and the hull is insulated so that the fish don't ever catch any of the warmth. I wanted the best insulation available for my new boat.

When I built the Katherine, most everybody in those days used cork to insulate. Cork is a pretty good insulator, but cork also acquires dampness, and the more dampness it gets, the less insulation quality. The year before I built that boat, I saw in a fishing magazine that Dow Chemical Company in Michigan had developed a new form of insulation - Styrofoam. I contacted them and found out they only made log shaped hexagon logs, ten foot long or something like that, but they said I could cut it with a regular saw, a circular saw or a band saw. So I ordered enough to insulate the Katherine. I had the first boat on the west coast with Styrofoam insulation.

During that time, Katherine worked in the Santa Cruz Hospital to keep some money coming in, so I was free to work on the boat. Katherine's mother, Mabel, came to stay with us and watch the children while Katherine worked. She was with us on and off for several years. Katherine also worked at a couple of other places for fifty cents an hour to help out. What a woman!

Katherine and I talked and talked about what to name that boat. We picked out this name, then that name, but her name was never mentioned. On the day of the christening in May of '49, I drove the family over to the dock at Fort Bragg where the ceremony would take place. We had to walk around a corner before we could see the boat. When we got to that point, and Katherine saw those big letters spelling out her name, she was surprised and thrilled and so very happy. With all the help and support she gave me, I felt she was certainly deserving of having her name on that boat.

The Katherine

There was a small gathering of local fishermen, and the Makela brothers waiting for us. The Makela brothers had brought some beer, and there was a bottle of champagne for Katherine to break over the bow. It took two tries for her to break the bottle. Then the boat was pushed into the water. That was another day I'll never forget and I don't think Katherine ever forgot it either.

When you put the boat in the water you still have to outfit them. That means the fuel tanks, the mast, the windows in the cabin, the engine, the propeller and propeller shaft, and the rest of the stuff are put in after you put the boat in the water. The Makela brothers helped, and they taught me a lot. It took seven months to build and two months to outfit.

When it was time to go fishing, I knew of a young man who had served in the Navy during World War II who was having a hard time finding a job because of a drinking problem. I hired him, but I told him there would be no alcohol on my boat. He went with me to Fort Bragg to bring the boat back to Santa Cruz, and he didn't have a drink on that trip. He worked all that summer and up until October when the albacore fishing was over. Then, I put the drag net on to fish for bottom fish, flounder and halibut and various. That guy stayed with me until February. He'd been sober on my boat all that time.

We lived at Santa Cruz when I got the Katherine built, and I fished almost a year in that area. I was having trouble selling all the fish at a decent price though. In that area, Monterey had a big fleet of boats, Santa Cruz' Moss Landing had a few boats, San Francisco had many boats, and Half Moon Bay had a few, so the markets were flooded with cheap fish. By moving down the coast to Port San Luis Obispo, we had Fresno, Bakersfield and Los Angeles, all pretty good-sized cities, only three hours away by car. Our competition wasn't nearly as great. That's when the family moved to Avila - in '52.

We couldn't find a house for some time, but I finally found a Greek motel with a vacancy, and my family moved into a little cabin there. My friend Roy Downing lived in a big house down on a creek, and when he found out that my family was living in that little cabin, he offered to stay at the fish buying station on the pier at Port San Luis and let us rent that place for forty dollars a month until we could find a place of our own. After a while, we moved into an apartment with two rooms upstairs and a garage downstairs. We made a bedroom for the boys in the garage. Finally, we found a house that was far better for our family, right on the same street.

When we moved there, Avila had about 350 residents. There was only one grocery store, two bars, two cafes, a barber shop and a fish and tackle shop. We had no service station. The road going down to the pier had been an old railroad bed. They had taken the train and rails out for the war effort, but the cross ties were still there. Going to that pier was a big job in the wintertime; there were mudslides and everything.

We got involved right away in trying to get the pier repaired. The original pier was built in the late 1800's. The people who owned it never maintained the thing at all. It was in such bad shape that a lady actually fell through some rotten boards and drowned. The first hundred or so feet had been improved so we could pull up and unload our catch there, but the rest of it was bad.

We wanted to form a harbor district which meant a part of the county's property tax money would be allotted to the district. I don't know how long it took us to get it on the ballot, but the first vote failed. Most of the county was occupied by farmers who did not want or need a harbor. My partner, Dick Kirby, knew how to go before the legislators and present our plans for the harbor district. He was the right man to represent us, and we got the harbor district approved in '54.

We formed a board to handle everyday responsibilities of the harbor district. That included clean, safe beaches, keeping up the road leading to the pier, repair of the pier and maintenance of all the piers in that district. Katherine was secretary of that board.

We were finally able to go to work on the pier. We had to start with the pilings. There was highway construction going on near Avila on Freeway 101, and a eucalyptus grove had to be cleared. The construction crew had to dispose of those trees some way. The smaller ones could be ground, but the larger ones had to be disposed of. We made a deal to purchase them at a reasonable price to use as support pilings on our dilapidated pier. And it was funny; the next year those eucalyptus trees had enough sap in them that they sprouted limbs and leaves. It looked really green under the pier; you couldn't see thru the growth. We had a number of seasonal boats from other ports coming in to sell their catch. Some of the fisherman asked if we were trying to camouflage our pier. It took a while but eventually we got that pier in good condition.

Right after the Korean War, I hired the best hand I ever had. Jack Rodin served in the Marine Corps, and when he got out, he came to work for me. He had just gotten married to a woman with a little boy about two years old. When they told me about getting married, she said to me, "I love him, but I don't know about marrying a fisherman. I don't know if they make enough money for us to get along."

I said, "Darlene, how much money do you think you need to get by?"

"At least six hundred a month," she said. (Remember, that was in 1953.)

"If Jack will guarantee me that he's ready to go fishing when I am, then I promise you he'll get six hundred. No matter how much we catch, he'll get at least that much."

Now, no fisherman will make that kind of guarantee because they don't know what they're going to catch. But I knew I had enough collateral, and my reputation was such, that I could take care of it, even if I had to replace an engine and it took three months to do it. And, I wanted Jack. His dad had worked for me, and I just knew he would make me a good deck hand.

An unexpected bonus came with Jack. He was left handed and I was right handed. There were lots of things we had to do when that came in handy.

Fish On!!!

I think it was '55 when Eileen and Phil went on a trip with me, and we got into the best fishing I ever saw. We were way down off the coast of Mexico, and for three or four days we had decent fishing. The fish were from twelve to twenty pounds usually. If you get a hundred fish in a day, that's pretty decent, and you're getting a few fish aboard. One day the fishing was terrible in the morning, clear up till noon. We were getting low on ice and fuel, so this was going to be our last day. We had a partner boat, owned by Bob Knapp, who worked out of the same port. He came on the radio and said, "I'm going to go north to look." Doug Britton on the Falcon came on and said, "I'm going try to the east."

I said, "Okay, I'll take the northeast. We'll scout this out, and if we don't find anything, I'm gonna head for San Diego."

I put it on auto pilot, and we started out. I told twelve year old Eileen I was going to rest a bit and she should keep watch ahead. I lay down in the state room. I hadn't even got to dozing when Doug Britton called and said, "Hey, I'm getting fish. Come on over." Eileen came and gave me the message. I jumped up and told Doug to come back real quick so I could get a direction on him.

He said, "Okay, but make it quick. This is costing me money."

"Thank you. That's all we need."

It just took two or three words to get what I needed. Since I made my direction finder myself, I knew how to use it quickly.

We turned that way and speeded up some, faster than our usual trolling speed. I went to lie down again, and I hadn't even closed my eyes when Eileen yelled, "Fish on!" She slowed the boat down, and I ran to the stern and started pulling fish. She came to help, and I let her pull on the inside where you don't tangle as much. But, she kept getting those lines tangled anyway, so I'd pull on my side and get it all clear of fish, then she'd pull on my side while I untangled her. I lifted four or five fish at a time, threw them on the boat, unhooked them, untangled her lines and gave them back to her.

Poor little Eileen, at one point she started crying and said, "Dad, they're like grapes; they're coming at me in bunches."

Phil, who was maybe six, was on deck too. He sat on a little hatch cover and watched a line to let us know if there was a fish on it. When we began to catch them so fast, he started moving the fish forward more and more. The deck had a ten inch step up to the cabin, but the fish were soon stacked so high they were falling off that and sliding into the living quarters. He got a lettuce crate and put across the door to stop that.

Eileen and I pulled fish till dark. We had over a thousand fish, and we caught those from two or three in the afternoon till probably eight-thirty - after dark anyway. We didn't have enough ice to keep all those fish, so after we got them put down in the hold about ten-thirty, I closed up everything, just left one small opening, and took a fifteen pound bottle of CO_2 fire extinguisher and sprayed it all over the fish. That puts a lot of cold in the fish hold, and we wouldn't open the hold until we got to San Diego. We had been at cruising speed for a couple of hours before we finished covering the fish.

I had pulled fish all that time without a shirt. Blood and scales were all over my back and cooked on by the sun. Eileen took the deck hose, which pumped salt water all the time, and washed my back to get the scales softened up and took a scrub brush to get them off. The next day she got the "stickers" off.

We kept running hard for two days and two nights, several hundred miles, to get to San Diego. We never lost a fish. At the cannery, I used a big aluminum shovel and took only two shovels of ice out. There was no more ice left – none. Things were cold enough though, that we had no losses, thanks to that fire extinguisher.

Doug came in just a couple of hours after we did. He didn't have as many fish as we did because his little schooner would only carry ten or eleven tons, but his boat was full also. We could carry eighteen tons, but we only had fifteen or sixteen tons because we didn't have enough ice and couldn't put more fish in.

That was sure good fishing. As I said - the best I ever saw.

Broken Hearts

When I had the little San Giuseppe I always hauled out in San Diego to clean the bottom and have the propeller tuned so we could catch more albacore. If you kept that propeller tuned, the fish would come right up to the boat, and you wouldn't have to pull a line that was a hundred feet long. When they were close, you pulled a line about six or eight feet, and then you could just lift them aboard.

In 1956, we were in Point Loma there in San Diego getting the Katherine ready to go into dry dock. Katherine and the children were there, and the older ones were helping me. Richard wasn't quite six then, and Susie was just a baby. I was sanding and painting the outside part of the boat I could reach while it was still in the water. One day Katherine and the children went to get groceries for the evening meal. I thought that all the children were with her, and she thought that Richard had stayed with me.

Richard was a sweet little boy, and all the boatyard workers knew him. One of them had carved out a little boat for him. He was playing with it on the opposite side of the boat while I was grinding and sanding away. But, I didn't know he was there.

It was toward evening when the others came back from the store. Katherine said, "Where's Richie?"

"Didn't he go with you?" I asked.

We always had life jackets on the children when they were on the boat. Richard had taken his life jacket off and left it on the deck of the boat, which was in the slip; he just reached over and dropped it on the boat.

We looked all over the boatyard and asked everyone we saw. Nobody had seen him. I waited till dark and called Red, a fisherman I knew. He was a diver and worked for the San Diego Harbor. I called the fire department of San Diego, the marine division, and they sent a boat over and diving equipment for Red. He dove down where Richard had been playing and brought him up over the slip. Richard was full of mud and stuff, and we hosed him off and took him to the mortuary.

I didn't know about it till the next day, but the night before he had asked Eileen, "Would you bring a map down?" We kept our maps and charts overhead. She explained the difference: a map is of land and a chart shows the water or the sky. He wanted a chart.

Eileen asked, "Why do you want a chart?"

"I want to see where heaven is."

I went to the funeral home the next day, and from there I went and bought him his last suit of clothes. He was the fourth boy, and he always had to wear hand-me-downs, so we didn't have any real good clothes for his burial. When I went in that Montgomery Ward store, I had just come from making arrangements, and there was a bustling crowd in the store, people all around, and my heart was breaking when the clerk asked me, "Do you want buttons or cuff links on the shirt?" To be questioned about the clothes, I just almost couldn't answer her. I couldn't tell her this was the last shirt I'd be buying for my little boy. It was hard.

The Church of the Nazarene took care of us and did everything they could to help and comfort us. One of our San Diego fisherman friends and his family, the MacLeish family had taken the children in and consoled them and fed them and bathed them and gave them beds at night.

After Katherine, Eileen and I went to bed on the boat that night, we talked. Katherine said it was her fault. I said no, it was my fault, and Eileen said no, it was her fault. Katherine was utterly devastated; well, we all were, but she was just not able to do the normal things involved with raising the children during that time. Eileen was very helpful, and Mabel came.

Richie died on August 3, 1956. He is buried in the Mount Hope Cemetery in San Diego.

Losing that little boy just about broke our hearts.

I left the boat in a slip and we came home. Katherine and I prayed a lot, every day, about what I should do. I didn't want to go fishing again. I was blaming myself, and I blamed the ocean for taking my little boy. I didn't want anything to do with the ocean. But, how was I going to feed the family?

Finally another fisherman, Roland, who lived across the street, said to me, "Travis, you're a good fisherman, and you have good equipment. Come on, and we'll fight this battle. Let's go down and get the boat and make a trip. The fish are still up north, and we can get some money coming in and see if you can get to feeling differently."

We did what Roland suggested and went to Point Loma to get the boat. When Richie died, they said we could leave the boat in the slip with no charge; it had been there for a month. We brought the boat up to Port San Luis to get it ready for a trip. Then we went out and caught a few tuna and talked to some of my friends. Some of them I needed to thank because when Ritchie died, they sent checks, a hundred dollars here and two hundred there. One of them had gotten on the marine radio out of Morro Bay and said, "Travis Evans and his wife have lost their baby boy. So, let's chip in." And, they did. The fleet gave us almost four thousand dollars.

When we first met Roland, he and his wife were sleeping in their car. He was having a hard time finding work, and I recommended him for a job on a fishing boat. I had helped him through a hard time, and now he was helping me through a hard time.

By the time Roland and I got back from that trip, it was at the end of tuna season. It was time to put in eight ton of salt for a ballast[3] and go bottom fishing with a drag boat. That trip with Roland turned me around. After all I had a family to feed and a partner who was depending on me.

The months after our little Richie died were tough times, but it strengthened our resolve. We had been going to church and Sunday School some, but I wasn't as committed as I became after Richie's death. The year after he died, I started visiting the prisons. But, that's another story.

By the Way

Katherine and I always tried to do our part in the community wherever we lived. In addition to the work I did on the harbor district when we moved to Avila, I joined a group of merchants and others who were trying to get the area improved, the Avila Civic Association. In a couple of years, I was president of the association, and one of our projects was to get the name of our little town changed. The sign out on the highway just said Avila, and who knew what Avila was? There was a beautiful beach, but the state wouldn't allow us to put Avila Beach on the sign out on the highway. Some of our mail was going to Avalon on Catalina Island, and we got some of their mail which only said Avalon. That was long before zip codes came into use.

---

3   Footnote for Landlubbers
     Captain Travis – Ballast:: any heavy material carried in the bottom of a vessel to provide stability.

Other communities had the same problem, Grover didn't say Grover Beach; it said Grover City.

Anyway, that was one problem I worked on. I went to talk with Postmaster Vincent Canet. He and his wife ran the grocery store and the post office in the back of the store. I asked him, "What can we do to get our name changed to Avila Beach?"

Mr. Canet said we needed to petition for the change with the postmaster general. So, I went around and got every voting resident of the town to sign the petition. It hadn't changed when my time to be president ended, but the lady who took my place agreed to continue the effort to get the name changed. As it turned out, we finally got it done in '57. Now, Avila Beach is a tourist town with hotels and motels, traffic signals and crowded beaches. It's booming and thriving – no longer a sleepy fishing village.

I also served as a member of the school board for a few years, one year as the president. Homer Odom was the superintendent then, and he was not happy with the way members of the board were spending money like it was going out of style. We made some corrections along those lines that year.

Besides her work on the harbor district, Katherine served as president of the Parent Teacher Association, was a Camp Fire leader and as the parade planner in our town. She made costumes, some of them fairly elaborate, for the kids to wear in parades and took them to parades in the different little towns in the area. She was always busy with our children and their different activities.

Richie and a friend

Besides all that, she worked some of the time, she cut fish for a dollar an hour, and she cut more fish than anyone, and faster. Mabel came to stay with us to help with the house and the children when Katherine was working.

Because I was gone so much of the time, I missed a lot of things at home, but the kids were always glad to see me. Well now, that wasn't always true. I remember one time in about 1952, I think I was gone fishing for five and a half months. Phillip was two years old at the time. When I got home, he wouldn't have anything to do with me, he'd run away from me, wouldn't come to me and wouldn't let me pick him up. It was because I now had a beard. I was fishing on the San Giuseppe at the time, and on a little boat you're short of fresh water. Shaving is not a priority. Anyhow, Phillip was not fond of my beard – or me.

I remember that well. That was before we moved to Avila. We were living in that rented house in Santa Cruz, up in the northern part of town and sort of out of town. It was a good place for the children. There was a country road in front of the house, and behind the house a little distance, was a shallow creek for the kids to wade in.

In 1955 our Susie came along. She was born in the French Hospital in San Luis Obispo, in the middle of the night. When Katherine and I got to the hospital, the doctor wasn't there, but the nurse took her to the birthing room immediately. I stayed down to do the paper work, and when the clerk came to Katherine's name she started it with a C. I corrected her. When I told her Katherine's maiden name, Kostaras, that threw her for a loop; I had to spell that for her. A little later after Susie was born, with the nurse assisting, the clerk asked what we were going to name the baby. I told her she would be named after her mother, and the middle name was going to be Sue, spelled S I O U X. That was just to throw her another curve. She laughed, but I'm not sure she wouldn't have preferred to box me one.

Sometime after we moved to Avila, my old friend from high school, Bob Elam and his family rented a house right next to the old school there, and we reconnected. By then, Katherine and I had four or five kids, and they had three, and so, we connected as family friends too. When Bob found out we were going to the Nazarene Church, he and his family started going there too. We stayed in touch after they moved to Oregon a few years later, but when they came down here, they'd be over to see us. I told you about us being in the same English class and being inspired to try writing poetry. Well, once in a while when they came, Bob brought me some of his poetry, and he'd ask for my latest poems. He wasn't as prolific as I, because he had a lot of other interests.

One thing we did for fun when we had a little time was, we'd pack up and go see my brother Rudy and wife Helen and their kids, two girls and a boy, for a couple of days. Katherine and Helen were very close, and Rudy and I were too. Their kids were younger than most of ours, but they had a good time together. They got to be with those cousins quite a lot.

We didn't have many vacations, but Katherine would put the kids in the car and come to where I was going ashore. We'd get to spend time together that way. As the boats got bigger, though, the loads got bigger too, and the unloading took longer. The fish were frozen, and they didn't come out easy one at a time - especially if you had twenty or thirty tons. Then, it takes a while to defrost and clean the boat, change the freezer filters and the oil filters on the diesel engines, get your laundry done, buy groceries and fuel and oil for another couple of months. Sometimes, we'd get to spend a week together, but we were rushing all the time to get me ready to go back out.

In 1957 we took the kids back to Oklahoma to visit Grandma Hulda. That was the first time we had seen her since 1944 when she came to visit us after Eileen was born. It was hot when we got to Oklahoma, and when we got to Grandma's house, she was sitting out on the porch with a wet wash cloth across her forehead and her feet in a pan of water.

Two years earlier, Grandma remarried; she married a Mr. Carr. It was a shock to the family. She had been a widow for nearly twenty years, and after all that time, no one could figure out why she wanted to be married. But Mr. Carr was a kind and gentle man, and his son was a good guy; even after Mr. Carr died, he took care of Grandma.

Anyway, that was a good trip and Grandma was happy to see us and meet some of the children for the first time.

All the kids went fishing with me from time to time, and they really didn't have to be a certain age. Tommy went when he was only three years old, and he didn't miss home at all. He minded well except for one time. I had told him not to leave the cockpit without permission. One day I was pulling fish, salmon I think, and all of a sudden the boat started making a slow turn. I thought – what in the world? I looked and there was Tom alongside the cabin where the engine is. When he stepped out of the cockpit, he stepped on a spoke of the steering wheel, and that started us on an entirely different course - going nowhere.

I took Fred fishing too, but he had eyesight problems, and he'd get seasick. The first trip he made was up to Fort Bragg which is a week's trip. He was sick every day. He was miserable; he'd have to lay in the bunk all day. To make it worse, when you're fishing salmon, quite often you'll get one that is undersized. When I got one like that, if he wasn't harmed, I turned him loose, and he'd swim away. If he was dead, maybe bitten off by a sea lion, I saved him and at night I cooked him in a pressure cooker. In the wintertime when the weather is bad, and you can't go fishing, you can break open a jar of salmon and have salmon patties or whatever. So I canned some of them. I did that a time or two on that trip, and when I took the lid off the pressure cooker, the odor made Fred so sick. He never wanted to go with me again.

The whole family went fishing with me every now and then. That was one way we could all be together for more than just a day or two that was spent mostly getting me ready for another trip.

On one of our family trips, we were not too far south of the border in Mexican waters. It was a nice, warm afternoon and very quiet. It was the fifteenth of June, the day before mine and Katherine's wedding anniversary. We always wanted to be together on that special day. Katherine decided she'd surprise me with a pot roast. She had a piece of meat in the oven and she peeled potatoes, carrots and onions. We had an adjustable rack on the stove with a clamp to hold the pan in place. She had the vegetables with water on the stove, but she got to feeling sickly, she had a real problem with getting seasick, and she went to lie down without putting the clamp on to hold the pan in place.

We got some fish on the line, and of course, you want to stay on that school of fish; so I put the boat in a figure eight pattern hoping to pick up the school again. In that pattern, you come across your own wake, and when it happened that day, the boat rolled a little, and all the vegetables for Katherine's stew spilled off and onto the floor.

As I went by the state room, she was lying there crying like everything.

"What is it?" I asked.

"All our food went onto the floor."

"Well, that's nothing to cry about."

"Yes it is. Tomorrow's our anniversary, and I wanted to make a special dinner."

Katherine just cried and cried. I felt so sorry for her.

I went and picked up the vegetables, put them back in the pan, washed them in fresh water, drained them, added fresh water, put them on the stove, moved the clamp, tightened it and went back to fishing. The stew came out alright, and we got to have our special dinner after all.

Once we were going to make a family trip, and Fred decided to go too, even though he knew he'd get seasick. I realized there were times on those trips when the kids got bored, so I built them a swing. They had a ball on that swing. Poor Fred would get so sick. He'd stay in his bunk until he finally got over it, and when he did, he took his turn on the swing. That was about the only fun he had on that trip.

Fred having a little fun.

Now, I've got to tell you the story of Umbriado. I'm not sure which one it was, but on a family trip, as we headed out to the fishing grounds, we went past Catalina Island, and a common housefly came aboard. There are no insects at sea, so it was quite unusual that he was on the trip with us. Katherine named him Umbriado. The kids made a pet out of him; he was entertainment they didn't ordinarily have on a fishing boat. They never swatted at him; in fact, they tried to tame him. When he landed on the rim of one of the kid's plates, they would brag, "Umbriado likes me best."

One day he disappeared. They looked everywhere to no avail. A couple of days later, I had to climb the mast to replace the light bulb, and there he was. They were all thrilled to have him back, and he stayed with us the whole trip. When we headed back to port in San Diego, he flew off to Coronado Island as we passed by.

PART VI
A CHANGE IN COURSE
1957-1962

What Now?

I fished the Katherine about eight years until I had a serious heart problem, and the doctors told me to quit. I was examined at the Marine Hospital in San Francisco, out by the Presidio. All mariners could go there free of charge, and there are qualified doctors, army and navy doctors. Once in a while, in a special case, they'd get a doctor from Walter Reed to come out. When I was there, it just so happened that two doctors from Mayo Clinic were there; both of them and two military doctors checked my heart. They all agreed that I shouldn't exert myself. One of them said, "Go sell your boat, sell your business and don't plan on working anymore."

I was feeling so bad that I couldn't even drive myself home. Cousin Homer drove me, but we thought it best not to tell Katherine all of that. We told her Homer just came for a visit.

I was still trying to pay off the boat, and I had a big family; there were a couple of new babies since I built the boat. So with all that, I think I was just working too hard. At that time we were still doing things manually. We didn't have any hydraulics; they hadn't been put on boats in our area. We had to do a lot of it by hand. If we had had then what we have now, I wouldn't even have needed a deck hand; I could have done it like I did until recently - alone. For the type of fishing we do, and the way boats are outfitted today, it is very safe and easy for one man to fish.

It was in about October or November they told me to quit. I didn't really want to sell the Katherine, but then, I didn't feel good either, and I had to do something. In 1959 I sold the boat and took half the money to buy a little grocery store, T&G Market, down on Grand Avenue in Grover City. It had a little meat market which I made into a fish market. I bought another little boat, the Golden Rule, so I could provide fish for it, but just not work so hard. We also had a collection agency in the store; we collected for Southern California Gas, Pacific Gas and Electricity and Bell Telephone. The only thing we didn't collect was the water bill.

Our family moved into a house back of the little store we bought. At that point I never thought that I would soon have a chance to go back to school. The way that happened was interesting.

When I sold the Katherine, the fellow that bought it wanted to keep Jack, my crew member, because he knew the boat; he'd been with me several years. It was probably a month or six weeks after I sold the boat, that Jack called and said, "Travis do you have a job for me? I'll work for half the price. That man I'm working for flies off the handle if something doesn't go just right. Now, he may not be mad at me, but he'll be mad at what happened, and he'll throw a wrench or hit a gaff hook on the rail or something. The other day he did that, he broke a gaff hook over the rail, and part of it flew and just missed me. I need a job, but I don't want to work for that guy anymore."

"Well, Jack," I said, "All I have is this little store, and there's not enough income for two families. Let's look around and see what we can find for you."

There was a onetime friend and fisherman I knew who

was foreman for a tug company. Jack got a job with him immediately working as a deckhand on a tug. Within two or three months, Jack called me and said, "Travis you're a good boat operator, and they need a tug captain in a hurry. All you'll have to do is turn the steering wheel – no work – no strain – nothing heavy at all. I really don't think it would hurt your heart."

He gave me a phone number to call. I got the job because I was a good boat handler and I knew the boss. When he heard I was available, he said, "Travis is available? Get him down here." Without an interview, he hired me. The superintendent said the two deckhands were there to do the work, and with my experience, all I had to do was turn the steering wheel. I went to work Christmas week for California Shipping. They owned and operated a fleet of tankers and tugboats. Jack was one of my deckhands; we were working together again.

The job was interesting and educational. Basically, the tugboats were there to help large oil tankers in and out of deepwater berths. Tankers have to be put in a mooring offshore because of the loads they carry. 300,000 barrels of crude oil displace a great deal of water, and those tankers have to have fifty feet of water to stay afloat. They are moored where there is that depth of water while they discharge their product and perhaps reload with gasoline or other byproduct of the petroleum industry.

It is necessary to have a tug alongside the tankers twenty-four hours a day in case of a disaster, an oil spill or a fire. The ship is there for nine or ten days, and it is dead in the water and doesn't have steam up to get out of the berth. It takes quite a while to heat a boiler and everything required to get the propeller going. You've got to be able to move that ship away from a pipeline that's pumping oil. So, we are destined to be alongside that ship as long as it's pumping or receiving a product.

I made it home for Christmas, all but one year when I was running the tug boat. It fell my crew's lot to take care of a super tanker. That year they didn't get to go home, and I didn't either.

From time to time I was loaned out to move a sand or rock barge on a sewer line project that Los Angeles had going. They were installing a huge sewer pipe line out into the ocean in Santa Monica Bay from a water reclamation plant. The pipeline was adjacent to the Standard Oil tanker moorings, and was so large one could drive a semi-truck through it. The barge I operated was carrying the sand and rock that would cover the pipeline; all concrete pipe had to be covered on the ocean bottom. That line is called the Hyperion Sewer Line and is near the Standard Oil refinery at El Segundo.

Actually, I was not licensed for what I was doing on the tugs. One day, Captain Melbe, the superintendent in charge, told me he wanted me to get a license. I had to go to maritime school to do that.

"But I've got to feed my family," I said.

"The Coast Guard requires all our skippers to have a license, and we will give our personnel time to get one if they enroll in maritime school. You don't have to worry about finances; we'll pay for the school, and you will keep your job. You'll work six days and be off three days, and you'll go to school on those days. You've been on the ocean all these years, you handle a boat well, and we have no complaints at all. We'd like to send you to school."

So, that's what I did. Jack and I both started the Coast Guard's maritime school in the later part of '60. I worked on the tugs and studied for the next two years to get a master mariner's license. That license will allow you to sail, but it has limits as to the size and duty of the vessel.

If I worked the hours they wanted me to and went to school there, that meant I could not see my family at all. I was working out of El Segundo, and Redondo Beach was a lot closer to my job. Katherine and I decided to move our family, and we found a rental house at Redondo Beach.

When I was home, I studied to take the test for my license, the master mariner's license. I did a lot of research, and Katherine helped me get ready using flash cards, and that really helped. The test for getting the license is tough, but I was well prepared.

When you take the test, you are seated in a glass enclosed area much like a phone booth. You have a black lead pencil with no eraser, and your sleeves are rolled up. You are observed for the next seven and a half hours straight. If you need to go to the bathroom, the ensign stays with you. All of those steps absolutely prevent cheating.

An ensign slips the test papers in to you through a slot with one sheet of paper and one question at a time. You ask for more paper if it takes more than one sheet to answer a question. Some are very complicated. It took twelve sheets for me to answer one.

On the master mariner's test, you have to answer

questions on thirty-two subjects. The subjects are as simple as boxing a compass, and as intricate as health and sanitation on a ship, and include navigation, weather mapping, aids to navigation, light houses and buoys, ship's business, signaling, Morse code, and so on. There wasn't much on mechanics; that's in the engineering department.

The first license is basic to all the others, and it is only good for twenty miles offshore. There are other licenses for more miles, different types of ships and their cargo. A test dealing with exploration wouldn't be as difficult as one for hauling people or for carrying munitions. The hardest of the overall tests was the one for carrying passengers. The tests are somewhat similar; once you get the original license, you have open book tests.

I passed that test and got my license and was soon studying for the next step up the ladder. Those were busy, busy days with work, church, studying, and keeping up with the kid's activities, so, there was little time for fishing, but we went when we could. I had the Golden Rule, a little thirty-six foot boat I bought when we had the market. It wouldn't have been safe to go offshore, but it was a good little boat, okay for gill netting[4]. The children, Fred and Eileen, and I also used it when we fished white seabass out of Avila.

The Wreck

I've got a story I want to tell you about the wreck of the Golden Rule. I kept the boat in Avila, and when we

---

4   Footnote for landlubbers
     Captain Travis - Gill netting: That's where you put a net down that looks like a fence; the
     fish will swim up to it and try to get through and the net catches their gills.

moved to Redondo Beach, of course, I wanted to put the boat down there. When I had three days off, I took the bus to go get it. It was in dry dock in Morro Bay where they had installed a new steering system for me. That was early in '61. I brought it around to Avila, went and bought some groceries and slept aboard part of the night. My friend, Bob Elam, was going to go with me to take the boat to Redondo Beach, but at the last minute he got a call to go to work. So, I wound up taking the boat down by myself.

Everything seemed okay when I picked it up. It was already in the water and it steered fine, but when I was about three miles offshore near Point Conception, I lost the rudder. Evidently the shipyard hadn't put nuts on the bolts that secure the coupling for the rudder. I was tired after six days of work and traveling for hours, so I took my mattress out on deck and went to sleep thinking I would jerry-rig something after daylight. When I woke up I was right in the breakers, and the boat was being shoved ashore by the waves. The Coast Guard station was just twelve miles above me. I didn't have a radio transmitter, but I thought I could send up a flare, and they would see me and send help. The next wave broke on deck and put water in the wheel- house. I couldn't even get down in the bow to get a flare because a wave could keep me in there. Remember, I don't swim. I started praying; I said, "Lord, what should I do?"

Somehow He got the message to me, "Well, you've got a life jacket, you fool."

So, I put on a life jacket.

By that time the front part of the boat was bouncing

on the sand. I went up toward the bow so I'd be clear of the boat, and when a big wave came by, six foot maybe, I jumped right into it. That wave sat me up on shore just beautifully. I knelt down on the sand right on the edge of the water and I said, "Lord, thank you for saving my life." As I was praying, I realized that I didn't have my dentures. They were hanging in a cup under a window right in the galley; I put them there when I went out to rest. While I was still praying, I felt something touch me on the shoulder. It's an unusual thing, but the boat had gotten up broadside on the beach, and that window was right there behind me. I just reached in there and got the cup with my dentures in it, washed them off with salt water and stuck them in my mouth. It was amazing.

The boat was on the sandy beach, a total loss, but I wondered what was in there that might be valuable. So, I climbed up and located my direction finder. I took it and jumped off into the sand and put it near the railroad track that runs right by there.

My clothes were soaked, so I went up by the tracks to dry out. It was a warm and sunny morning. I took my shoes off, wrung my socks out and laid them out on the rail to dry. Way over in the distance to the north of me, I could see a farmhouse, a barn, and a little bit of smoke. It was five or six miles over there. When I got up the courage, I decided I was going to walk up there. I thought about my direction finder, but that thing probably weighed thirty pounds. It was up high and dry below the railroad tracks, so I decided to leave it, and I took off walking.

It probably took an hour or more to get up there. It was

about ten o'clock in the morning, and the sun was beating down on me by then. As I went by the barn, there was a water trough that had a float on it to help keep the water supply up, and I pushed it down to get water, got a drink and washed the salt off me. When I got to the house, it was fenced in, and there were flowers here and there in the yard. I heard a motor that sounded like a lawn mower coming from the back yard. I knocked on the front door and didn't get an answer, but an old dog came out from around the house.

I was a little skeptical at first, but I called him Shep and patted him under the chin, and he went to wagging his tail. After I petted him, he went around the house and came back with a tennis ball in his mouth. There was a fence about four feet from the house with a narrow walkway from the front to the back of the house. I walked around there with that dog following me. As I got around the corner where I could see into the back yard, there was a lady mowing the grass and going the other way.

I hollered, but it didn't do any good with that lawn mower going. So, I went back and sat down on the front porch in the shade and began to pray. I heard the lawn mower motor sputter a little bit. She'd run out of gas. I called out, "Anybody home?"

She answered, "Just a minute. Just a minute."

She went through the house and opened the front door. I visited with her and told her what had happened to me. She made a phone call to Katherine at Redondo Beach and told her about the wreck and my situation and gave her directions as to how to get to the house. "Now write all this down or you won't get through," she said. Katherine would have to come through Vandenberg Air Force Base where there was a gate with a lock, and she gave her the combination; then there was another gate, and she gave her that combination; and there was a rock laying by the post of another gate and a key under the rock. There were a lot of stops, but that was the only way to get out to the ranch. Katherine got all the information, and while we waited for her, the lady and I got acquainted.

Her husband was foreman of the ranch; about four thousand acres, I think. He was on a trip to Long Beach to bring back two horses in a trailer, and was due back sometime that day. The ranch belonged to two very wealthy sisters who lived down south of Long Beach. There's a little area down there that's very secluded and remote; only the wealthy live there. The sisters raised Appaloosas there on the ranch, and had bought two more.

The lady gave me something to eat, and we got to talking. One thing I asked her was how she got her groceries. She told me they went to town about once a week. Then I asked where she went to church.

She said, "We were raised Catholic, but we're so far from anything out here we don't go to church."

She had two girls, so I asked her about them.

"They go to a Catholic school, and that's all the spiritual training they get."

Anyhow, I witnessed to her about Christ's teachings, and I prayed with her. She put Jesus in her heart. We must have talked for two hours or more.

Just think – out of the catastrophe of losing my fishing

boat I had the opportunity to witness to that lady about my Jesus.

I was very tired after all that happened. The lady said, "It's going to take three hours to come from Redondo Beach and stop and open all those gates. Why don't you stretch out on the couch?" So, I slept for a while. I didn't get to meet her husband; he didn't make it home before Katherine came, and we left to go home.

That's the end of the story and the end of the Golden Rule. I had that boat two years before it wrecked. I didn't have insurance on it, but it wasn't a very expensive boat, probably $3,000. Anyway, I was out of a boat for a while.

A little later, I bought a government surplus boat. Actually, Katherine bought it. I went to San Diego and looked at it and was going to bid on it at the auction, but I got a call to take a tugboat out. I really wanted that boat. It had just come out of the shipyard and had a lot of brass and was all polished up, and oh, it was a beauty. The admiral had gone back and forth to the ship in it. They called it the "Admiral's Gig."

I sent Katherine to the auction. I gave her the number on the boat and told her not to go over twelve or thirteen hundred dollars. A lot of boats had sold by the time the one I wanted came up for bid. The admiral, being a government employee, could not bid on it, but he hired someone to place his bid. During the bidding, he'd go up fifty dollars, then Katherine would. It got up to eleven hundred, and when he went to eleven-fifty, Katherine went to twelve. He had a little pad and a clipboard, and at that point, he threw them down and stomped out.

The tugboat company I worked for had a boatyard where we worked on our boats. I hired a fellow with a big trailer to bring my boat from San Diego up to that boatyard. Then I went to work on it and named it the Sir+, or the Sir Plus. At that time I was going to maritime school and studying, but there were a few days I could work on my new little boat, and it didn't cost anything for it to sit there. When I got the Sir+ finished I took it up to Avila and moored it there. Harbor fees were much more expensive in Southern California than in Avila. I could moor in Avila for twenty-five dollars a month.

When Phil or Tom had a little time off, they'd take it and go fishing just for fun.

By the Way

Every summer for years and years after Homer got out of service, he came and went fishing with me. Sometime in there, I don't remember just when, we were fishing salmon in shallow water close to shore, eight miles or less, and quite often only one mile. That close in, the sea lions are terrible pests; they come and take the gear and cut your fish in half or tear them off the hook, so we kept a shotgun or flares to scare them, but it didn't deter them much. They are very opportunistic feeders, and they'll feed wherever they find food. The end of a fishing line means they don't have to chase it very much, and they like that.

Homer and I had been fishing for salmon when some of the boats found albacore offshore, only twelve miles or so. So we took the salmon gear off, put albacore gear on overnight and went and bought ice. With salmon fishing we deliver daily, so you don't bother to take ice, but with albacore, you have to take ice because you're offshore a day or two. You don't put a hot blooded tuna down in your ice; that melts it too fast. So we just put wet gunny sacks over the fish on deck. In the evening, we opened the hatch and got the fish iced down before we went to bed.

The two little bunks didn't have much headroom; you had to get undressed and then sort of roll into the bunk. Along in the night I heard Homer call out, "Travis!" I woke up and turned over, but he didn't say any more, and I thought he'd probably had a dream. I turned back over and went to sleep. The next morning he had a big red crease across his forehead.

I asked, "What in world happened to you, Homer?"

He said, "I was dreaming, and I thought those sea lions were taking our fish, and I sat up too quick."

He had hit his head on the 4 x 4 inch deck beam above him, knocked himself out and fell back down on the bunk.

He said, "I've got the awfullest headache this morning."

Sometime in the summer of '57, we, the family, were fishing way offshore and it had been pretty good. But, poor Katherine had been sick every day – every day. One day I was really feeling sorry for her, so I said, "If the fish aren't biting good tomorrow, I'll take you ashore."

We were close enough to Hawaii I could have taken her there. When I told her she could go there or to San Diego, she said, "The car is in San Diego, and I don't want to be without my car."

The next day we headed in. When we got in, we started

unloading the younger children's clothes and packing them in the car. Then I went to get in line to unload the fish, and she went up to the Marine Hospital. When she came back she said, "Put the clothes back on the boat. The doctor said the rabbit died, so I may as well go fishing." She had been seasick <u>and</u> had morning sickness at the same time.

That was when we were expecting Jan, our third girl.

Our precious Jan was born the following spring. That little girl loved music from the beginning, and as time went by, we realized that she had a real talent for it. Katherine and I thought she needed a piano to develop that talent. Now here's a real coincidence that allowed that to happen. Sometime earlier, we, the family, were in Long Beach and we happened upon an   auction in progress. I bid on a man's diamond ring and got it. We were able to trade that ring for a piano. By time she was four, Jan had learned to play that piano well, and she played it all through college and she still plays it. It's in her home today. She sings and plays piano in our church. We're all very proud of her.

PART VII
GLOBAL
1962- 1970

Another Door Opens

In 1962 the tugboat company promised me I could have time off to go albacore fishing, so I leased a boat from a friend in the San Francisco Bay area and went fishing. When I came back the company was unhappy with me and scolded me because they had called the house trying to get ahold of me; they had work for me. Katherine said, "He's at sea; I can't get ahold of him."

When I got back, they told me I should have checked in.

"Well" I said, "You told me I had a hundred days off."

"Maybe that's what the foreman told you, but that's not what we understood."

"If you're not satisfied with me, I can always get a job somewhere else."

He said, "No, no, you don't want to do that."

"Well, let me think about it." And that's what I did. I thought about it and decided I could do better.

I called the Los Angeles Harbor Department where they had postings for companies needing crew. I put my name in with four different companies that worked in the oil and tugboat business; Global Marine, Inc. was one, Western Offshore Drilling and Exploration Company, otherwise called WODECO, was one of them, and there were a couple of others. All of them were on the New York stock exchange. Global Marine called me and asked me to come in for an interview. I gave them my resumé and was interviewed by Captain Grant Allen. He liked what he heard and asked if I had any reservations about taking the job.

"Yes," I said, "I'd rather not work on Sunday.

"Well I don't know that we can arrange that, but would you be willing to work every other Sunday?"

"I can make that compromise," I said. And, they hired me.

Global Marine, Inc. worked for, I'm just guessing, about twenty-seven oil companies; there were the Hawaiian, the Standard, Conoco, City, Humble, Richfield, Phillips, Texaco, Union and a bunch of others. Global was not an oil company. It rented its rigs, equipment and crew in drilling operations. Sometimes two or three companies would go together on a project, and we'd have that many superintendents on a ship to keep happy. I had experience with that later on.

The first ship that Global Marine built was the CUSS I. That stood for Continental, Union, Superior and Standard. Those companies put all the money together for the first drilling ship on the west coast. The CUSS I was used when they drilled the Mohole project in 12,500 feet of water in an attempt to drill through the earth's crust. The job was done through the National Science Foundation back in '57 or '58.

There's an interesting thing about the name of that ship. Sometime later, when they were drilling for British Oil, they found that CUSS was a dirty word in the Arabian area, so in the Mideast they changed the name of that and other Global ships to Glomar, though on the west coast it was still the CUSS I. When they built the second ship they called it the Glomar II, and then the next one was Glomar III and so on. Later, I worked on the Glomar IV at Hartlepool, England.

Global did a lot more than drill oil wells. They had a part in the mining of gold and diamonds. In the late '60s, they sent a ship to Alaska to mine for gold, and before that, they mined for diamonds off the coast of South Africa. A few years after I left the company, Global sent the Glomar Challenger to drill and take core samples of the Mariana Trench, which is the deepest part of the ocean in the world. The company also drilled and took core samples in several other places. We did a dragline survey for the Mexican government for minerals near Cedros Island. We found a lot of manganese deposits there. It would be viable mining if they wanted to do that. Later, that manganese was used as a decoy. The company claimed that the Glomar Explorer was going to be used to mine manganese, but it was really going to be used in an effort to raise a Russian submarine that sunk somewhere off of Hawaii. The work was requested by the CIA, and it was a hush, hush project. Working for Global was a learning experience, and I didn't know half of what they were doing.

I went to work for Global around Christmas in '62. I was hired to run a personnel boat, the Cathead, which was used to take people out to the drilling ships and back to shore. I was on duty seven days and off seven, and I ate and slept on the ship when I was on duty. The captain of the ship directed me as to other jobs I needed to do.

One day I picked up four or five men, in business suits carrying brief cases, going out to the CUSS I. After we got out a ways, one of those guys came up on the bridge and sat down beside me. I said, "Did you read the sign? You're not supposed to be here." He assured me it would be okay, he just wanted to talk for a few minutes. It was a several mile trip, and I didn't have anything to do but steer the boat, so we talked.

He said, "You're new here aren't you?"

"I've only been here a couple of months."

"How do you like your job?"

"I like it alright, but I see some things that I believe could be better."

"Like what?"

"Well, I've noticed when those guys come up from drilling, they've got a lot of mud and grime on them; and the stairs, they're just steel, and I think they should have safety grating on them, and the handrails should be painted a bright color so they could see them better."

"Those ideas just make sense," the man said.

By then another fellow had joined us, and we just had a conversation about how certain things could be improved, everything from safety drills to having a newspaper to be circulated on the ships and to families of the workers.

One of those guys, asked me, "Anything else?"

I said, "Well, yes. The men on a ship like this one ought to have a place to go on their time off to have prayer and meditation, a separate room where they can be alone without everybody milling around and watching television and everything."

"That's a pretty good idea, too," he said.

By then we were at the ship, and we said our goodbyes. They went their way and I went mine, and I didn't think any more about it.

The next Wednesday night the expediter called me from

the dispatcher's radio and asked me to stop by the marine superintendent's office when I got off work on Thursday at noon. Captain Allen was in another room on the phone when I stopped by the office. The expeditor asked me, "What have you done?"

"I don't know what I've done," I said.

"Well the marine superintendent doesn't call you in for nothing. You must have crossed somebody on the ship."

He had me nervous. I'd only been with the company a short time, and I wasn't sure of all the dos and don'ts. Pretty soon Captain Grant Allen opened the door and had me come in and closed the door. "Do you know Bob Bauer?" he asked.

"No, I don't. What ship does he work on?"

"Bob Bauer is the president of the company. You never met him?"

"Not that I know of."

"How about A.J. Fields?"

"No, I don't know who he is either."

"That's the vice-president of the company. You took them out to the ship sometime this week. Evidently Bob Bauer was pretty impressed with you."

He showed me a paper and said, "This came down from the top." It read something like this: To all marine superintendents: Captain Travis Evans is hereby made chaplain of this fleet of ships and men. If a man has a problem of any kind, he is to see Captain Evans, and Evans is to be available whether he is on duty or not, night or day to counsel anyone in our personnel. He is to have a full expense account for travel needed for that counseling. He is to take care of the ship's people when they have personal problems.

I would have been nervous if I had known who I was talking to that day on the personnel boat, the president and vice-president, but I always have tried to treat everybody the same, whether they were a big shot or a peon, it didn't matter to me, they were treated the same. Telling them we ought to have a prayer room, and we ought to have safety drills, and we ought to have a newspaper was exactly what I thought, and evidently, it was the right thing to do because of all the good things that came about. I was not expecting to be made chaplain of the ship.

I counseled many men in my office aboard ship in the time I served as chaplain. I counseled company personnel and the personnel of the companies who were aboard. I was called out a few times.

Once I was called to a home about three hours away. I took Katherine with me, just for the company, but she was a big help when we got there, and that was around ten o'clock in the evening. A husband and wife were in heated dispute. They were shouting at each other with much profanity. She was throwing clothes into her suitcase, and he was packing his work clothes. Katherine and I started talking to them, trying to calm the situation. Katherine took her in the kitchen while I talked to him. We talked and prayed several times, until two or three in the morning when we all had breakfast together. Before we left Katherine helped her put her clothes away. The man told me he didn't want the company to know about the squabble. I told him not to worry about that. I never turned it in to my expense account. I don't know if they made it or not. I never looked into it. But, he did show up for work the next week.

Later, I befriended a man and took him back and forth to work for a while. When he called me at home one day, I could tell by the way he sounded that he'd been through some really frustrating experience. He was in a hotel somewhere, but he wouldn't tell me where. He told me that one of his children had been arrested. We talked, and I prayed with him and gave him some scriptures to look up. He said he didn't have a Bible, and I told him to look around, he would probably find one there in the hotel room - the Gideons, you know. At one point, I put my hand over the phone and told Katherine to go next door and trace the call so we could locate him. Katherine had the car ready when the call was finished, and we drove to a town about fifteen miles away, to a hotel in a sleazy part of town.

When I asked the clerk if he was there, she said he was not. I described him, and she said he was on the second floor. We went up, and knocked on the door. He said "It's open. Come in." We walked in to find him sitting on the bed with a Bible on his knees and a pistol next to him. We spent time with him, talking and praying, and he seemed okay when we left. He didn't come back to work again, I never knew what happened to him. But, I believe to this day we saved a life that night.

I volunteered to help train the marine crew after their work hours, so they could get a higher license and advance from able bodied seaman to boatswain, from boatswain to third mate, and so on. It takes proof of a year's sea time at each level to sit for tests for the next license. The men on the crew worked their twelve hour shifts, then went to the wheelhouse where I drilled them on all the subjects I knew were going to be on the Coast Guard tests. Global hired retired Coast Guard and American Bureau of Shipping officers. They needed their experience in qualifying the seaman they were hiring and also for building the ships they were building. Because of their training, we were able to get our licenses upgraded without having to take four of the tests before the Coast Guard. If they thought a man was lacking in some area, then he could go to the Coast Guard, and they would give him an open book test.

During that time I got promoted right up the line. In fact, when I went to get tested for higher tonnage, the company sent a letter to the Coast Guard stating "Captain Travis has spent enough time on our ships that he is qualified to get his license for higher tonnage if you find him adequate to the test." So, just like that, I climbed the ladder.

I became captain of a mineral and exploration ship in about 1965. I was pleased, but there really wasn't much cause for celebration; my pay didn't increase all that much, but it increased my responsibilities and certainly matured my thinking. The captain of a ship is responsible for the safety of the crew, the vessel, and the cargo. Can you imagine this uneducated farm boy with the responsibilities of a big family having that top heavy load of responsibility added on?

However, I wasn't nervous at all about taking the captain's position even though the mortgage on the ship they put me in charge of, the CUSS I, was $21,500,000. I had company manuals, plus I had the alternate captain's logs, and I had prepared for the job and was confident that I knew what to do. I had only been with the company about a year and a half when I was skippering their ships with forty or fifty men aboard.

At that time we were drilling along the west coast and the Channel Islands near Santa Barbara. We drilled a bunch of oil fields in that area. I never kept a record of how many, but we drilled for several companies in that area.

The main thing in the operation of a drilling ship is to keep it moored in one spot. There is a twenty-five inch hole in the base plate on the ocean floor for the drill to go through, so the ship must be moored in one spot regardless of the weather conditions. We are moored by eight anchors and chains.

There were only about twenty men who were marine oriented onboard a drilling ship. The other twenty or twenty-five men were on the drilling crew. There was a drilling superintendent, but I had authority even over him. If I said, "You guys bring the drilling gears out of the hole, we've got to secure for a storm." nobody questioned it. They secured all the drilling operations.

The specialty people included Schlumberger who stuck stuff down the hole to check the density of the terrain, Halliburton people who did the cement work, Kodak camera people, mud people who found the right mud mixture to use to case the drill stem and lubricate the bit. All of those people weren't there on a daily basis, but sometimes in certain stages they might be there for a week. In emergencies they came in on a chopper, but mostly they came in on the personnel boat. We had rooms for the Halliburton crew and for the Eastman camera people and other specialty people. They ate and slept on the ship.

Any vessel with over twelve persons had to have a hospital, or a designated area for a hospital. Even though we had service people aboard, sometimes for long periods of time, Global vessels only employed the marine and drilling crew. There were no paying passengers on our ship, so we never had a hospital aboard. We had a medical dispensary for minor ills. We had a chopper and were close to shore, and we could take them in if necessary.

If someone needed medical assistance, as captain, it was my duty to diagnose the illness, disease or injury and dispense the proper care. Sometimes it was splints and bandages and medication, and sometimes I sent our helicopter ashore with the patient; other times I was forced to put them to bed in the dispensary and play nurse along with my other duties. I was furnished medical books and supplies, and I studied the latest journals and books the pharmaceutical companies furnished with each medicine. The books described symptoms, false symptoms, dosages, side effects, emergency methods, longtime methods, the cure, and possible reoccurrences.

Most of my experiences were with minor injuries, burns, heat strokes, flu, and viruses. Over the years, I also treated venereal diseases, as you can imagine with thirty to fifty personnel going ashore in foreign ports, and then coming onto our drilling ship.

One time during an outbreak of a new strain of Asian flu, my crew didn't get shore leave for ever so long. After their tour of duty with me, instead of getting to go home, they were asked to crew another of Global's ships. All its crew was hospitalized. Another ship had to stop operations altogether for even the officers were sick.

Some crew members who worked on the CUSS I, during the Mohole Project, were still working when I became captain of that ship. They had quite a story to tell about a writer who was there to observe and report on the project. I'll tell the story they told me as best I remember it:

They said you couldn't hold a conversation with that man; he had an abstract mind and just couldn't stay with you. He wanted favors all the time. The ship had four meals a day, at six in the morning, at noon, at six in the evening and at midnight. He'd go to the head cook, the steward, and want a certain thing prepared for his meal. He didn't want to eat when the men did, and he didn't want what they ate.

He was not liked by the crew. Here's an example of why: One night he asked the radio operator to call his wife. In those days a call had to go through the ship's operator to a marine operator in San Pedro, San Francisco, Portland or Seattle. At night, men on the tuna boats down in the Galapagos, Peru, and that area called home to their wives. Sometimes it was a pretty long wait, but you had to wait your turn.

That guy was down on the drilling floor and every once in a while he would call up with the ship's intercom and say "Have you got my wife yet?" He was getting pretty impatient.

"No," said our operator, "We're having to wait our turn."

That went on for an hour or two and finally, when the operator got through and got her on the line, he called the guy on the P.A. system and said, "We have your wife on the phone."

He didn't get any reply. After waiting for several minutes, he took off and went down a series of stairs and across the deck and found him watching the work that was going on and making notes. When he looked up and saw the operator, he said, "Oh, just tell her I'm busy, and tell her I'm okay." After pestering that seaman so much, that was all he had to say.

Every door on the ship was all metal, and each room had a porthole which provided the only ventilation if the door was closed. All the doors had two hooks, one about three or four inches long and another about nine inches; you could hook the shorter one and crack the door for ventilation, or the longer one for a little more air.

One night some guys found a seabird, a cormorant, swimming in the moon pool[5]. They got a little net and caught him and slipped him through the crack in the writer's door while he was sleeping. That bird messed all over the floor. When that guy got up out of his bunk to go to the bathroom, he slipped on that bird manure and fell. Then he went into the galley in his undershorts and all messy, and started hollering at the chef, of all people, who was busy making breakfast.

I was told that to this day no one has admitted guilt.

---

5   *Footnote for landlubbers*
     Captain Travis – moon pool: A diamond shaped hole about 24' to 28'feet cut in the bottom of the ship, usually in the middle of the ship, the most stable place. Sides are built around it to make the ship watertight. Most of the drilling equipment goes down through the moon pool. Larger equipment is floated alongside the ship and taken under the ship by divers. The moon pool is right under the drilling tower.

They had all gotten tired of that smart aleck. Anyway, that brought him down a notch or two.

I worked on drilling ships off the coast of California and, at the discretion of the company, wherever I was needed, sometimes for a short time, mostly just a week. I might be on four or five ships before I had time off, and that meant four or five weeks before I could go home.

Once Global needed me to take a vessel to Juneau, Alaska. We took the La Ciencia to the delta regions off of the rivers that run down in southeast Alaska. We went there to mine for gold. Our engineers had figured out a way to go up and down on exact coordinates of the ocean, suck the sand and bring it up and onto a big wheel. The wheel was mercury laden and the gold adhered to the wheel, and the sand, rocks and other debris fell back into the ocean. I can't remember the name of the company that contracted with Global to do the work.

I just delivered the La Ciencia to the site, and another captain was responsible for anchoring and searching for gold. The crew had to use the anchors on the stern of the ship every time we moved at the end of a day's run. When our crew, with that company's guard, not Global's, went back to work the anchors, the guard had to unlock a chain link fence back where the mercury and the shaker tables and all of that were.

When it was determined that the process was a viable way to get the gold, Global's stock doubled on the New York Stock Exchange overnight. The ship was only leased for three months, but Global's stock had really gone up by the time the ship got back to Tacoma, Washington.

We never did know how much gold there was, but it produced enough that the company paid a huge amount for that equipment. The La Ciencia was a 137 foot government surplus wooden minesweeper when Global bought it and converted it into a shallow water drilling vessel. They only had $130,000 invested in that ship, but the leasing company bought all the rights to the equipment, the transformer and pumps and all that. Then, they gave the ship back to Global. It sat at the dock in Tacoma for a long time, and was finally sold for only $35,000. It had three big diesel engines and a couple of smaller ones, and it had radar and everything else. It was a good, good ship that sold for peanuts.

I don't know if they are still searching for gold like that or not. Before that though, in about 1963 I think, Global rigged a ship to mine diamonds off the coast in South Africa. It was originally called the Rock Eater. I believe the diamond kings of the world now own that ship. Our company bought it for $100,000 out of the mothball fleet up in San Francisco Bay. It sucked up rocks and diamonds and there was a shaker back on the stern that separated the debris from the diamonds, and then the diamonds were gathered. I was told that the diamond company that leased the ship wouldn't let us have it back. They paid big, big money to keep it.

A Dud

I took the CUSS I up to Alaska to a little island called Fire Island in the Cook Inlet, way up by Anchorage, to drill a well for a big oil company. When they assigned me that job, I told the marine superintendent I didn't think that vessel was capable of going up there. He agreed, and we put the ship in the shipyard and reinforced and widened it. The company spent $300,000 restructuring the ship so that we could carry more load. We would be taking casing, drilling pipe for deep water, and heavy equipment, plus two automobiles on the chopper deck.

When the work was finished, we got underway. I arrived at the Corps of Engineers dock at Homer in Cook Inlet on April 3, 1966. The ice was so heavy on the inlet no vessel was going to go up it. I kept sending the chopper out every day to see if we could find a crack or anything. I had a fifteen hundred horsepower tugboat standing by. In fact it was pushing the calves twenty four hours a day – that's what they call breaking off the edges of glaciers coming downstream. Without that, the glaciers would have bumped up against the ship, and that was dangerous. We sat there and sat there at Homer.

Finally around the first of May, I got permission to get a U.S. Coast Guard ice breaker. The Kinnick Bay is a big ice breaker ship. It runs up on the ice, pumps its liquid ballast forward and breaks through the ice, pumps ballast aft so that the bow of the ship is out of the water, runs up on the ice again at full steam, and repeats the cycle. I had a Pacific Mariner tug in front towing on the CUSS I, two tugs on the port side, two on the starboard and one astern pushing to get me up to the site.

By that time all the girly magazines had been read a time or two, and all the movies had been seen a time or two. Those were long days because up there it was daylight until midnight. The drilling crew was getting bored and antsy because we were not underway.

The crew members on the drilling ships were sent to me by the company, and there was one man, Jimmy, I had some doubts about; he had been in prison for several years. Jimmy was the bedroom steward, known as BR in ship's language; he saw to it that the sheets and stuff were clean, and he kept the floors clean.

As I said, I had doubts, but Jimmy turned out to be one of the best crewman on the ship because of his lighthearted personality. While having the CUSS I towed up the frozen inlet, ice would come up on our decks around the moon pool so that even our water tight doors could not be opened. To access anything on the stern, we had to walk on a narrow deck alongside the deck house. On the blackboard in the galley one morning, Jimmy had posted a sign stating "For anyone lounging around the moon pool, please return your lawn chairs and sunglasses to their proper storage." Different crew members would walk through to get a cup of coffee and double up laughing. Another time the blackboard read: "A famous European conductor will be bringing his troupe of musicians and dancers to perform next Friday night on the chopper deck. Please check with Captain Evans for your tickets. You don't want to miss this occasion!"

I questioned whether Jimmy would or would not be a good crewman, but he turned out to be a real morale booster on the ship.

From April 3 to May 10 - it took that long to get to the drill site. We were finally on location near Fire Island, which is just below Anchorage and right off of Turnagain Arms where the wind gets very strong. Once we got on location the wind was blowing eighty knots[6] out of the east, and there was six to eight knots of current. That inlet is more than two hundred miles long, so that's a great body of water that's moving. There are four tides every twenty-four hours, two high and two low. About every five hours and fifty-six minutes, you've got fifteen minutes of slack, before it goes the other way. With the wind and the current pushing the barges, they would actually get ahead of the tugboats, so the tugs had to swing around and steer into the current lightly, just enough to keep steerage, and let the current take them back up to where they needed to be. It was something.

When we got to the site, we had to anchor the ship eight ways with that eighty knots wind coming out of Turnagain Arm. It took some time to get the thing moored; actually, we put down nineteen anchors. After they put the base plate with a blowout preventer down, we could finally start spudding.[7] By then, I had been at the wheel ninety hours without sleep.

The only experience the superintendent of the drilling crew for that company had, was down in the swamp area of Louisiana and Mississippi. He was a terrible guy to get along with; he wanted it done yesterday; he was awfully impatient. His room was right next door to mine, the captain's quarters. He was pestering me every day. "Do something," he'd say, or, "Get this thing moving." And he was

---

6   Footnote for landlubber
     Captain Travis – knot: A knot measures speed and is one nautical mile per hour. A nautical mile is about 1.15 miles. [In landlubber language - that wind was about 92 miles per hour.]
7   Footnote for landlubbers
     Captain Travis – spudding: spudding is the very first drilling.

calling my office down in Los Angeles all the time. We were up in Alaska. What did he think they could do? I just couldn't get along with that guy.

Off the California coast out at Point Conception and Gaviota, we drilled a well every eight days or so and found oil and gas at four thousand feet. Up at that location, we went to seventeen thousand feet. That superintendent said, "Let's keep drilling." So we did – day, after day, after day.

After twenty-six or thirty hours of continual drilling to cut through the rocks and stuff, the drill bit got worn down, so the crew had to change it. There was a joint about every ninety feet on the drilling stem, and the crew broke them at those joints and laid them on a rack out on the deck. After we changed the bit, we reassembled the drill pipe and put the bit back in the hole. When we were drilling at great depths like that, it took a good crew twenty-four hours to change the drill bit.

We were on that job from April to October, and we never found oil. That superintendent kept wanting to go deeper and deeper. Our contract was up September 19. I didn't want to be up there after the equinox, September 21. That's when the weather changes from bad to <u>worst</u>. We were using diamond drill bits by then, and that kept us from having to come out of the hole so often. Anyway, the company negotiated a contract to keep us there longer.

When we finally left in October, there was a blizzard like you wouldn't believe. I couldn't even see the towboat untying us to get us off location. I couldn't talk to the captain because there was so much static from the storm. The only way we could talk to each other was with the ship's whistle to signal. Fortunately, I knew the tugboat captain, and he was good, really a very efficient man.

We finally got out and on our way, but we got right out into a gale of a wind. It was a rough trip, but we finally got home the day before Thanksgiving, well not home, but to Port Hueneme, California. I left the ship and went home and got there in time to be with my family for Thanksgiving.

We could lay at that port to take all of that oil company's stuff off and outfit the ship for another company. The ship itself wasn't damaged, but the seas were so bad there was about $300,000 worth of damage to the deck's cranes. Of course, Pan Am had to pay that.

I started this poem while crossing the Gulf of Alaska in a storm in October, 1966. I was never satisfied with it and re-wrote it several times. Finally in 2006, I tackled it and hopefully finished it.

Hebrews 6:19
An anchorage for storm tossed souls

Sometimes mariners at sea are caught in a gale,
And fearful hearts tend to fail,
But there is a calm, away from harm.
'Tis only found in the eye of the storm.

'Tis there the seasoned mariner would fly,
Where raging winds would pass him by.
At times, life like a storm would over us fly.
Take refuge, dear friend, centered in the Master's eye.

Usually riches, power, fame would lure us there,
Into life's swirling troubled stormy snare.
There is a refuge where no storm clouds fly,
Secure my soul, centered in the Master's eye.

So take heart when Life's storm cloud's blow
Bringing swelling troubled tides of woe.
Find refuge, dear heart, in a safe retreat,
Always found at the Master's feet.

Isn't God awesome?

After my week at home, I went back on the ship and started getting it ready for another contract. I spent another month, a week on and a week off, there in Port Hueneme.

Then I was asked to take a supply vessel out to a drilling site off of Westport, Washington. Once again I went to the marine superintendent. I told him that the vessel should not go around Point Conception, near Santa Barbara. Point Conception is called the Cape Horn of the Pacific. Cape Horn off of Africa is known for its stormy weather and rough seas, and Conception has a similar change of land mass - seven islands which draw winds – always. I had skippered the vessel down there in calm waters, but when the water was a little choppy, I could feel the boat twist. I told him the vessel wasn't safe, and I wouldn't take it.

He got my alternate skipper, Bob Davis, to take it. Bob got around Conception in good weather and got up as far as Point Sur, a good hundred miles above Conception, when the bottom of the front end of that ship dropped down into the water. The boat nearly sank. They almost lost the vessel and ten or twelve men. Fortunately, there was a bulkhead that kept the engine room from being flooded. The Coast Guard sent a tugboat down with pumps, and they got the ship to a shipyard.

One of the places Global sent me to do a job was Gaviota, California. There's a refinery there on shore and a bunch of operating wells just offshore, about two miles. I had to put anchor from my ship there so drilling equipment could be taken off the ocean floor. The well head was surrounded by about a dozen others, and they were at risk too. I had six big anchors to anchor the ship so the divers could unhook the blowout preventer platform and so forth, and I had fifteen or sixteen men to help bring the well head up. In a situation like that, anything brought up from the ocean bottom had to go straight up. If not, it might disturb other oil equipment.

It was a dangerous job and one that needed to be done quickly. None of the other captains wanted to do that because of all those other well heads. But we managed to get the ship on location, do the job within a day or two and bring everything back to Santa Barbara with no damage to anything. That was a pretty quick job we did out there, and after that, they gave me the kind of jobs they didn't trust others to do.

There's a little manmade island, Rincon Island, with a couple of palm trees, a causeway going out to it and a short narrow pier. It was built specifically for well drilling and oil and gas production. I took a supply boat in and out of there. In fact, I was the only one in our fleet that could come into that island. I was running a surplus government landing vessel, and we took some pretty heavy equipment in there and used a big boom to help unload it. I had to come in at high tide and get out while it was still high tide. When I called and told them I was coming alongside, they got everything ready so they could get me in and out quickly; if they didn't, there wouldn't be enough water to get us out.

My son-in-law, Fidel, who worked on my crew, was with me a couple of times when we went in. The first time he said, "This ship is as big as the island. I don't see how you can get in there."

"But, there's a way." I said.

The ship had three propellers. So, that meant I could walk that ship broadside with two engines pushing me out and the other engine holding me from going forward or backward. I could just move it broadside, not real fast, maybe three knots, but we made it.

There were several oil wells and pipelines right below Santa Barbara. We put in three or four more wells down there in pretty shallow water and some in deeper waters.

Global drilled an oil well at San Miguel Island, one at Anacapa Island, about six for Texaco at Gaviota, some for Phillips right off of Refugio and some for Standard Oil. I can't tell you the number of offshore wells Global drilled in other areas.

England

While I had time off in 1967, Katherine and I served as delegates to the Southern California Nazarene convention in Pasadena. On Friday, we were in session when our pastor came and told me there was a phone call from my office. The dispatcher said, "We need you to skipper the Glomar IV in the North Sea."

Pastor Scharn took me to LAX where I boarded a plane and flew nineteen hours to Heathrow Airport, London.

Global had the Glomar IV, a drilling ship, down off the west coast of Africa where the winter months are fine. But, those months aren't fine in the North Sea. They put the ship in West Africa for the winter months and brought it back to the North Sea in the summer.

My job was to bring that ship up from the coast of Africa to Hartlepool, England and get it and all its equipment in shape and get it out on the grounds as quick as I could. I had to fly to the Canary Islands, off the coast of northwest Africa, to pick the ship up. I was over there in June when the Six Day war between Israel and Egypt, Jordan and Syria took place; really, the whole Middle East was at war. We needed to get our ship and personnel out of there, and we did, as fast as we could.

The ship and its equipment were getting pretty well run down. It had been in Africa under a two year contract, and had been there probably a year or more. The company wanted someone who would stiffen things up and bring things back up to par. That job proved to be a challenge.

After we got back with the Glomar IV, a supply boat was supposed to put the anchors down. They got four of them down, remember, we have eight, when one of the engines went out. While they got the engine out of the supply boat so it could be taken to be overhauled, I took four 2,000 foot anchor chains into Hartlepool to get the studs welded. There's a stud on the center of each link, and each link probably weighs fifty pounds. When a chain is strained on over the years, some of the studs will loosen, and they have to be re-welded. I hired a hundred welders and a hundred helpers.

In Hartlepool it was drizzly and misty and rainy, and every time it got a little drizzly, those guys would stop to have a cup of tea. We weren't getting anything done. I threatened to fire them, and one of them said, "That's okay. I make more money on the dole than I do welding anyway."

Really, I couldn't fire them; I needed to get those anchor chains out to the ship. We were having to pay demurrage, that's payment for a ship's staying longer than agreed, until we got the ship ready to work.

I thought we would have to take the ship into a port at a little town called Eaglecliff on the Tyne. The Tyne River separates Scotland and England up above Newcastle. I was told when I was studying my Coast Guard classes to never enter an unfamiliar harbor without local help, so I decided to drive over there to check things out. I got some of my deck hands to supervise the work, and I borrowed a company car, a tiny thing with the steering wheel on the wrong side.

Now that was an experience; those big lorries, that's what they call big trucks over there, going the other way with their drivers way over there, and there I was on the wrong side of road way over here in my little old car. Besides that, their roads were not nearly as decent as ours unless they were marked A. If they were marked B or C they could get pretty rough. I'm not sure, but I don't think that was an A road. That drive was an experience!

Anyhow, I made it up to Eaglecliff on the Tyne. It's a city with machine shops and foundries and all that sort of thing. They burn peat and coal, and everything is really smoky, and that day, really foggy. I went down to the dock on the river, and I couldn't even see the mouth of the river, it was so foggy.

When I was in Hartlepool, my company put me up in the Grand Hotel, one of a chain of hotels in England. That chain had a hotel in Eaglecliff too. I thought I'd go over to the hotel and visit with the locals and find out a little about the system for bringing ships in and ask how long they thought the fog would hold on. I was going to have to bring the ship in there, and it was all strange to me. I had the charts, and knew the approximate water depths, but I didn't know their system, and I needed some local knowledge.

As I drove to the hotel, I had to go on a roundabout that had a park in the middle of it. On one side of the park there was a beautiful bronze statue of a lovely young woman; her hair looked like it was wet, and her clothes were sticking to her like they were wet. It was a little larger than life, and there was a scripture inscribed underneath it. There was an old man nearby feeding the pigeons. I wanted to know more about the statue, but I thought I ought to get back to the ship. I planned to come back the next day for it was only a few hour's drive.

That night I looked up the scripture on the statue. It read: "For she hath done what she could." That verse was from Mark 14. I read the whole story that night; it tells about a woman, probably a prostitute, who came with an alabaster box of oil and poured it on Jesus' head. Some of the disciples, and especially Peter, spoke up and complained. Jesus said, "Leave her alone, she has done what she could. Wherever this story is told, it should be to honor her because she did what she could."

Anyhow, when I went back the next morning, I saw the same old man feeding the pigeons, so I found a place to park and walked over and spoke to him. "Hello, me lad," he said.

After we greeted each other, I asked him if he could tell me about that statue. "I was just a wee tad when it happened," he said. And he told me the story. This is the way I remember it:

In 1919 a large ship was going to come up the Tyne River with passengers, and it ran aground on a reef offshore. It was awfully foul weather – so foul that the Coast Guard couldn't get through the breakers on the river to get out to the ship. But there was a lighthouse on an island just offshore of the entrance to the river where the lighthouse keeper, his wife and young daughter lived. The ship was laying there wallowing in the reef, blowing its steam horn trying to get help. The daughter went to her father and said, "Can't we launch our lifeboat and go help them?"

"Oh, we couldn't do it in this storm. We wouldn't survive."

But the ship was getting more and more worn and torn, and finally he decided they would try to make it. He said, "It will take you too, daughter, I won't be able to row against these seas alone." He told his wife to gather up pails they could use for bailing and all their wool blankets and store them in the life boat while he greased the skids.

So his wife and daughter went to work and did their part, and he did his.

He and the daughter got into the life boat, the mother cut the rope, and they went out into the storm and the turbulent waters. They managed to get alongside the ship which had put rope ladders over the side. Nineteen women and children managed to get into the boat and then to safety. The others on the ship perished. The father and the daughter survived after having saved those nineteen lives. But two or three days later, the girl got pneumonia and passed away. So that statue was built in her honor.

When I got back to the ship that night. I could not sleep. I was far, far away from home and oh, so lonely. I thought about my family and how glad I was that I would be going home soon. I got to thinking about the story of that statue and I thought – in my life have I done what I could, all that I could? Had I spoken up when I should have? Had I always made the effort I should have?

That was one experience of many in my seaman's life, and it impacted my life in a powerful way. I tried to make some life changes.

As it turned out, the company decided to have Caterpillar mechanics come to the ship and make the repairs, so I didn't have to take it into that town after all.

When I took that job, Global promised they would bring me home in time for my twenty-fifth wedding anniversary and my youngest son Phillip's graduation from high school, both of which were going to be on the sixteenth of June. When it was time for me to leave to go home, there I was up in the northeast of England, almost in Scotland; I didn't have the job finished, and the other captain hadn't shown up yet. I called our office, and talked with John Evans, the North Sea Superintendent. He said, "No, you're going to have to stay."

I said, "John, get on the telex and talk to Grant Allen. He made me a promise that I wouldn't miss my anniversary and my son's graduation."

"Okay," he said, "but I want you to stay aboard the ship till the other captain gets there."

Within two hours he called me and said, "Travis, get on the train and meet me in the office here in London."

When I got there he said, "The head office told me to get you on a plane and get you home on time."

Katherine and Fidel picked me up at LAX, and we went right straight to the high school stadium and got in line for a seat. Within an hour Phil was graduated.

It was good to be back home with my family. I don't think I told you that home was now back in Grover Beach. A couple of months after Kerry, our youngest daughter, was born in July, 1964, we decided to move from Redondo Beach back to Grover Beach.

Back Home

When I went back to work, I went aboard the CUSS I; we were outfitting it for a different client. And after that, we began a job for seventeen oil companies just south of Point Dume, west Santa Monica Bay, just a short distance from the LAX Airport runway. So, I was on a drilling ship for some time in that location.

While we were drilling there on January 13, 1969, a Scandinavian jet crashed about a mile off our stern. There were forty-five people on board; fifteen of them died. The survivors were moved out onto the plane's wings and were picked up by the Coast Guard. Global crews helped to retrieve and identify victims and recover passenger's belongings for well over a week. The CUSS I became a holding place for body parts and luggage. We were more or less a morgue.

That was an experience that no one would want to have, but less than two weeks later another jet, a United Airliner, crashed just after takeoff in somewhat the same area. There were no survivors. The television show, Bay Watch, had a couple of rescue boats, and some of the show's crew came to help recover luggage and body parts which filled the decks of the CUSS I. Once again the Global help was tremendous. That was a month I'll never forget.

That same year, we were drilling up at Carpenteria, California, when the Global vessel, the Rincon, had a blowout. The petroleum engineers had suggested only casing to 4,000 feet. They were wrong. That was not deep enough, and their decision resulted in a blowout. I had to get the ship off the hole. It was a dangerous situation. Fortunately, we got the divers down to turn off the blow out preventer in time to prevent a fire. We got peppered with mud and rocks blowing up through there, but we got the ship moved before a fire got started.

Going back a few years now, I want to tell you about my first steel boat. Global told me I could have tuna season off the summer of '66, so I started looking around for a boat to lease for three months. I found a boat named the Yankee Girl up in Moss Landing; it was owned by Dave Gibson, an American Airlines pilot. When I called him, I told him I had the summer off and wanted to lease his boat. He said, "Yeah, the boat is for sale, but I really don't care about leasing it."

I asked, "Do you know any fishermen on the West Coast?"

"Yeah, this is my second boat, so I know a few."

"I'm not gonna tell you to talk to any one of them, but I am gonna tell you to ask any fisherman about Travis Evans."

He called me back the next day and asked me, "You still want to lease the boat?"

So I took the Yankee Girl and Phillip, my youngest boy, and I put it in dry dock and went to work on it. It was July, and a few tuna were already being caught, but we had to get the boat in shape, with fresh paint, a new propeller, and a few other things. When we got it ready, Phil and I went albacore fishing off the Oregon and California coasts. We had quite an experience on that trip. I don't know just when I did it, but sometime later, I wrote this story about it, but I never titled it.

On a warm, sunny afternoon in August of 1966, Phil and I were about seventy-five miles offshore of Central Oregon in the fishing boat, the "Yankee Girl." The albacore tuna were biting like crazy, and we were very busy landing fish. Looking up I saw huge billows of white smoke pouring out of the exhaust stack. I dropped everything, and holding my breath, I dove into the engine room. A refrigeration pipe had sprung a leak, and the escaping Freon was threatening to smother and stop our diesel engine. I managed to disengage the reefer compressor clutch and escape to the deck and fresh air. I got a little too much of that Freon, and it made me sick. After throwing up and laying on deck a few minutes to get stabilized, I headed the boat for shore to make repairs and sell our fresh catch.

Shortly after dark we ran into heavy fog. Not having a radar unit, we were forced to slow down and both stand watch, me at the wheel and throttle on the bridge, and Phil on the bow. About two a.m., we approached the entrance to the Yaquina River and Newport Harbor. The fog was too thick to risk entering for I could hardly see my son on the bow. Via radio, the U.S. Coast Guard advised us to wait. We decided to drop anchor and wait for daylight. I was reluctant, not knowing our exact position, the bottom structure, sand, rock, mud, etc.

Phil and I were both on the bow, wet and cold, tired and sleepy, preparing to drop anchor, when he said, "Dad, we haven't prayed about this." We both knelt there on the cold wet bow, and told God of our desperate need. You know, our fish were perishable and the family needed money. We would have to hire help to repair the reefer with a quick turn-around to finish the season. I don't know how long we prayed. Not long, I'm sure, for we were drifting in very thick fog in an unknown location. After the "amens," we stood and looked, and the moon had broken through the fog, and I could hear a faint foghorn. There was a dim path of light leading inshore, and we could just make out the red light on the south jetty about a quarter mile away. Starting inshore quickly, we could soon see the green light on the north jetty. God had answered our desperate prayer, and we were soon secured to a fish buyers' dock awaiting daylight.

The reefer repairs were finished the next day, and we began outfitting for another tuna trip. The fish buyer gave us several five gallon cans of small, unmarketable shrimp and shrimp carcasses which we used for chum on the tuna. After running all night, we were on the tuna grounds with the rest of the fishing fleet shortly after daylight. The shrimp chum helped us to get a good catch, so that it was as if we had never lost any fishing time.

You can be sure this old Dad and his young son will never forget how God answered our prayers - and then some.

Well, that was a while back and that young son is not so young nowadays. He lives in Alabama and is a ship's captain in the petroleum industry.

It was along about Thanksgiving when I took the Yankee Girl back. It was clean, freshly painted, the oil was changed, everything was up to par and ready for the next year. I think that impressed Dave, and too, we had done very well in the seventy days we were out fishing. Anyway, Dave asked me to be his partner. "Look, I've got some money to invest," he said, "Would you like to come in as my partner and build a steel boat?"

"I've still got a house in Redondo Beach, and if I could sell that and get my money, I'd do it."

About December or so he called and said, "Well, I've got the keel on the ground in Moss Landing, and I've got Martin Allen, a boat builder up there, ready to start building the boat."

I said, "Wait a minute, Dave. I haven't got enough money just yet."

"I've got the money and I need a place to put it. I can write it off if I put it into a commercial boat. When you can, come up and help Martin get it laid out the way you want it."

I started to work on the Seeadler right after Christmas when we laid the keel.

What happened with Global was – when I told them I wanted to build a boat, they said, "Stay on with us and go on and work on your boat." I worked for Global one week on and one week off. In the fall of that year I asked if I could have the next six months off to get the boat finished for the next tuna season. They told me they had some ship deliveries to make, and if I'd be available for that, they could keep me on the payroll with all the health benefits and everything, but if they called, I had to lay down my tools and go. They said they had a ship, the Submarex, they were going to send to Peru and another going to the Bay of Carpentaria in Australia and another to New Guinea.

My boat was almost ready when they asked me to get the ship ready to sail to Peru. I agreed to that and went down to do the work. A ship has to go through Coast Guard and American Bureau of Shipping inspections before it can be taken out of the country. That means it has to be put in the shipyard where all the fittings are checked, along with the bearings, the propeller and all that stuff. And, we have to put sacrificial zincs on all underwater metal to protect it from electrolysis, a chemical reaction. Dissimilar metals and salt water make electrolysis that will eat the steel, so if you put the sacrificial zincs in, it'll eat the zincs before it gets to the metal. That will only last for about two years, so you change them out every two years. My job was to supervise all the work to get that ship ready.

I asked who was going to be the skipper, and was glad to hear it was a fisherman who was a friend of mine. I got ahold of him and said, "I'm going to be bringing a crew of men to work on your ship; they gave me about eighteen or nineteen men to do the job. May I bring my new boat, alongside and work on it when I'm off watch?"

He agreed, so I kept the Seeadler right alongside the Cuss I and worked on it when I was off. Some of my days off, the tugboat company hired me. Another company, General Transport, was doing seismic work looking for oil bearing sand in the area. I was about the only guy around that knew how to read their government surplus equipment, and they'd call me sometimes. I worked for them some of my days off. That helped my finances.

Global allowed let me use their machine shop on the CUSS I to get a lot of the work on my boat done. I had the outside finished, but not the inside. I had hung a couple of navy pipe bunks, and I had a refrigerator, but I still had to put refrigeration in the fishhold and put paneling up inside the cabin.

John Sheets, a Christian friend of mine, had a refrigeration shop just a few miles or so from where the ship was tied up at Pier D, berth three in Long Beach. His shop was close by, and it took him fifteen minutes to get there to work with me. He came down and helped me put the refrigeration in and install the generator plants and some of that stuff.

A retired preacher, George Pestana, who was a great cabinet maker, came and lived aboard the ship, and worked on my boat, thirteen or fourteen hours a day, doing the carpentry and finish work.

I have to tell you a story about George. Every once in a while, he would get into a tight place and he'd call me. "Brother Travis, I have a problem and we need to pray about it." John and I would take our hats off and go up to see the problem and pray about it. George would go back to his job, and we'd go back to ours, below deck in the engine room.

John was helping me mount a generator and doing some other machine work. There was just a small entrance with a pipe ladder to climb down into the engine room where we were working, and it was a real tight place down in that hole. One day John and I were working, and George hollered down "Brother Travis, Brother John, would you come up? We need to pray about this." So, we went up and prayed about it and went back down to our work. That happened three or four times in about four hours. The last time he called, I said, "Again?"

John knew that the albacore fleet was already out and that I was interested in getting out there, and he saw how exasperated I was. He put his hands on my shoulders, I was about fifty years old, and he was seventy or so, and he said, "Now Brother Travis, I know having to stop what we're doing here bothers you, and we've had to go up several times this morning, but I want you to consider this: you're getting the best cabinet maker you could find, a good Christian man and a conscientious man for $6 an hour, and I'm only charging you $3 an hour. Now, where do you think you could get a good cabinet maker, a good machinist and the Lord all for just $9 an hour?"

That quietened my nerves. We went up and we prayed, and I was okay.

George finished his part a little before John, who worked clear up to the last week of July when we had the boat good enough. And, the ship was ready to go. And, I was too.

I named my boat the Seeadler, which is a particular kind of sea bird, and I want to tell you why. If you ever, ever want to read a good book, read the story of Felix von Luckner. During World War I, he was sailing out of Germany with a ship called the Seeadler. Wilhelm II, the Kaiser of Germany, ordered it to be taken to Norway and converted into a ship that could change its appearance in a short time. That included masts that would stand up and sails that could be pulled up so it would look like a sailing ship. Or, they could pull the mast and sails down, put lumber on the deck, and it would look like a lumber carrier; or they could stow that stuff, and it would look like an oil tanker. They were so successful that von Luckner once sailed through the British fleet with a load of lumber on deck. He went right thru their warships with no recognition.

On the bulwark were hidden cannons, so they were able to come up alongside another ship and signal that it was a friendly vessel. When they got up close, they lowered the bulwark so that personnel of the other ship could see the cannons. Captain von Luckner didn't think it was right to sneak up on people and kill them. He asked them to surrender, and signaled a message with flags - if they surrendered, they could come aboard and be taken to a neutral port, and their ship would be sunk. Then he said, "If you prefer to get in a lifeboat, I will tow you to a neutral port, but I am going to sink your ship."

He never took a human life, but he sank more allied ships, French, British and American than any other German captain, including the submarines of the German Navy. After the war the Germans promoted him and gave him the title of Baron Felix von Luckner. Because he was such a humanitarian, I named our boat after his ship.

Back to fishing. The year we finished the Seeadler, I worked up until July for Global Marine, and they gave me the rest of the year off; I had earned that time. I hired a crewman, Rollie, who was building a steel boat and needed the money, and took our daughter, Susie, age sixteen, and we headed for Oregon. When we got out to sea, I could feel a thump, thump, thump. I could not figure out what the noise was; I knew I had aligned the engine and propeller shaft up good. When we got as far as Eureka, I talked to Katherine on the marine telephone. She told me our son Fred and his wife and their two children just came in from Alabama for a visit.

I said, "I've got something wrong with my propeller shaft, and I'm going to pull into Eureka to get it fixed. Why don't you guys drive up and stay a day or two so I can see them?" So they met us there, and we stayed in a motel for a couple of days and had a good visit.

When I first got into port there at Eureka, I disconnected the propeller shaft and checked the alignment. I connected everything back up, but I still got the same floppy noise. Come to find out, as we laid for so long beside that ship I was getting ready for Global, we picked up some little barnacles that came from foreign ships. There were barnacles on the propeller. I couldn't figure that out. I never had that problem before. The propellers are bronze and they aren't usually painted because they're moving all the time and the paint wears off, but if you're laying still in a harbor for a month or two, the barnacles will start growing on it. They won't grow on the bottom of the ship because they don't like the paint we use nowadays. Rollie was a hard hat diver, and went down and scraped some of the barnacles off of four blades. It didn't completely eliminate the problem, but it improved it enough so that we could go fishing.

We, Rollie, Susie and I, took off and headed out to sea, and the family, Katherine and daughters, Jan and Kerry, went home, and Fred and his family went back to Alabama after our short visit.

Before the boat was finished, I had to borrow money for some of my electronics; I was flat broke and in debt. On the first day of August in 1969, we got the first tuna blood on the deck of the Seeadler. We had several tons of fish on the boat when we went home for Thanksgiving. We got right outside our home port at Avila Beach, anchored and left the deck light on. From our house in Grover I could see it. I spent Thanksgiving Day with the family and left at midnight that night. By daylight I had more fish, albacore tuna. By the end of the day I had another ton of fish. I stayed right there within twenty miles or so from home port until the first of December. After that, the fish slacked off, so I took my catch to the cannery at San Pedro on December the third. I delivered nineteen tons of fish for the season. The boat was paid for, and I had enough money to order the steel for a bigger boat.

Dave, my partner, said, "You go ahead and build another one and you take it, and I'll take the Seeadler."

He loaned me enough money for other expenses I would have when I started on the boat, so before I went back to fishing, I ordered the steel. As it turned out, by the time it was built, Dave had made other plans. I paid him back the money when I could - no schedule and no interest. Now, that's a good friend.

I took our youngest son, Phil, fresh out of college, and went to San Diego with the Seeadler. I outfitted it again, and we left on the first day of January to fish yellowfin tuna in Mexico. We normally made thirty day trips into Mexico, but with Phil we made it kind of a vacation and stayed out fifty-six days. It wasn't real profitable, but the money we did make was needed since I ordered steel for another boat.

I worked part time for Global getting ships ready to sail after we moved to Grover City. I drove clear to Long Beach where we kept the ships when they were on standby or not on duty. I got a ship ready for them in late '70.

Sometime that next year, I had a conference call from a high official in the company and our marine superintendent, Captain Grant Allen. They wanted me to take a ship, and I forget now where they wanted me to go. They had given me the rest of the year off. I said, "Well, I'm in Oregon, and I have to finish this season. And, I have this time coming to me."

The vice-president of the company wrote Katherine a letter that said something like this: "When Travis finishes the fishing season he definitely has a job with us, and we think we'll have a place on the ship Global Discovery." I contacted them and told them I was building my second steel fishing vessel, and I wouldn't be coming back.

I may have lost my claim to fame right then. On the front page of Life magazine that month there was a picture of that ship, and the labeling underneath it said, "The Ship That is Rewriting the History of the Earth." They were doing a lot of core drilling, and had taken samples from the deepest Venezuela trench in the Caribbean. They had a contract with the government through the National Science

Foundation. They had several other projects that brought a lot of fame to Global Marine.

I worked for Global eight years, and I worked wherever they wanted me to work and did whatever they needed me to do. And, they were good to me, oh, so good to me, and I left on good terms.

But, isn't it amazing that they took a fisherman, made him a captain and gave him the opportunity for such varying and interesting experiences? Being a ship's captain was never anything I planned. I believe God had something to do with that.

PART VIII
ABOUT FISHING

No Regrets

I have never regretted the decision to leave Global and work as a commercial fisherman for those many, many years. Fishing is a dangerous business; in fact, some sources say fishing is the second most dangerous occupation in the world. I've been in many perilous situations out on the ocean, but with God's help, survived to fish another day. Fishing is hard work, and I've done plenty of that. The unusual lifestyle of a fisherman is a real hardship for the family. I missed a lot of family things being gone so much, and the family missed me some too. As I said, Global was good to me, and I could have stayed with them, but I chose fishing as the way I wanted to provide for my family, and I'm pleased to say that I was somewhat successful.

Honestly, some of my success really has been out of necessity. By that I mean I had to keep striving to be a better producer in order to care for my large family. I don't think I was so smart, but when I knew what was expected of me, then I could usually get it done. My love, my life partner, my Katherine deserves much of the credit. All through the years, she was my helper, my sounding board, my encourager – my backbone. I couldn't have done it without her.

There is more to being a good fisherman than a lot of folks might think. Besides knowing where and how to catch fish, you've got to have at least basic knowledge of mechanics, refrigeration, electronics, navigation, ocean winds and weather and on and on. There's also a lot involved in the maintenance of your boat and equipment. And then there's the business end of it, which means keeping records. I did my own bookkeeping, with some help from Katherine. I even did my own income tax returns, until a friend at church went into business doing that kind of work. I gladly handed that part over to him.

There are plenty of rules and regulations for fishermen. You've got to have a license and permits and you have to register your boat and so on. Like any other industry there are laws for commercial fishing, and a wise fisherman will know them and adhere to them.

In the mid-sixties and early seventies, the United States only had authority out to twelve nautical miles, so Japan, Russia, China, Thailand and other countries began plundering the USA seamounts[8] and the crab and fish population. In 1976 Congress passed the Magnuson-Stevens Fisheries and Conservation Act which eliminated foreign vessels fishing so close to our shores. It also enacted a management policy to two hundred miles, and financed patrolling enforcement policies. The Magnuson-Stevens law is the primary law that governs and sustains our fisheries.

The powers that be in Congress decided that since each geographical area of all our coasts was different in fish populations, and since it was apparent that some of them were being overfished, they would institute several geographical fisheries management councils, twelve, I think.

Since we can't micromanage the many species, it was decided that giving limited entry permits to active fishermen and their boats might be the best way to manage fish production. To be eligible for a permit, a fisherman had to have produced a certain amount of fish in a limited time.

---

8   Footnote for landlubbers
     Captain Travis – Seamount:: similar to onshore mountains, but located deep under the
     ocean surface.

There are permits with variable prices for the different species. Some permits sell for as much as two or three thousand dollars, and some are priced as low as thirty dollars. State permits vary as to the state's fishery needs. Federal permits remain pretty evenly priced. Permits are required for most fisheries.

I served two 2-year terms on the groundfish[9] panel of the Pacific Fisheries Management Council which manages fisheries in four western states, California, Oregon, Washington and Idaho. Though Idaho has no ocean, they are included in that management council because some fish, such as salmon, shad and trout live most of their lives in the ocean, but travel upriver to Idaho to spawn.

Because all the travel to meetings every month was curtailing my fishing, I did not accept another nomination for the Pacific Fisheries Management Council. I did, however, serve as a groundfish advisor on the California Fishery Council for about ten years. At the same time I was doing that, I was also serving on the San Luis Obispo Energy Task Force. I took that position because the petroleum industry was trying to take over some of our productive fishing grounds. I think my work on the task force made a difference because of my experience.

I also served two years on the Monterey Bay Marine Sanctuary Board as a Commercial Fishermen's Association representative. Monterey Bay Marine Sanctuary is a federally protected marine area. I'm so glad I served on that board, for like all government entities, they tried

---

9   Footnote for landlubbers
     Captain Travis – groundfish: fish whose habitat is on or near the ocean floor.

to expand their authority. I have firsthand knowledge of their antics and have testified several different times to stop them from invading our fishing grounds. We can't even fish groundfish by trawl[10] in Monterey Bay, which for years has been a very productive area and has brought millions of dollars into the area. I also spoke at harbor meetings in favor of leasing the former Union Oil Pier in Avila to Cal Poly University for a marine education center. I was one of the founders of the harbor commission back in the early 1950s, so again, I think my voice carried a little weight.

I wish I had kept a journal. I have worked with scientists, bankers, university professors, petroleum engineers and others to promote fishing as a viable sustainable resource. I have also worked with Coast Guard personnel helping to save lives out on the ocean. All that exposure gave me many opportunities to show brotherly love through and for Jesus Christ.

I was a mariner for seventy-five plus years, but most of that time it was as a commercial fisherman. It was hard work, but it was fun and educational, often dangerous and sometimes profitable. There have been many ups and downs, but praise the Lord there have been more ups than downs. I feel blessed that I have been able to contribute so much help to the industry that cared for my large family for so many years.

---

10   Footnote for landlubbers
     Captain Travis – trawl: Trawl fishing is dragging a net to catch fish, not to be confused with trolling which is line fishing.

"Cousins" on the Ocean

I cannot emphasize strongly enough the strength and support that's found in the comradery we fishermen share.

We stick together. We're "cousins" on the ocean. And, like cousins, there's many a deep lifelong friendship among us. There's also lots of foolishness that goes on between us. I was reminded often that I was an Okie, and I picked up some other nicknames too. Albacore Farmer was one of them, Mickey Mouse was another, and Preacher Boy another. We had some fun, but we worked hard too.

We tried to be as self-sufficient as possible. Out where we fished, we were so far from anything, and you know, you can't just run down to the corner garage. At six or seven knots it takes a while to get into port, and then you try to get a repairman who might not be able to get to the job till tomorrow, when you really needed it done yesterday.

Everybody carries a lot of redundancy of equipment in case of a problem, but every now and then there comes a breakdown or troubles that are unforeseeable, and there's no way we can repair it ourselves out there. Then we have to depend on our buddies. One fellow broke down, and Wayne Smith towed him sixteen hundred miles to get him back to shore. I've left my fishing and run two days and a night just to take a part to someone. That's the kind of help we give each other, where in another occupation we might be competing with each other for a job.

At the time I started fishing, we had cardboard funnels that we used to communicate. We'd put it up to our mouths and ears to talk to each other. 'How many fish did you catch today?" one would holler. The other might answer "Oh, I got so many." Sometimes, we used hands to answer, holding up our fingers. That was before there were many diesel engines that are so loud; we still had gas engines, and they weren't so noisy. Still, our conversations were not lengthy.

Sometimes you wouldn't see another boat for a day, but if the fish were biting, there might be a dozen boats around you. But, we respected each other's tack, and we respected each other's territory. We were competitive; we wanted to catch more fish than the next guy, but we also wanted to help each other catch fish.

The radio was a great help in creating a closer relationship among the fleet. There were three or four of us in the fleet that everybody called "prospectors." We'd go out further and get away from the common grounds to look for other schools of fish. Sometimes we wouldn't see another boat for a week. We were just looking and radioing the information back to the fleet.

The closed circuit cell phone has destroyed much of that comradery. One fisherman can call his buddy and say, "Get over here. I'm catching." And nobody else can hear that.

One time there were four of us, Ward Wilber, Don Hart, Bill Windbegler and myself, tied in Noyo River, and we planned to go the next morning to Shelter Cove about thirty miles up the coast. Bill and Ward decided they needed to change oil and get spare parts in Fort Bragg, so Don and I started out before daylight, about four in the morning. At daylight we saw bird activity in the water off Westport,

California, and we decided to slow and put the gear in the water. From the time the first lure went in the water, the salmon tried to eat us up. We were so busy landing fish, there was no time to clean them. Around eleven, I saw Bill coming up a mile or two behind us. I kept pulling fish, and when Bill got close enough he gestured by spreading his arms, which meant "How many?" I answered by spreading all my fingers many times. He ducked into his cabin, he had a radio transmitter, and he called back to Ward. He said, "Get up here! That dang Okie has got a hundred and twenty fish on deck!!"

I had to quit about two-thirty in the afternoon and anchor up to clean fish - till way into the night. The next morning, all of us had gear in the water before daylight, but not a fish to be found. About the middle of the morning, Don and I gave up and took our fish to the market.

Not long after we first got radios on our boats, I started a nighttime program so we could communicate our needs better. After we shut down and got the dishes done and our fish put away, we'd get on a separate channel, even a different radio, such as a citizen band radio if we had to, but one that would reach further. Generally, they depended on me to host the night time radio talk program because I had a pretty good radio; it reached a little further than most. There were times when I'd still be busy putting away fish, so someone else would be host.

We'd invite people who had a problem of any kind to talk about it. It started out as a fisherman's needs program, but it evolved into a combined Christian and fisherman's needs program. Often we prayed about personal problems, a family member who was drinking or using drugs, someone who was sick, even someone who had financial problems. Sometimes we'd go to midnight or even later, talking about family problems, and what God's word said about it. I kept a Bible, a concordance, a topical index, a pen and a notepad on the console next to my radio to assist in finding what God's word said. After the session, there was a unison of prayer amongst those who were in talking range.

At noon each day everybody quits talking on the radio. Otherwise there would be jabber, jabber, jabber all up and down the coast from San Diego to Alaska, and you'd be overriding people. So, at noon everybody stops. The day before, a master of ceremonies is chosen for what we called the "silent hour." The first thing he asks is, "Does anyone have a need?" If a guy calls in and says he has a refrigeration problem, or maybe a guy calls and says his automatic pilot isn't steering, or he has an alternator out, or whatever, the master of ceremonies for the day asks if anyone knows about that problem. Someone might come on and say, "I've had that problem and this was my solution...."

During that hour the emcee says something like: "Can anybody in this area give us a report?" then someone in the fleet tells what the weather conditions are in the area where he's fishing, what the water temperature is and about the fish he caught that morning, the size of them and so on.

Sometimes the "silent hour" will run into two hours. We go ahead fishing, but we respect one another enough to pay attention; we're getting information and giving others information. That's the kind of fellowship that goes on out on the grounds. A lot of times we never meet the people we talk to, but we know we can depend on each other. We stick together. We're "cousins," you know.

We were probably fifteen hundred miles at sea one time, when I got a call from a fellow who said that he was going to have to head in to San Francisco even though he only had half of a load of fish. He said his refrigeration had a leak. He had the old fashioned ammonia refrigerant in his pipes. That stuff is very dangerous to work with. You don't want to breathe it for long.

I asked him if he could get at the leak. He said, "Well, it's hard to get at, but I know where it is. I pumped the ammonia down it, and I've got the lines cleared, but I can't do the welding."

"Okay," I said, "When we shut down tonight I'll come over in my life raft, and we'll see what we can do."

So that night we shut down about a quarter mile apart, and I went over to help him. I located the leak way back close to the compressor. He had all the vents, the hatch and the back door open, but it was hot in that engine room when I crawled up there, lit my torch and welded on that ammonia pipe for probably two hours. I thought I had it sealed off. Then we cranked it until we had frost on the pipes and discovered we still had a tiny leak. So, we had to start over, pump down and weld again, and after that, we welded again. It was nearly daylight when we finally got the leak stopped to where he could fish and finish his trip instead of running fifteen hundred miles and losing out.

Another time I came across a fellow way down near the Guadalupe Islands in Mexico. He had been drifting two days and two nights because of a dead battery which meant no radio to call for help. He saw me coming and went out on the deck waving his flag. He also had an American flag hanging upside down on his mast which is the signal for distress. I went over, slowed my engine and kicked the boat out of gear and asked him, "What's your problem?"

"My outside throttle shorted my battery during the night."

He had a little switch that he used to change the speed of the engine from the cockpit. It got moisture in it and shorted the battery. He had no way of charging it. I asked him what kind of engine he had, and he told me it was 671 diesel Detroit. I'd had some experience with a Detroit engine.

"Do you know how to release the compression?" I asked.

"There's no way to release it," he said.

I explained to him that those engines only have exhaust valves, there's no intake valves because they're two cycle engines. If you put a thin object under each exhaust valve, then the compression will release.

I asked him, "Do you have any pennies or dimes?"

He did, so I told him to take the valve cover off, lift those valves and put coins underneath all of the valves but one – just one. If the engine turns over, it will fire that one piston. So he tried that while I laid by there, just circling. He finally said, "No it's not going to work; it'll go rrrump but it won't turn over. My battery is not strong enough to turn it over."

You know how on shore we tow a car or truck, but out

on the ocean, we're working in fluid, and you don't have a wheel on the ground to create the friction you need.

"We'll try this," I said, "I can tow you, and I'll get you up to the fastest speed I can, and when we go over a swell, you're going to get more speed, so you have that engine ready to go. When I blow my whistle, you hit the button and put it in gear at the same time. If that works and you're running on one cylinder, you don't need to tell me; I'll see your smoke."

So we did that, and as we were coming off a big swell, I gave a toot on my emergency air horn, and he hit the button and put it in gear and baroom, baroom; it was running on one cylinder. After we slowed down a bit, I told him to go get his pliers and go down and start pulling those pennies out from under the valves. Every one he pulled out, that cylinder fired and start running. All of the cylinders started running, and when he got the valve cover back on, the generator started to charge his battery, and he was able to go fishing.

He was fairly new on the ocean with a Detroit engine that was government surplus. There were more of them on the ocean than anything else at the time. Sometimes it takes a little bit of ingenuity and a good bit of experience to help someone who is just getting started.

One time we were fishing yellowfin tuna six or eight hundred miles below San Diego and a fellow called and said, "I've got to head for port. I've been losing fresh water every day, and it's going to be getting low. I'm going to have to go in."

I asked him, "Where are you losing it?"

"I don't know. I think it's in the keel cooler."

"How much are you losing?"

"Probably a couple of gallons a day."

"I'll tell you what; I've got some Bar X Stop Leak, and you put that in your tank, and as it circulates and gets warmer, it will fill any hole."

I always had a couple of jars – part of the redundancy. It was no problem getting it over to him. I dropped the jar in a plastic garbage bag that inflated itself; then he came along with a gaff hook and picked it up. I've transferred bread and meat and engine parts and all sorts of things that way. Anyway, he was able to get on with his fishing, and we finished the trip together days later.

On one trip I had my family with me, Katherine and our six children, including our youngest who was a little over a year old. We towed a boat in from Mexico. There were two brothers, Laddie and Gene Haldeman, who had been divers on the east coast, I think New Jersey, and they heard about abalone, a shell fish that is pried off the rocks in shallow water. They came out and bought a little twenty foot gasoline powered boat, the type used by divers, and they planned to make their fortune; but they came at the wrong season. It's closed except for the months that have an *r*, and it was summertime. I wondered if someone suggested they fish for albacore and they got it confused with abalone.

When they found out that the season was not open, they decided to go ahead and fish albacore, and they caught a few the first and second days, and drifted at night. Nobody told them what the currents would do to them with a northwesterly wind. After drifting a couple of nights, they were so far out they couldn't see land. They began to worry about getting low on gasoline and thought they should head back in. They didn't have a radio, so they hailed a boat and asked which way it was to San Diego. The boat was the Blue Skies owned by a couple I know, Jim and Mary Butler, good people. Jim pointed and said, "It's up there and it's going to be a twenty-four hour run."

"Oh, we only have enough gas to run maybe two or three hours."

Jim said, "We'll have to get a boat to tow you in. I heard the Katherine is going in. Let me see if I can contact them."

So, he called me and said, "I came across two young men on a small boat, and they're out of gasoline and food. I don't have any gas on this diesel boat. Could you tow them in?"

"Yeah, but since they don't have a radio, how am I going to find them?"

"I'll stay close to them today, and in the morning you call me and get a bearing on them with your radio direction finder."

So we did that, and I ran in their general direction during the night, and we found them easy enough. We gave them some potatoes and a loaf of bread and a gallon or two of water. I had my drag winches with wire ropes and cables to rig it so we could tow them in.

I told them, "Put your lines out. We'll be traveling at tuna speed and you'll catch some fish. I'm going to put mine out." Sure enough, they caught more fish than I did. They didn't have the noise of the propeller, nothing to scare

225

the fish, and their boat was back in the wake of my boat which created a little turbulence, and fish are attracted to that, so they did have some advantage.

We towed them all that day and all that night and early the next morning, we were at Point Loma Harbor. They said they had enough gasoline to make it to the cannery, so we turned them loose and never thought much about it. Every time they got near us after that, they treated us like heroes. I was dragging out of Port San Luis a year or two later when one of them contacted us and said, "We're going to be in your port, and we're diving abalone. Would you like some?" So they gave us abalone, and we gave them fresh fish. If they saw me out fishing, dragging for halibut or sole, they'd go by and toss over a couple of abalone. Anyhow, we became pretty good friends.

Sometime after that they got a job diving for the oil companies that found oil and started drilling in the Santa Barbara Channel. Where they were, in shallow water, it's necessary to have a diver hook up the pipe lines, blowout preventer and all that. They began to make big money doing that work for oil companies, a lot better than abalone could ever be.

They were both good thinkers, and they developed a different kind of underwater bathysphere with two chambers. Union Carbide Company saw a future in it and paid them a million or more dollars for their patent. Those boys went on to become pretty wealthy and retired after Laddie was disabled by the bends, a diving hazard.

The last few years, I've been training my grandson, Danny, to go into fishing full time. He is fishing my boat the Lucy L now, but he will eventually own it.

A while back he was fishing and was ready to set the last trawl, which usually takes about two hours, when he saw that a fisherman, a very good one too, was adrift about thirty miles below him. The boat had a Cummins engine that was getting pretty old, and it broke down. A northwest wind was blowing, and he was drifting farther away from port. So Danny picked up his gear and went down to get a line on his boat and bring him back to harbor. Since they were going against the wind, Danny could only make about five to six knots, and by the time he got there, the fellow was fifty miles from port. So Danny towed him the rest of the afternoon and all night long to get back into harbor.

The Lucy L

He missed a day's fishing by doing that. Naturally, he was exhausted when he got in, and he went to sleep on the boat. He woke up sometime in the afternoon and went home. Somewhere around two or three the next morning, he got up and went fishing.

Danny has learned a lot and will learn more still. One of the things he learned early was seeing how we helped one another. He knew if someone needed help that he should be there. And he also learned that we don't expect anything but a thank you. I'm very proud of him.

Along with the Fish

Jack Rodin and I shared a lot of experiences during all those years we worked together. We brought all sorts of things up out of the ocean. Once we drug up a big granite stone, about sixty pounds; well, it wasn't too big considering that we brought up stones that weighed tons. And, you know, I'm not real certain that stone is granite, but it's real, real hard. It is a green stone, and what makes it unusual is, it has red garnets. When I put a little water on it, the red shows up just beautifully. They are large garnets, as big as the end of my thumb, where most garnets are no bigger than the end of my little finger. I've worn out two diamond blades trying to cut that thing. I'm cutting off a piece for my daughter Eileen.

One time we were fishing longlines for black cod in deep water. We were in the San Giuseppe which was only twenty eight or twenty-nine feet long, and we hung up a little bit. We thought we might have gotten into some rocks. When I felt the lines get tight, I stopped the winch and backed the boat up. I had to take maybe a ton of fish off of the line before I could get to the hook that was hung up. I found out that there was not one hook hung up, but two or three. The only thing I brought up was a boot, one of those pilot's boots, and it was laced part way up. So, there was probably someone down there that my hooks got into.

Jack and I also brought up an airplane, one the government used as a drone; they flew it remotely, and somehow it had gone down. It was a huge thing with a wing span of twenty-five or thirty feet. I got it in the net with the wings still intact. We had it hanging from the boom just swinging around, which was not good. We took it into a rocky area, so that when it went back into the ocean it wouldn't be an obstruction to other fisherman. It was a kind of dangerous way to go about it, but we got the job done.

Another incident comes to mind about things that came up in the net. We were fishing right off Vandenberg Air Force Base where they sent missiles up. One of their missiles had malfunctioned, so they aborted its flight, and it fell back into fishing grounds in deep water, about eighteen hundred feet, where we were fishing for dover sole. The missiles are made of fiber glass, and they're not very heavy. The circumference is probably thirty-six to forty-eight inches, but they are long, about sixty feet.

We got the thing up using the boom and hydraulic winches, but we couldn't put it on the boat; it was twice as long as our boat. We secured it, tied it down where it wouldn't bang against the boat, and towed it into the dock at Port San Luis. When we got there, a man in the harbor department called the airbase to tell them we had their missile. They asked where it was, and he responded that it was tied onto a boat, and we were going to set it on the dock. He was told to cover it and not to let anybody go on the dock, and they'd be up the next day. When a colonel and a team came to pick it up, they brought a big old semi-truck with a crane on it. It took about an hour just to back it up on the dock.

Our boat got some damage getting that thing to shore. It got into one of our propeller blades and bent it. We explained the damage to the colonel, and he said for us to have the propeller fixed and send them the bill. Then he said something that really helped, "You lost some time fishing, so make it about twenty-five percent more than what you actually spend on it." It was helpful to get paid for lost time.

Once when we were fishing Dover sole in deep water, we brought up a World War II mine. Not knowing whether or not it had been exploded, we had to use extreme care. We took the boat at a slow speed on the course that we thought would be the steadiest. Finally, when we got to deep water, I was able to push it out the stern slot where the fish net came in. Of course, all that time my two crew members were up on the bow of the boat praying that the thing didn't blow up before I could get it overboard. It was a great relief when nothing happened when I pushed it over.

We picked up all sorts of things in the nets. We got a full case of old glass milk bottles; remember those that used those little cardboard stoppers in the necks? The wooden case fell apart when we dumped it on the deck, but I saved the bottles. We picked up lots of things that fell into the category we called "Katherine fish." She had a collection of things like pitchers, plates, mugs, coke bottles, creamers and other things we brought up. When we got something like that, I'd call Katherine and tell her I had a "fish" for her, but I wouldn't tell her what it was. She'd get excited about what it might be. Once I brought up a Red Star Line plate, which is very rare these days. If it hadn't had a chip, it would be worth thousands of dollars.

Another time we brought up seats from an old airplane. It evidently came apart when the plane crashed. The seats were made of leather, and the springs were made of brass. The leather kind of disintegrated, so those springs sprung out and went all through our net. It took a couple of hours to get them out so we could go back to fishing. We fished in that same place quite a bit and brought up scrap from that plane time and time again. The fish will hang around wreckage like that, because those pieces will get a little growth on them that the fish like to feed on.

There was a write up in the paper about the giant squid that Freddy Johanson, my crewman, and I brought up in the early fifties. We were between Port San Luis and Point Sal fishing for halibut, sole, and sand dabs. The squid we brought up weighed between two and three hundred pounds. It probably reached twelve to thirteen feet in length. The next day, Disney Studios called and asked us to hold and refrigerate the squid. Some of Walt Disney's engineers came up and took measurements to help them make a big rubber squid for their movie *20,000 Leagues Under the Sea.*

Once I brought up a small black deep water member of the ray family that is called a saucer ray because of its size and shape. Its habitat is so deep it has no eyes, only very short side fins and a very small tail. I gave it to Cal Poly Marine Sciences Department who kept it in formaldehyde. They said they only knew of one other creature like that, and it was in a Hawaiian marine college. We also caught a very large sea turtle and donated it to the Santa Cruz Municipal Wharf.

During an El Nino year sometime in the nineties, a couple of times we caught a mantis prawn. We donated one of them to the local fish and game aquarium and another to Cal Poly. They are very colorful creatures, blue and green on top and bright yellow underneath. They are beautiful, poisonous and very aggressive. Each side of their tail is thorny, very sharp like a lobster, only sharper and faster. One of them put a hole through a quarter that we dropped in the tank. Another one put a hole through our aluminum shovel as we were trying to move it from the boat deck to a water tank.

I brought up a number of parachutes over the years. I saved all of them that I could because they can be used for sea anchors during rough weather. I just gave the last one to a neighbor. To make a sea anchor you rig it so that it's sucking water instead of air, and that creates a drag that acts like a brake and slows the boat down. The sea anchor is fastened to a line that's let out from the bow, and from that position it helps keep the boat straight up into the wind, so it doesn't turn broadside and cause a rollover. After the storm, we can fold that thing up into something about the size of a Coca Cola box, and it sets out on the deck till the next windy day or night that we need it.

That makes me think of another little trick of the trade. If it's a really rough night, we take a roll of paper towels and dip it into cooking oil, and we have a stabilizer. Flopper stoppers, we call them. If we put those out on our lines, they put a little sheen on the water, and why I don't know, but that keeps the waves from breaking on us. It makes it more comfortable to rest during the night as we are drifting. It's amazing how great that works.

The Perils

I was gone so much of the time and oh, I missed my family. And, while I was missing them, they were missing me. So, in order for us to be together, a lot of times the whole family went fishing with me. One time back in the fifties, I had them all with me, Katherine and our six oldest children, Eileen, Fred, Tom, Phil, Richard and Susie, who was just a baby at that time. We were quite a ways offshore, and it had been pretty good fishing that day; we were putting our catch down in the hold. Eileen and Tommy were dropping fish to me and counting the day's catch as they dropped. I was down in the fishhold placing the tuna in the ice, or like I told the kids, putting the fish to bed.

Katherine was at the wheel. We were moving to a different fishing ground because we heard on the radio that there was better fishing to the northwest of us. I was still placing the fish when Tommy called down to me and said, "Dad there's a bait boat over there." I knew something was wrong. Bait boats work close to the shore, and I knew there wouldn't be one as far out as we were. The fishhold is over my head, so I jumped up and grabbed the hatch cover and got out as fast as I could. There was a big ship crossing our path.

I ran in and threw the pilot out of gear and put the wheel hard over. As that ship went by, I could read right on the stern:

USS CONSTELLATION
HOSPITAL SHIP
TWIN PROPELLERS
STAY CLEAR

The ship was so close I had to look almost straight up to read that.

There was a Plexiglas panel on the window side where Katherine was sitting and it obstructed her view. She had not seen that ship. Another ten seconds or so and the whole family would have perished. Way out to sea like we were, nobody would have ever known what happened to us. That ship was probably a six hundred foot ship. When a ship that size hits a little wooden boat, they don't even feel it.

We, Jack and I, were on the Bountiful one time when we brought up just the guidance system off of a rocket that the Air Force was sending into space. Something went wrong, so they had to abort the flight. There was ten or fifteen feet of the fuselage, made of fiberglass, still attached and all tangled up in my net. It was all of the guidance system, and all the wiring that goes up to the nosecone is made of pure gold. I wanted to bring that small structure up; it was small enough that I could have laid it on my deck, but we couldn't get the tail fin up. We were working to get it out of the net when here came a huge ship, a car carrier bearing down on us. It was just getting dusk. I had a three million candlepower strobe on the mast, so I got up in the wheelhouse and put the strobe on, thinking they might give me a few minutes to work on getting the wiring up. I figured if they'd just give me ten minutes, I could get that thing out of the net. But they kept bearing down on us pretty rapidly, about eighteen to twenty-two knots, and they weren't changing course. I had a choice of getting hit by that ship or cutting the net and letting the nosecone go. Time was precious.

That ship never did turn, and would have run us over if I hadn't cut the net to let the thing fall back into the ocean and hurried to the wheelhouse to turn the boat. He was bearing right down on me, not knowing or looking, and I had no choice; I had to move. I could read the name of the ship on the stern as it went by. It was that close. It was a Japanese ship, and I don't remember the name of it right now.

A year or so later, a friend and his two crewmen were fishing in that same little canyon when a car carrier ran them over. It happened at about the same place we were. The ship never stopped. It was seven or eight in the evening

when the boat was hit, and it tipped and rolled. They barely had time to get the life raft which was loaded with water, fishing line and flares.

Those car carriers, built for twenty or twenty-two knots, with several hundred automobiles stored on the deck and below, travel at high speeds. Oil tankers can carry up to a hundred thousand barrels of oil and are built for only eleven or twelve knots. That ship might have rocked a little bit when it hit the boat, but the men aboard wouldn't have thought anything of it.

Anyhow, to finish that story, there was a company in San Diego named Kelco that had a license from the state to harvest kelp all along our seashore. One of their ships was in the area.

Those guys in the life raft were really fortunate. They saw the Kelco ship passing inside them and sent up a flare. Sometimes, the man on watch in the ship would be down getting coffee at that time of the morning, but that night he was up on deck and saw the flare. Those things only go for three or four minutes. During that short time, out of the corner of his eye, he saw it.

Anyhow, about three or four in the morning, after eight hours in the life raft, the Kelco ship picked the three men up and took them into Santa Barbara. The fishing boat was out of Morro Bay which is ninety-five miles away in the wrong direction from the port. When they got ashore, the captain called the owner of the boat. The owner called the Coast Guard and told them his boat had been sunk by a car carrier. He asked them to be on the lookout for that ship. The only information he could give about the ship was that the men remembered seeing the name of a Japanese hail port[11] on the back of the ship.

The Coast Guard sent men out to all the docks, in San Pedro and Long Beach, and they found the ship unloading autos, but all they had to identify it was the hail port. Several ships sailed from that port, so that was really no proof. They questioned the captain and crew, and they all denied hitting a boat. The Coast Guard asked what time they were at the point where it happened, and that coincided with what the boat captain had reported. That was not really proof either.

Those car carriers have big, big wide doors that also serve as ramps, so they can just open the doors and drive the cars off the ship to a parking lot before they go out to the different agencies. The Coast Guard was aboard the ship when the crew was getting ready to start unloading cars. When that big side door was opened and the ramp lowered, there was the fishing boat's bridge, which is the top of the cabin, with the boat's name on it. It had hung up on a portion of the ramp. Some of the apparatus from the bridge fell on the dock right in front of the Coast Guard. They couldn't hold the ship because there were no lives lost. The ship finished unloading and went on to San Diego. The ship's insurance carrier compensated the boat's owner, but not the crewmen who had to find another boat to fish on.

On one trip, sometime in the early seventies, my crew was my pastor's eleven year old son. Little Ronnie Scharn was tall and fast, and he would go on to make one of my best

---

11 Footnote for landlubbers
Captain Travis - hail port: Every ship has to have the name of their home port on their ship.

tuna crew members. We were fishing up near the Gulf of Alaska, following the tuna. My friend, Ralph Rhineholtzen, had a boat named the Platinum. He called me when he was down off the Juan de Fuca Straits, Washington, headed up to where my fleet was working off the Queen Charlotte Island.

He said, "Have you heard from the Margie H?"

"No, I haven't. Why?"

"My brother, Jim, leased the Margie H for the summer, and we set up a schedule to make contacts on the Canadian channel. We agreed to make contact every other hour. I've been trying to call him ever since I left Newport, Oregon. I haven't been able to raise him. You're further north, up in the area where the fleet is. Would you call him at odd hours and try to raise him?"

"Yes, I'll try, Ralph." I said.

I knew the Margie H and the men who built it, and I knew Jim's dad, but I never had met Jim. After a day of trying, I called Ralph and said, "I can't raise him. We need to start praying about it, though."

So, I kept trying every odd hour with no luck. Every time we called and didn't get him, little Ronnie and I prayed for Jim and his crewmen.

After a day and night, Ralph got ahold of the Coast Guard to see if they could send a plane up to search. They refused. They said since Jim was in Canadian waters, they couldn't do that. They told him to call the Canadian Coast Guard, so he did, and they refused because it was an American boat in international waters. It was a dilemma. However, after the Canadian Coast Guard refused to go, the U.S. Coast

Guard men in Washington got permission from their commander to send a C130, a big cargo type plane, to go out from their base on the Washington Peninsula to search.

On the third day that plane came out and flew right over us, and I was able to talk to the pilot on the Coast Guard frequency. They went on searching, flying in a big circle till almost evening. By that time Ralph, who had come up the Oregon and Washington coast, was getting up close to us. The pilot of the plane contacted him and said, "It's getting dark, and we're running low on fuel, so we have to head back. We're going to make one more circle, and we're going to expand that circle in case those fellows are in a life raft. They may have drifted farther than we calculated."

It was after dark when he called back and said, "We found a flashlight beam, and when we turned on our landing lights we saw that it was three men in a raft. We put down water and food they can reach, but we <u>must</u> leave now."

The pilot gave me their coordinates, and said, "Remember, there's a southeast wind blowing, and they'll be drifting quite a ways, so you want to account for that."

I said, "I'm headed that way right now - full bore."

After we finished our conversation, a Canadian Fish and Game patrol boat called and said, "We're closer to that position than you are, and we've got two big engines, so we're fast. Let us go get them."

I was getting the gear in the water the next morning when they called and said the men were aboard Ralph's boat. A little later, Ralph called and told me he had someone who wanted to talk to me. It was Jim and he said, "I understand you've been keeping a vigil and praying for us. I just wanted to thank you. Here we are safe, wrapped in warm blankets, and we've got hot coffee and we're going to be okay. Ralph is going to take us back to Washington."

I asked what happened, and he said, "When the cook went to light the propane galley stove, it blew up. It happened so fast we couldn't get a Mayday call in, but we were able to get into a life raft."

When I talked with Jim, I told him that God had given him a second chance and he ought to be in church and trying to live his life for Him.

They had been in the water three days and three nights. God answered our prayers, and three lives were saved.

Little Ronnie and I went back to our fishing. The only problem I had with him was, he drank all the soda pop, and chewed all the gum and ate all the candy he could find. I couldn't keep enough food on the table for him. It got to where even the freezer supply was getting low. When the meat got low, I cleaned a fresh tuna, and put it in the oven. By ten it was sitting on the galley table. By noon it was bones. That boy could eat a twelve pound tuna in nothing flat!

I knew Ronnie's dad didn't make a lot of money as a pastor, and there were two siblings older than him. I was sure the boy wasn't going to be able to go to college without help. I only paid him a hundred dollars for school clothes, and I put the rest of it into a trust fund that he couldn't touch till he graduated high school and enrolled in college.

That trip lasted about thirty-eight days. When it was

over, I got Ronnie into Sea-Tac Airport near Seattle and on a plane in time for him to be there to register for school. That was the first time he had been on a plane. He went home a happy kid, and he came back the next year. I think he went with me three summers. One summer I had him and Jan and Susie. By that time he was thirteen, Jan was fourteen and Susie was maybe sixteen. Those kids had a ball.

One of the worst experiences I've had in all my years on the ocean was back in 1962. I had accumulated some time off at Global, so I asked my bosses if I could have sixty days to fish albacore. They agreed, so I leased a forty-five foot wooden boat, the El Marue, for the season. Eileen was married by then, and the boys were going to school, so none of them could go with me. My handicapped brother, Bill, lived with us at that time, so he and I took that little boat fishing albacore.

On Columbus Day, October 12th, 1962 there was a storm – a tropical storm – a bad one. It started in Mexico where they call those storms chubascos. By the time it reached Point Conception, fifty miles below Arroyo Grande, it was gale force.

There was a fleet of us, probably fifty boats, quite a ways up from there, outside of Farallon Islands to the west, about a hundred miles out of San Francisco. We were doing pretty good, catching some fish. I had refrigeration on the boat, and we had between eight and nine tons of frozen fish aboard.

That storm kept moving up, and moving up. At that time, we could only get weather forecasts from the marine operator at eight a.m. or eight p.m.; there was one in San Pedro, one in San Francisco, one in Portland and one in Seattle. You had to get the forecasts by short wave radio. The operator we got didn't give a full report; she just said there was a small craft warning with winds up to thirty miles an hour from a southeasterly direction. I battened down the hatches so I would be prepared in case the storm came while I was sleeping. Some of the guys didn't even bother. When we woke up in the morning it was gale force; that's between thirty-five and forty miles an hour. Some of the boats that didn't secure the hatches had cockpits full of water and were calling for help.

The rain and the wind got so bad we couldn't even see any of the other boats. I had to keep Bill laying on the floor up in the cabin. I couldn't trust him down below; I just wanted him with me.

You can't buck the kind of wind that came with that storm and make any mileage. That boat only had a little four cylinder Detroit engine in it. It would only make about six miles an hour in good weather, and against that wind you couldn't make three miles an hour. Along about midmorning we made contact with a navy ship that was forty or fifty miles from us, and the operator told us the wind was blowing 125 miles an hour where he was. He said, "If you can, seek shelter."

I decided to try to make Bodega Bay, the port above San Francisco. My home port would be back southeast, but I couldn't buck that southerly wind. There's another port above Bodega Bay called Noyo River at Fort Bragg. I decided I'd head for Bodega, and if I couldn't make it, maybe the wind would set me toward Noyo River. It was blowing hard and raining hard and getting stronger all the time. A Coast Guardsman had called the fleet and told us, "Don't call us unless it's a life and death matter; we've got a lot of boats in trouble."

I had to wear oilskins at the steering wheel, and when daylight came my hands looked like they had been soaked in a bathtub all night. We had a bilge pump running off the engine, but it couldn't keep up with the amount of water coming in. I went out every fifteen minutes and hand pumped water out of the bilge, just to make sure.

Fortunately, the El Marue had a small underpowered boat motor that wouldn't let me drive it too hard. I could only maintain steerage and let the sea push me where I wanted to go. If I'd had more horsepower, we probably wouldn't have made it. I might have driven the boat hard enough that it would have torn a plank off; then we'd have sunk. Another thing, we would not have stayed upright if we hadn't had that nearly nine tons of fish in our fish hold; that was good ballast. Otherwise, we'd have capsized. Several boats did.

We fought it all that day and all that night. The next morning we were in radio contact with a vessel, the Elsinore, owned by a friend out of Eureka. Shortly after talking to him, a mayday came on. I immediately swung the direction finder loop and determined the mayday came from the direction of the Elsinore. The captain there had done likewise and determined the vessel was toward us. I called for the vessel in trouble to talk a minute so we could determine his exact position. The troubled captain came on the radio and said, "We have to leave the boat! The three of us are getting into a large skiff!"

I answered back, "Don't get into the skiff, you'll never survive!"

The next moment the Elsinore called out, "We've got 'em!"

The captain told me his deck hand was standing at the cabin's back door and saw the skiff's bow rope, grabbed it and wrapped it around the base of the Elsinore's mast. Three wet fisherman were saved by a miracle. We just had to praise God for that!

The day we were getting close to Fort Bragg, the El Marue was being tossed, and was getting some damage. Back then, when they built those boat cabins, they painted the top of the cabin, and while the paint was still wet, they stretched heavy wet canvas over it good and tight and tacked it down. Then when they painted the canvas, it shrunk right to the wood. The canvas on the El Marue got completely ripped off that night.

When we got within fifteen or twenty miles offshore my engine kept wanting to die. I had to keep changing fuel filters to get it started again. Along in the afternoon, I was down to my last filter, so I called the Coast Guard and asked if they could help us.

I told them I didn't know how long I could keep the engine running. The man I talked to said that they were towing a boat over the Noyo River bar.[12] Then he said, "Don't

---

12　Footnote for landlubbers
　　Captain Travis - Bar: When the tide is up, the ocean floods the river and at high tide it sends water up a mile or so. If the tide is ebbing, where all that water flows down and meets the swell of the ocean, that's called the bar. It is it very dangerous.

try to take your boat over the bar. As soon as we get this fellow in and tied up, we'll come back out and put a tow line on you. It might be forty-five minutes."

When we finally made it into port, Bill and I were hungry and so very tired, but my first concern was to let Katherine know we were safe and in the harbor. I talked to a friend, who was a ham radio operator, and asked if he could contact someone in southern California; we were living at Redondo Beach at that time. I really wanted Katherine to know we were safe. Come to find out, down in southern California, she didn't even know about the storm.

The storm sank a drilling ship, the Wodeco I, near Point Conception. It was a small one, only 204 feet long. All the lives on that ship were saved. A supply boat and a personnel boat took all the crew off the ship. Many in other vessels were saved by the Coast Guard.

I'm not sure how many died in that storm. There were approximately fifty boats in our fleet that day, and it sank eight of them. One boat had three men on it, and two of my buddies from Moss Landing went down on another one. If a man wasn't a good seaman, he wouldn't have made it through that storm at all, and some who were good seaman perished.

The Columbus Day storm was the worst I've seen in all the years I've been in the area. It went all the way up the coast. It was destructive from San Francisco to Vancouver, British Columbia. Before it calmed down, it did great damage in Astoria, Oregon and the Puget Sound area, and then turned inshore to a ski resort, called the Whistler, up above Vancouver. It is called the Storm of the Century.

Bill never went with me again. It wasn't that he was scared. I was.

By the way, as far as I know, the boat we were in when that storm hit, the El Marue, is still fishing. I saw it out here not too long ago.

Fishing is a very dangerous business. Sometimes a man would go out and never come back in. That happened to a friend and neighbor. His name was Richard Wagner. At one time, he only fished salmon and albacore, but there's a long period between those seasons that you're not making any money. So, he put the same kind of gear on his boat that I had on the Katherine and came down and fished alongside us for a year. The following year, he was on his way north for tuna when he and his boat disappeared. We never knew what happened to him. His boat was a small one, about the size of the boat I have now. They never even found a part or anything from that boat, or him. I think a ship ran him down.

Besides the loss of our precious little Richie, the ocean would claim another member of our family. In 1993 our daughter Susie's husband, Ken Morton, called me and told me his net was hung up on some rocks, but he was hoping that during the night, the current would change and perhaps allow him to break free. He also called Susie and talked to her and the children. It was the last time. The next morning when he put the boat in gear, there was a loud noise. A cable broke and it flipped the boat. Ken was trapped beneath it and drowned.

That was a horrible loss, not only to Susie and her two children, but to the whole family. Once again, the ocean left us all with broken hearts.

About the boats

While I was still working for Global, I leased the Yankee Girl from a good Christian man, Dave Gibson, and we wound up in a partnership that allowed me to build two steel boats. I told you the story of the first one, the fifty-two foot Seeadler, which was finished in '69, but I don't think I told you much about the other steel boat.

Right after Christmas in '71, I started to work on the new boat, a fifty-nine foot steel boat. We worked right up here in San Luis Obispo at the end of a narrow gauge railroad that was no longer in use. There was an old railroad round-house that had eight foot thick concrete floors. I needed a good foundation to lay my keel so it wouldn't sag or move when the weight of a fifty-nine foot steel boat was placed on it. I rented the space for sixty dollars a month and went to work on it when I wasn't fishing.

The new boat had a wooden house, or cabin, because I wanted the comfort of wood. I made that wooden house as strong as if it had been steel. You could have lifted the boat with that house. The boat would carry sixty tons of frozen tuna. It would also carry nineteen thousand gallons of diesel fuel. I could have gone to the Philippines without refueling.

The year I started the new boat I worked on it till the end of May when I took the Seeadler and went north to fish tuna again. We usually fished tuna from the middle of June till Thanksgiving. I did that for about five years before I got the new boat finished. Because of the way I had to work on it, it took some time. It was the summer of '76 before it was finally, finally finished.

We called it the Bountiful because the Psalmist said in Psalms 13:6, "He hath dealt bountifully with me."

The Bountiful

I have owned a few boats since I started fishing back in the forties; I'd guess fifteen or sixteen, something like that. Some of them I owned outright, and others I owned in partnerships. I fished most of them, but some were bought as investments, and I bought a couple for my sons to fish.

I've kept up with several of the boats, but have lost track of others. All of them has - or maybe had - a story. When Hank retired, I bought his half of the San Giuseppe and fished it for a while before I sold it to twin brothers who were married to twin sisters. They did well with that little boat and later, they bought a big double ender with a Caterpillar diesel engine - the envy of most of us. Those boys were lost in the Columbus Day storm.

I fished the Katherine for eight years. It took a lot out of me, though. The work was hard; much of the gear was mechanical; there were no hydraulics on the Katherine. I had to sell her because of health problems. I didn't make a big profit on her; I sold it for what I had in it, but, she had taken care of my family for those eight years. As far as I know, the Katherine is still fishing out of Crescent City. The last time I saw the owner, he was fishing her, but they had a tsunami come through there a few years ago, and I haven't seen her for a while. I can't be sure she's still fishing.

After I sold the Katherine, I bought the Golden Rule to supply our little store with fish. I had it for a couple of years and then I had the wreck…. Well, I told you that story.

I was working on the tugs when I sent Katherine to the auction to buy the surplus boat that we called the Sir+. I never really got a chance to fish it much. It was a good little boat, but not really what I needed for the kind of fishing I wanted to do. So a little later, when I got a chance to sell it, I did. I only had $1,500 in it, and I sold it for $3,500, which was a pretty good deal.

After they married, our daughter Susie and her husband Kenny Morton wanted to go fishing. They had worked as deckhands on the Seeadler before they even started dating. When they decided they wanted to fish, I had a friend with a wooden boat, called the Nona May, and I leased it for them. We sailed as partner boats, me in the Seeadler and

Susie and Kenny in that one. They had a good year. Susie was raised on a boat and was very capable. In fact she was a better boat handler than Kenny; he hadn't had the experience. And too, his glasses were pretty thick, and the salt water would fog them up so bad he couldn't see. I had to laugh at them; when they tied up at a harbor, he'd holler for Susie to get this line or that line or whatever, and Susie would holler right back. Everyone in the harbor could hear them.

Susie and Ken took over the Seeadler in 1978, the year their daughter Christina was born. She was a little baby when they took her to sea with them. They had the whole bow full of disposable diapers. That baby didn't see land for months. They fished the Seeadler until they decided to buy a boat called the Corsair, and they fished it for a while. After their son Danny was born, Susie felt it was too dangerous to have their children aboard, so she quit.

Sometime in there, my partner, Dick Kirby, and I bought the Blue Jay, for practically nothing, and had it rebuilt by two local boat builders. We bought a four cylinder Detroit diesel engine and had it installed. Dick owned the San Luis Fish Company, and when he sold it, we decided to sell the Blue Jay that we owned as partners. A local high school teacher bought it, and I lost track of it.

One time I turned the Seeadler over to Jack. It was a real good boat – everything top notch. He and his cousin made about a ten day trip. When he came back, he told me, "I'm not made to be a skipper." And that was that. He went to work for the Port San Luis Harbor operating the mooring vessel, and worked there until he retired. We figured out one time that we worked together twenty-six years. Jack passed some time ago.

Dave Gibson remained a partner on the Seeadler until we decided to sell it in the mid-eighties. We sold it because I could not manage and maintain it and fish the Bountiful too. We sold the Seadler for about what we had in it. The people who bought it put over a $100,000 in making it ready to fish crabs.

I'm not sure what year I bought the Penny Lynn, a thirty-eight foot wooden boat that had salmon and crab permits. That boat had been used by an insurance company for its television program. You may recall the Mutual of Omaha television series *Wild Kingdom* with moderator, Marlin Perkins. It was a popular show that ran from 1963 to 1985. When I bought the Penny Lynn, it had been modified into a fishing boat. It needed a lot of repair. I repaired the deck and fishing gear and fished it for only a part of one salmon season. Then I sold the crab permit, for more than the boat cost, and I sold the boat and the salmon license for twice what I paid for it.

The Tralee was a sixty foot trawler that was built during World War II. I bought it from an old friend whose health was failing. He wanted me to have the boat, for he knew that I could repair and restore it. Phil and I repaired everything, but we never took it fishing. It turned out to be a good investment.

In 1990 I bought a fifty foot boat called the Saturnia. It was built by the same one who built the San Giuseppe, and was named for a town in Italy. It was built in 1926. I had fished on it a trip or two back during the war in the forties when I was fishing with a group of the San Francisco Italian men. We were fishing for soupfin shark. Their liver provided a highly potent vitamin that the government needed for the troops. So we butchered them on the boat to remove the liver for the government; then the last day of the trip we sold a limited number of the carcasses for human food.

The Saturnia was a good riding boat, one of the best I was ever on. When I had a chance to buy it, I did, and I made money on it. After I fished it seven months, paid my son-in-law a crew share, and met all the expenses, the boat was free and clear. After I bought the Saturnia, I asked my son Phil, who was working in Alabama, but wanting to fish, "Would you like to come and fish the Bountiful? I'll fish the Saturnia right alongside of you to steer you clear of snags and put you on to the fish."

He came out, and we fished together for a while, and it didn't take long for him to start producing. He did really well on the Bountiful in Monterey Bay. Sometime later, his brother Tom decided he wanted to come out and fish too. So, I started looking for a boat. I had a chance to buy a really nice one, the Sierra Madre; it was just like the Katherine except it was fifty-six foot instead of forty-five foot. Tom was working with his brother Fred, who was in the medical gas business in Oklahoma City. It would be a year before he could get loose and come out. So, I hired another fisherman to fish the boat part time. He had his own salmon troller and only wanted part time work. He did well, and in one year he and I caught enough fish to pay for the boat, plus his wages and all expenses, which included seven thousand dollars' worth of insurance.

During the time I was finding and getting and hiring someone to fish that boat, Tom fell in love and married. When he and his new wife, Sharon, finally made it out here, I left the Saturnia on the mooring while I showed him through the ropes, took him out on the Sierra Madre and fished with him for about a month and got him producing.

I fished the Saturnia for two or three years. It was a safe and dry boat, and it didn't leak at all. I went to Alaska for Global Marine one summer and was gone for forty-one days. When I came back, there wasn't five gallons of water in it. I sold the Saturnia and the permit in the mid-nineties. It was still being fished out here in the harbor the winter of 2019 when a storm drove it up on the beach and wrecked it.

Sometime in the early nineties, I took the Bountiful and went tuna fishing. I went up as far as the southern edge of the Gulf of Alaska. That was my last tuna trip. At my age, close to eighty, it was not hard to make the decision to stop long distance fishing. When I fished tuna I was a long way from home and medical care, and I knew I could make as much money fishing local. The best part of that decision was, I could be home every night.

Not long after that, I sold the Bountiful to a friend and took a comparable wooden trawler called the Kincheloe as a trade in on the deal. It was well outfitted and had good power, but it had no permit. I knew a man that had a permit, and Phil worked out a deal with him and went back to fishing.

Altogether, I had the Bountiful for about eighteen years. The man who bought the boat from me sold it, so there's a different owner now, and I don't know him, but I see the boat once in a while. It looks to be kept up well, and the main engine has been replaced. It is still fishing out of Crescent City. It fishes crabs in the winter, and in the spring goes to shrimp trawling and in season fishes albacore.

After Tom had been fishing the Sierra Madre, I'd guess about a year, the government offered a buyback program. That was in 1995. The government claimed that fishermen were overfishing or not fishing in a sustainable manner. And, I have an opinion about that: I don't think the legislators have a clue about fishing or the environment of fishing, but are eager to make more money by keeping the lobbyist donations coming in.

Anyway, Phil and Tom both decided it would be a good time to get out of fishing. When they told me, I said, "Good, we'll put a bid in to the government."

We sold both of those boats, the Sierra Madre and the Kincheloe, and their permits. The government actually wanted the permits more than the boats, and what that boils down to is, they are limiting permits and American commercial fishing. Anyway, they took the boats, but they just looked at them and gave them back with the caveat that they would never again be used for commercial fishing anywhere in the world. They could be used for sport fishing or recreational fishing or to live in, but never for commercial fishing.

I bought the Lucy L in 2002 and fished it for about five years before Danny came aboard for training. I went out with him quite a bit for the first few years he was fishing. He is still fishing the Lucy L.

In May of 2012, at age 89, I bought a good strong fiberglass boat called the Peggy Jean from a very successful local friend. It was a fine boat, but I had to have hip surgery the year after I bought it. The freeboard made it hard to get aboard, so I had to sell it. I wish I still had it.

I never insured any of my boats except one, and I insured that one only because I had a hired captain to run it. None of the boats I ran had insurance. It wasn't necessary. If you are a prudent seaman, accidents aren't liable. Carelessness is the most common cause of accidents. One of the main subjects that the Coast Guard drills in us is prudence.

Some of the places I took the Global Marine ships – well, there wasn't another captain in the fleet they would trust to put a ship where they asked me to put it. And when I retired from Global, I had the Safety award for the captain who had the least lost time job related injuries. I thought all that was enough insurance. The mortgage on one of those Global ships was $21,000,000, so why should I insure one little old fishing boat?

PART IX
WALKING IN THE LIGHT

The Walk

Your witness is very important, but sometimes you need a friend to critique it. Doug Britton was such a friend, and I'll never forget him. He was a Christian man, and one day when I made an unseemly comment, he said to me, "Travis, I don't think you're walking in all the light you have."

You know, it's a real friend that will do that. It awakened me; it awakened me to a closer walk with Jesus. That had such an impact on my life.

Katherine was always my partner in the closer walk, and later when Doug got a fatal disease, emphysema, we were able to help. The disease got so bad he couldn't even go into one of the larger ports like San Francisco or San Diego or Seattle because of the smoke and smog and stuff. It just put him under. He had a little schooner boat that he tied up in Morro Bay, about thirty miles from us, and he lived aboard. When I went over to see him one day, he was alone, bedfast and struggling to breathe. I felt so sorry for him.

Around then our son, Phil, was serving his internship in our little thirty bed hospital. He had graduated with a degree in pulmonary medicine. I asked him what we could do to help Doug, and he said, "You make a little tent with cardboard or newspapers or whatever, and you get a container of water hot enough to make a steam, add a little vodka and put that under the tent. When he breathes, that vodka will help clean out his lungs." It's a trick that a lot of hospitals use even today.

So I went over with a pint of vodka. I went down in the bow of the boat where he was sleeping, heated some water, poured some of that vodka in it, put a paper shield over his face, and stayed with him a while. It helped him, so Katherine and I did that for some time.

Once when I went over to see him, he was having teeth problems. I was fishing locally, but I asked Katherine to go get Doug and take him to my dentist, and of course, she did. He was so weak he couldn't even get out of the car. Katherine went in and told the dentist, and he went out and carried Doug in his arms into his office and took care of him.

Soon after that we got Doug into a local nursing home, closer to us, and Katherine got the doctor to prescribe that particular breathing treatment with the vodka. He began to improve.

Doug's son had fished with his dad on their boat, called the Falcon, when he was seventeen or eighteen years old. One time I went to see Doug and I asked about the boy. Doug said, "Oh, we haven't spoken for years."

Doug's wife was a nurse, and while they were married, he was gone a lot, and she couldn't live with that and they divorced. They had two children, a boy and a girl. I don't know any details, but the children hadn't had any contact with their father for years.

Somehow or other Katherine and I found the son's address, and I wrote him a letter and told him a bit about what I wanted, and asked him to send me his phone number. When I talked to him, he was reluctant to come visit. He said, "It's been a long time since we've had any contact; my dad probably wouldn't even want to see me."

I said, "Son, you're mistaken there. When I talked to him

about you, he said, 'Oh, I'd love to see him, and I've got grandchildren, and I'd love to see them too.' Son, you've got to come down. You come and bring your family, and you can stay at our house. We'll take you down to see your dad. He is close by."

They came in a little Volkswagen bus. There were three children; the oldest might have been eleven. We took them down to see Doug, and they had a wonderful reunion. They came another two or three times before Doug passed away.

I felt I owed that to Doug because he awakened me to my loose walk and brought me closer to Jesus. That was forty something years ago, and the closer walk has been a beautiful thing.

Katherine and I always knew that helping others was a part of walking the walk, and we have helped a lot of people in all sorts of situations through the years. We've had people that misused us too; one of them cost us thousands and thousands of dollars when he filed a lawsuit against us. But then, when I read the scriptures I'm encouraged because Jesus said He would bury all my sinful past in His Sea of forgetfulness never to be remembered again. He removes our sins as far as the east is from the west. To me, that means that forgiving is important for us too. I may not do it instantly, but I don't hold a grudge against anybody in this world.

We have lived in this same community for sixty plus years, and attended church here for fifty years or more. We have stayed busy in the community, mostly in our church, but we were active in other things too. We thought if you were interested in the people that lived around you, then you should be involved in some of the organizations that benefited them, such as, PTA, Boy or Girl Scouts, school boards, civic committees, and so on. Katherine served on the county election board for nearly fifty years.

I was involved in the Gideons for a long time. I worked in the distribution part of it placing Bibles in hospitals and motels. I was not allowed to go into public schools, but I stood on sidewalks near the street and handed many a copy of the New Testament to students at high schools and colleges.

There is a sculpture of four dolphins at Port San Luis that honors those who lost their lives at sea. One man claimed I was the "primary instigator" of its getting erected. Since we lost our youngest son, our son-in-law and a number of friends to the ocean, I was especially interested in seeing it built and did what I could to help. I picked the inscription for it from Psalms 107. It reads: "They that go down to the sea in ships, that do business in great waters, they see the mighty works of the Lord and His wonders in the deep."

I couldn't begin to list all the jobs we've done in the church over the years. We taught Sunday School in nearly every church we ever attended, and, of course, worked in the other programs that needed helpers. We visited the sick in their homes, hospitals and nursing homes and served communion when it was appropriate. We also took collections for our church and for missions. Katherine sang in the choir, sometimes took care of the church nursery and, at one time, was the church secretary. I've served terms on the board in some of the churches and was honored to represent our church at conventions.

We became members of the Nazarene Missionary Society in 1957. It seems we were on the mission team at our church forever. I'm glad they kept asking us to serve on it. We really enjoyed it. The mission team went on work and witness trips to help build and establish churches. Some of the trips would be for just a week or two, but others would last longer. Katherine went on some of the mission trips, one of them to a Navajo reservation; she really enjoyed that. The Church of the Nazarene, throughout our nation, sends teams all over the world to help spread the Good News. It was a blessing to be a part of such a team. We stayed on it until Katherine passed.

I helped build the Community Church on Ramona Avenue in Grover Beach, or at that time, Grover City. When they dismantled the military base at Camp Cooke, we got two of the buildings that were Protestant chapels, one for our church and one for the parsonage

We moved back to Grover Beach in 1964, I think, and first thing you know, I was teaching Sunday School again, and during our regular church services I prepared and delivered what we called "Sixty Second Sermons." I was only able to do those things every other week because of my work schedule at that time.

The year we moved back to Grover was an important one for the citizens in our little town. The city council wanted to incorporate the city. We all had septic tanks, even the businesses, and if the city incorporated, that meant they would put in sewer lines which would increase our water bills. It was put up for a vote, and it passed by eighty percent or something like that.

After I made the trip to England, I had some time off and spent part of it working on my new boat, the Seeadler. Also, it just so happened that the Nazarene Church in Arroyo Grande was building a new church over on Eighteenth Street, and I spent quite a bit of time working on that. The property we, the church, owned was on the side of a steep, steep hill that needed to be levelled. It's interesting how the solution to that problem came about. More of God's handiwork!

The city of Grover was working on the sewer lines that we voted on a couple of years before. In digging the ditch big enough for the sewer line, the city had to haul a lot of dirt away. They had big bottom-dump trucks to do that.

The city was renting one of my buildings, an outbuilding on the property we bought for the T&G Market, so I knew the street department foreman, Morgan Page. I talked to Morgan and asked him, "What are you doing with all that dirt?"

He said, "We've got to haul it clear out to Nipomo Mesa. It's costing us an arm and a leg."

"How would you like to put some of it up on Eighteenth, just five blocks away? We're building a church, there, and there's a steep hill that needs to be filled in and we could use that dirt."

He said, "We could do it, but we'd probably have to have a bulldozer."

"I've got a friend that has a bulldozer."

I borrowed it, and they started bringing dirt in there

with a truck and those big bottom-dumps. I worked on that bulldozer every day from five o'clock in the morning till ten o'clock at night, and then I put the sprinklers on the site. I kept the water on it at night and got up early and went to work on the bulldozer to compact it. By seven-thirty or eight in the morning, here came a load of dirt.

My work helping build churches continued for a number of years. In 1985 I helped expand the Arroyo Grande church by welding the upper beams and doing the plumbing that was needed. A couple of years later, I helped pave the parking lot and install fencing at the campus of Pismo New Life Nazarene Church, the church that I've attended for many years.

I received a lay pastor's license from the Church of the Nazarene in '67. I was asked a series of questions that had to do with our church's beliefs and practices to verify that I was qualified for the position. I can conduct weddings and funerals and fill the pulpit when it's needed. As a lay pastor, I have been interim preacher in Redondo Beach, Grover City, Arroyo Grande and Mission Valley churches.

I do several funerals each year, both on land and at sea. I am asked fairly often to take ashes out to sea to be scattered on the ocean. When I do that, the bereaved family usually goes with me. At a certain distance from shore, I stop the boat, and conduct a little ceremony. Then we pray, and the ashes are scattered and wreaths of flowers are placed on the water.

I have been asked to give talks at different churches elsewhere. I once spoke on a radio talk show, and shortly after my talk, my grandson Chacho called me from Afghanistan to tell me he heard it. Isn't that something?

My witness as a Christian fisherman is still being carried on at my church. Not long ago I was asked to give a talk about how God works. I told the story of the wreck of the Golden Rule. People seemed to like it. I was also asked to make a film at Christmas time. I didn't speak. They just filmed me walking into a room with a Bible, reading it and sitting silently to meditate on what I read. I'm so honored that the people of my church respect me and my witness.

Studying the Word

I don't believe that we have to go to church to live a Christian life, but we assemble together because the Bible tells us to, and because it increases our faith and gives us a community of like believers. We go to church to worship and to be strengthened by His word. His word just fills my heart, and sometimes I feel like it's bubbling over. The spirit within me just wants to bubble over. In a poem I wrote called *Happy Thoughts* I said:

> *To think that because of His great love,*
> *All my sins have been removed,*
> *As far as the east is from the west.*
> *That starts a wild beating in my chest*
> *And my dancing feet give no rest.*

I don't have to go to church to have that feeling. But to go to church and worship God with a community of other believers is reassuring to me. I recommend it!

Prisons

We became much more active in our church after Richie died and that led to spending a lot of hours with prisoners. The first time I went to the prison was Christmas of '57. I went because Eileen and Fred were singing with the teens in the Choraliers, a choir from our church. They were going out to the California Men's Colony, a minimum security prison, to sing, and they needed chaperones. The prisoners seemed to enjoy the Christmas program the choir gave. I met some of the guys and heard some of their stories. I thought maybe I might help convert some of them and help them get to know Jesus, and I asked for permission to visit.

All the inmates there were crippled, some were paraplegics, most were in wheel chairs. They were housed in an old Corp of Army Engineers barracks from World War II. There were ramps at each end of the buildings so they could run their wheel chairs up to their bunks.

I've worked with a lot of prison programs since starting out there at the Colony. During the1960's, after the maximum security prison was built, the director of the M-2 program called me. M-2 stood for match two,

or match a civilian to an inmate. I took training through the program to go into the prison to witness, council and pray with the prisoners. I taught a Bible Class there on Sunday afternoons. Katherine went with me sometimes. She wasn't allowed to go to class, but she could visit the inmates one on one. If I went ahead of time for my class, and she hadn't gone with me, I went to the visiting room and visited some of the other fellows. I never asked a question of a prisoner about their past criminal life; a lot of them are shysters and you might not get the truth if you did ask.

When I was with that program there were two of Charles Manson's gang there. They had taken part in that killing rampage. I don't think Charlie Manson was ever in his right mind, and I don't think the people who were in the gang were thinking at all. I think they joined up for the easy source of drugs. There were half a dozen women in the gang too, and I'm sure they signed up for the same reason – drugs. That's what took them into such deep trouble.

When I was counseling with one of the men from the Manson gang, he was doing well and his family was attending church, his wife and two or three children. I don't know if he was married when he was sent to prison or not, but he could have had children after that. The state had opened conjugal visits - even at the maximum security prison. What they did was put in two trailers, and the inmate had to wait his turn, then his wife could come and spend the weekend. So he might have had those children as a result of those visits. I met with that man a number of times and talked with him about his relationship with God, but I don't know if he ever became a Christian.

The other man from that gang, we'll call him James, married a woman who had been visiting him for a while before they started allowing those conjugal visits. When they made those visits available, they decided to get married, and they had a child from those visits.

He was in prison nearly ten years before he became a Christian. He was interested enough that he asked for us. A Nazarene friend of mine visited him first; I was committed to another lifer who was in for murder. When that man was paroled to a halfway house I was free to counsel with James. I was with him when he gave his heart to the Lord. He has been clean and a good prisoner for a long time. He has even been asked to preach on Sunday mornings in the Protestant chapel. After twelve or so years, they stopped the conjugal visits; they were stopped because of one rotten apple, but James' wife still came out on Sundays. I'd see them out in the courtyard reading the Bible and talking.

Some of those guys just could not obey the rules. One of

them I counseled with, as part of his training, worked in a department where he built a device that maintained some of the equipment that the guards used. They'd leave the things that needed attention with him overnight or over the weekend and he'd work on them. That was all well and good, but he started charging them for it. When it got out to the state that an inmate was using state equipment to do that, that he had disobeyed those rules of the prison, he was sent to a higher security prison, and I never saw him again.

I was in the M-2 program for eight or ten years before it disbanded. The last governor who approved the state furnishing monies for that sort of thing was Duke Deukmajian. He and I did sort of a commercial trying to get more people involved in the program. It worked for a little while, but another person who was evidently in there just for the dollar was installed, and he caused the program to be disbanded. There would never be a program that the state got more out of. After the state dropped out of the program, I continued to go every Sunday that I was ashore. The chaplain asked me to teach a class on Sunday afternoons. I called the class Practical Christianity. Some of the hard core prisoners, the ones I call lifers, were under my charge in that class, so I got to know quite a few of them. Several accepted Jesus.

Some of the prisoners I counseled still correspond with me, and I am pleased with what I am hearing from them, and from the prison personnel I see when I get to visit. In one of the letters from a man called David, he said, "I don't know why it took so long for me to get it, but Jesus is in my heart because of you."

I get Christmas letters from several of them every year.

Two of them are on the list of inmates who have a possibility of getting out soon. I write to the board of corrections telling them of my history with the inmate. I think that has helped some of them to get out. After M-2, there was another program on the move and growing. It was called Friends Outside. It was a private organization. They had a building outside the state grounds where the wives who went in to visit could leave their children. They even had a playground for the children. I went a time or two, but I never did join that organization. I still have my M-2 pin. It's part of my collection.

There was a youth prison, California Youth Authority or C.Y.A., about forty miles away at Paso Robles, and I also went up there and taught marine science for two or three years. I taught subjects like fish species identification, diesel engine overhaul and maintenance, net repair, net patterns and net building.

A lot of those kids in that prison didn't even know who their fathers were. They were put in there and considered incorrigible. When someone took their time to go in there and teach them something like marine sciences, really anything else they were interested in, well, it meant something to those kids.

Some of them never had any discipline at home, and it was rather hard to make any discipline stick, so we devised a reward system. I tried to give them the kind of discipline that said, "If you don't do right, you're out of the class, but those who work and do good will be rewarded."

The reward for the top students who completed my class was, I'd take them fishing for two or three days. We could sleep seven, and that included a prison guard. They'd have to put the net in the water, bring the net back in, sort the fish by species, cook all the meals, wash the dishes, come in and unload the fish, clean the boat - everything that you would normally do in the fishing occupation. A kid that had been raised with a silver spoon in his mouth would never even want to go and do that. But overall, the program was quite successful.

A legislator from San Francisco, Senator Hayakawa had a program to recognize and honor persons who were making a difference in the lives of young people in his district. Katherine wrote to his office telling of my activities at the youth prison. That resulted in several phone calls from the senator, and an intern from his office visiting the prison and interviewing me. A little later, she informed the prison officials of an award coming to me. In my honor, a huge barbeque was held, and attended by graduates of the course. My pastor, local public officials, radio, television and newspaper people were also there.

A little more about Senator Hayakawa. Even though he was of Japanese descent, he always wore a Scottish tam o'shanter. As part of the reward I received, he gave me one. I still have and treasure my tam, the very first he ever presented.

I could not stay in touch with those kids like I did with some of the men in the maximum security prison. In fact, I didn't even know any of their last names; it was against the rules. One or two called for a job referral, but I don't know what happened to them. I like to think that experiences they had in the class made a difference in their lives, that they lived better lives because of that program.

In 1996 I was honored with the Outstanding Service Award from the California Men's Colony because of all the time and effort I had given to help the prisoners there. For more than forty years I worked with the needy and often forgotten men in the prison system. The reason I quit was that my hearing got too bad. It was a joy to share the Good News of Jesus with those who needed it so badly. I think that was part of His plan for me.

A Position

As I've stated before: your witness is very important. I wrote about that once.

What is your position?

Every prudent seaman knows the value in the answer to that question. The accuracy of your vessel's position can be the difference between life and death. That is why the first question the U.S. Coast Guard usually asks in an emergency is: "What is your position?"

In an emergency, whether it is your vessel or another, it is essential that you know exactly where you are. You could be in a position relative to an emergency that would allow you to save lives sometimes when no one else is close enough to help. Or, just knowing your exact position could help rescuers save you.

This is true in the spiritual realm as well. In First Peter chapter 3, verse 15, God's word says, "Always be prepared to give an answer to everyone that asks you to give the reason for the hope that you have." By knowing and stating your exact position you could be the one to help someone into a beautiful relationship with a loving, all wise God, our Creator.

I believe if we are always ready to give our position, then God, in His wisdom, directs the needy soul our way.

In Second Timothy, chapter 1, verse 12, Paul writes, "I know in whom I have believed, and am convinced that He is able to guard what I have entrusted to Him." If you are sure of your position, state it. Throw out the life raft! You may be the only Christian that is close enough to help that needy person.

THINK ABOUT IT! WHAT IS YOUR POSITION?

Now, I don't believe that you have to know the Bible front to back or have a bunch of memorized verses to quote in order to tell of Jesus' love and how it can make for a better life. I believe that God creates many opportunities and many ways for us to witness right where we are.

My brother Bill and his wife Beulah were faithful to their calling to witness. They lived in San Bernardino. Both of them were handicapped; he couldn't talk plain, and she couldn't either. Neither of them could work, neither of them could drive a car or ride a bicycle; they didn't have any money; all they had was a little welfare check from the state. But, they looked for a way to witness, and when they could, they'd buy rubber bands and ten dollars' worth of Bible Tracts. They'd go on a city bus for fifty cents, and sometimes they had to get transfers, but they took those tracts all over the town of San Bernardino which had probably a hundred thousand people. They'd leave the tracts under the windshield wipers of cars, put them on the screen doors of homes. She'd take one side of the street, and he'd take the other, and they'd go up and down witnessing in their way. They wanted to show Jesus what they had in their hearts.

I have never been bashful about sharing about Jesus, and as a result I've been blessed in seeing some of the results of my witness.

I met Bill Szabo at a cannery before we even had marine radios. It all began back years ago when Bill was standing in line for a shower at the cannery. I was waiting too, and we got to talking and got acquainted. He told me they had just lost a son. He had a little boat just like mine with a gasoline engine, and the little boy had been asleep down in the foc'sle, down in the bow of the boat where the living quarters are, when the exhaust pipe sprung a leak. The boy died from carbon monoxide. I was able to console and pray with that father, and that created a lifelong bond between us.

Years later, I was coming out of the Columbia River at two o'clock or so in the morning and the marine radio air was busy. There were hundreds of boats out looking for albacore and trollers out looking for salmon. That meant a lot of radio traffic. Way off in the distance I heard someone calling the Seeadler. I got a little break in the air traffic and said, "Will the vessel calling the Seeadler please stand by. Traffic is heavy. I'll get back to you when I get a chance."

Then I heard someone say, "Travis has got a call, I'll call you back." Pretty soon all those around close to me quietened down so I could make my call. I got on the radio and said, "Will the vessel making a call to the Seeadler make it fast? People are standing by."

Bill Szabo came on and said, "The Lucky Strike here. Travis, I just wanted you to know that Cecily and I accepted Jesus as Savior and our children are following in our footsteps."

The whole fleet heard that. I heard a guy saying to him, "That's the best news you'll ever tell us." And others began calling in with encouraging messages.

Bill and Cecily and their children were friends with our family for more than forty years. Every time the Szabos were in our port they would come in to see us, do their laundry, have meals with us and take my truck to go get groceries. We were almost like brothers and sisters.

After Bill and Cecily passed away, their children invited Katherine and me to come to their family reunion up at Loon Lake in Oregon, and that's nearly a thousand mile drive. They insisted we come, saying "We have a cabin rented for you, and we really want you to be here."

Bill and Cecily had eight or nine children, and of course,

by the time of the reunion, there were grandchildren and one great-grandchild. Altogether, there were forty-five family members there. All of the Szabo children were devoted and had good testimonies.

On Sunday, they asked me to lead the devotion. The whole family and I were out around a campfire. I told them, "I remember when your mother and father, or grandparents to some of you, accepted Jesus many years ago. I want to know how many of you have accepted Jesus as your Savior." Every hand but one went up. After that, we had our devotion.

When the reunion was about over, one of Bill and Cecily's younger sons, who was a grandfather, came to me and said, "Which way are you going back to California?

"Well, we came up on Highway I-5."

"Our daughter goes to Humboldt College and lives at Eureka on Highway 101. She doesn't have a ride."

"Good," I said, "We can go that way. We'll take her."

Well, guess what? She was the one who didn't raise her hand. That girl was of the hippie class – she didn't even have a suitcase; all her clothes were in a gunny bag. Of course, I talked to her about Jesus, but there were many, many things in her background, and she had not accepted Him by the time we got her home. But, she did promise to think about it.

I don't know if the girl ever changed her mind, but God is in charge of that. He doesn't guarantee the results. Still, he asks us to be faithful.

I met a man when I was on the tugboats, we'll call him Ed, and I introduced him to Jesus right on the Challenger where he was working. At first he said something like, "Oh, I can't serve the Lord with this crowd bringing liquor on board and....." He went on and on making all kinds of excuses, but somehow the Lord made sure that I got that ship into the berth every forty days three different times. There were other tugboats that rotated to bring ships in, but I was assigned that ship. Finally Ed accepted the Lord and became His witness. For instance: When he had an appendicitis attack in the Singapore straits, they had to take him off the ship in a helicopter to a hospital in Singapore. While he was there he was reading his Bible and one of his little Chinese nurses said, "You Christian?"

"Yes, I am," he said.

"Tell me about Jesus. They tell me in the orphanage when I was a little baby about Jesus, but I don't hear more."

So he introduced her to Jesus.

After he was well and coming home from Singapore, the plane stopped in Hawaii; the next stop would be LAX. On the way there, he was sitting by a well-dressed man in a suit and tie. Ed was reading the Bible, and the fellow said, "Mister, are you a preacher?"

"No, but I am a Christian."

"My dad's a preacher, and I just can't believe all that stuff."

Ed began to tell him of the love of Christ. He talked for an hour or so before he finally said, "I'm going to get down here on my knees and pray for you."

"In front of all these people?"

"Well, we're sixty thousand feet closer to God right now, and I think this is a good place to pray."

The man finally came around and accepted Jesus.

When that plane landed at LAX at two o'clock in the morning, I got a phone call from Ed. He said, "Brother Evans, I'm at the airport and I'm going to be here for a while. Come and see me. I have something to tell you."

So, I drove down there, and he told me those two stories. He was very excited about his witnessing to those people, and I was oh, so glad to hear it.

Do you remember when my friend's brother, Jim, was missing in Alaskan waters, and little Ronnie and I prayed for him and his crew? Years after that, on a Wednesday night, I was attending the Nazarene church in Astoria, Oregon at Seventh and Niagara, way up on the hill. Since my hearing was not too good, I was sitting down near the front. It's traditional in our denomination for the pastor to ask for testimonies, so I stood up to tell what was going on in my life at that time. When I sat down a man in the back of the church stood up and said, "I have never met that man, but I will know his voice from here to eternity."

Then Jim Rhineholtzen told the story of his rescue. He said "I followed the advice Travis Evans gave me that night, and my wife and I went to church with my brother, and we knelt at the altar and gave our hearts to Jesus."

Now, that right there is joy.

At one time Eileen and Fidel were living in Lompoc where they were teaching. Eileen was talking with the fire chief one day, and she told him the story of the Golden Rule. That was several years, maybe four or five, after the wreck. The chief was a Christian, and he wanted all of his men to become Christians.

He asked Eileen, "Do you suppose your dad would come and speak to us?"

Of course, I spoke to the group, and later, when another meeting was planned, they asked me to come and speak again. That meeting was held at the largest and nicest restaurant in town, and there were a lot of people there. After I spoke, an Air Force Colonel gave his testimony. He told how he had been saved and how the Japanese had been so receptive to the Gospel when he spoke to them. When he finished speaking, he said, "Now we're going to have a little altar service and anybody that wants to attend is welcome."

The lady on the ranch I went to after the Golden Rule wrecked had heard about the meeting and came and brought her husband. Sixteen or eighteen people came to accept Jesus that night, and her husband was one of them. Later, after they left that ranch job, they moved temporarily to the town where Fidel and Eileen lived and started attending New Life Church which I attend. They both had a beautiful testimony.

I have to tell you, this was an unusual work of God. I was fishing off the coast of Washington when I helped a fellow and his two crewman from having to go into port. Billy Rhodes was his name, and it was his first trip out with his new boat, The Charlene. He said when they built the boat one of the workers had not tightened a clamp on the fresh water tank and there was a gradual leak. We were only about a hundred miles from shore, but it would still break the trip if he had to go in. I had a fifteen hundred gallon fresh water tank. So I said, "Bill, I've got plenty of water."

"Well, how are we going to get it over here?"

"I've got a five gallon plastic bottle, and we can ferry it across. When we get our lines aboard tonight, you talk to me, so I can get a bearing on you with the direction finder."

We met up like we planned so I could give him the water. I tied the neck of a water bottle in the middle of a line, and threw one end of the line to his boat while holding the other end. We ferried fifteen or twenty gallons of water over to him. He had tightened the clamp, and was able to continue his fishing.

By the way, I opened a strand in the rope and tucked in some Sunday School pamphlets. We always had Sunday School on the boat. The next day he called me and said, "What are those papers you put in there?"

"That's some devotionals."

"I don't think I needed those. My crew is sitting back there reading; they're not watching the lines."

"Well, it might help you in the long run," I said.

He finished the trip three or four days later and went ashore. He planned to be finished by Saturday night and go back out. He asked me to turn on my radio at midnight on Friday, so he could call and get a bearing to help him get back to the fleet where we were catching fish.

I called him at midnight on Friday and got no answer, at 1 a.m., no answer, in another hour, no answer, and at 3 a.m. the same thing. So, I turned my radio off and went to sleep. Saturday night I tried again with no results, and Sunday night, the same. Finally, on Monday night I turned the radio on and saw that he was calling me. He said, "Travis, I have to apologize for not calling you Friday night. We were hurrying around to get ready; one of my crew was in town getting groceries, my wife was doing the laundry and I was changing the oil. I got my hand caught in a belt on the engine, and it cut it so bad, I couldn't even get off the boat. One of my crew came and helped me and took me the seventy-five miles to the Longview, Washington, hospital, to get sewed up. Of course, my hand was all bandaged up, and the doctor said I couldn't go fishing.

"I went to church with my wife Sunday morning for the first time in years. I went back that night, and all the people of the church gathered around me and prayed. I want you to know that I accepted Jesus that night. I went back to the doctor today, and he said if I kept a rubber glove on that hand, didn't handle any fish, didn't pull any fish, let my crew do the work, then I could come fishing."

Isn't that something? Giving him water, witnessing by sending those Sunday School papers to the crew, papers that he also read, then the accident a week later which allowed him to be there to go to church, exactly at the right time. It just blows my mind! God supplies miracles.

Katherine, Phil and I were walking on the pier in Seattle one time, a big U-shaped pier that has a little sidewalk restaurant with a canopy. We were just walking along talking when a fellow came and touched me on the shoulder. I turned around and saw a man in a grey suit with a white shirt and a tie who looked a little familiar. He said, "You're Travis aren't you? I heard your voice and I thought I recognized it."

Then I remembered. He was married to the daughter of a man I knew pretty well. When I told him I remembered that they were married, he said, "Well, I was married, but after I accepted Jesus she couldn't accept the way I wanted to change some things in our lives, and we're divorced now."

"You accepted Jesus?"

"Yes, I never commented on it, but some mornings I'd hear you say, 'Fellows, the ocean is calm this morning, so we can circle today. Let's thank God and get with it.' Or, if it was windy you would say, 'Fellows, there's a little chop on the water today, so the jigs are going to be bouncing good, and that'll entice the fish. So, let's thank God, get on a tack and start pulling fish.' You always had that positive attitude, and you always thanked God, and that attitude appealed to me."

We talked a little more, and he told me he was a captain of a big fish processing ship up in Alaska, was doing well, and trying to live a Christian life.

On another trip I went into the Columbia River to the fish buyer, and when I went up to sign in with the weigh master and get in line to unload. I heard the loud speaker in the big cannery warehouse come on and say, "Bob Clark, get ready to open your hatch. You need to get started unloading." He was tied up on the outside in his boat, the Ina Ruth.

I was standing in line and pretty soon I heard them call Bob Clark again, so I thought to myself that I'd just go see if I could find Bob Clark. I had never met him, but I had talked to him on the radio for fifteen or twenty years; he had taken part in the radio Bible study group. Anyhow, I started out across the warehouse, and here came a fork lift with flashing strobes on it, and I waved at the operator and said, "Have you seen Bob Clark?"

"Yeah," he said, "He's right back there," and he pointed to a man and he hollered at him, "Hey Bob, they're calling you to unload."

"Just a minute," Bob said, "I saw the Seeadler over there, and I want to go meet Travis."

I hollered back, "Hey Bob, I'm Travis."

He came over and hugged me and introduced me to his grandson, Bobby. I had talked with him when he was just a boy, but he was, by then, attending college. Bob and I talked for a minute. He told me that he and his wife had become Christians, and a lot of it was due to the Bible Study we had on the radio. He told me that Bobby had just become a born again Christian too.

Those things are the rewards of my willingness to use the opportunities that God made possible.

Here's one more example of that - Jack Rodin, my longtime crewman, and my young son Tom and I were out near the Urban Bank, which is about fifteen hundred miles southwest of California toward Hawaii, when we blew a piston in the engine and couldn't navigate. I called the Coast Guard for help. We were probably eight hundred miles from the vessel, the Ticonderoga, which was a huge two hundred foot ship; mine was a forty-five footer; it probably had two hundred and twenty men aboard; there were three of us. We couldn't move, so we just laid adrift till they could get there. We had to wait two days and two nights for them to get to us; they had been on a weather station way out there somewhere.

The skipper was so considerate. There were two of us to steer, and you really don't have much steering to do if you've got someone towing your vessel. But that skipper insisted on putting two of his sailors aboard my boat to assist us. Well, I stood watch with one, and Jack stood watch with the other; then we rotated, so I got to speak to both of them. By the time we got to port with my boat, both of them had given their hearts to Jesus.

You can't tow a vessel at high speed. The Ticonderoga probably towed us sixty hours to get us to our home port where we got the necessary repairs made and went back to fishing. After the captain got back to Oakland he wrote me a letter. He wrote, "I thought I was going to have to discharge those boys from the Coast Guard, but their attitudes have changed since your talk with them."

I want to emphasize here that God made those opportunities. How could I ever have talked to those two sailors if the captain hadn't insisted that I take them on my boat? I believe it was God's intervention that caused our paths to cross to fulfill a part of His plan for me – and them.

PART X
CATCHING UP

Friends and Family

God has blessed me with wonderful friends throughout my life and I thank Him for that. Some of the friendships have lasted a lifetime. Bob Elam was a good, good friend to me for close to eighty years, from the time we were sophomores at Redwood High in Visalia, until he died a couple of years ago. I think he was the last of my classmates to pass.

Pastor John Wylie's boys are friends I've known even longer than Bob. They were younger than me, but were in the school at Farmersville at the same time I was. The youngest boy, Paul, the one who rode on his mother's cotton sack, served in the Korean War. After he came back, he became a preacher like his dad. The next youngest brother was Jim, who was one of the two boys who were supposed to be watching Paul so his mother didn't have to carry him on her cotton sack. He also became a preacher, and at one time he had a big fancy church. They both preached over in the San Joaquin Valley for years and then went to preach in Oklahoma, near Lawton. We are still in touch. Isn't that something? After all these years.

Bill Codiga, my old boss' son I used to babysit, became a very successful lawyer, and owns a couple of shopping malls. He's past eighty now, but he still remembers when he was six and I was eighteen. He had a little boat at one time, and one year when salmon season was going to open in February for recreational, he called to ask me where he should go and what weather condition should he look for, and so on. If he was going to do anything, say mend the propeller, he'd call me. Any time I needed legal advice, like when our son-in-law capsized his boat, I called him. Who else would I call? He's not practicing full time now, but we are in touch often.

Remember those abalone divers we towed in? Laddie and Gene and I became good friends, and we have also stayed in touch. Here a few years ago, Laddie called and he said, "We're having a big reunion party at our house in Santa Barbara; we're going to have some of the divers and old fishermen over for a get together. I'm going to send a chauffeur up to get you and Katherine."

His home was a palace – I mean a palace. I can't begin to describe it. And, there was a great big buffet with a special chef, and you can't imagine all the fancy food they had. Anyhow, it was a fantastic evening.

I'm the only one left in my immediate family. I never knew when my birth mother passed away, nor where she was buried. My dad and my step-mother, Rosella, are both buried in the Exeter, California, Cemetery. All my aunts and uncles have been gone for some time now; and most of my cousins are. I've lost track of some of them.

My brother Rudy was drafted into the army during World War II and served two years. When he got out, the war was still going on, so he enlisted in the Navy. He suffered an injury to his foot when his ship was attacked. After his discharge, he married Helen Leatham, and they had one son and two daughters. He died on May 26, 2004. He had a military funeral, with taps and the rifle shots as a salute, the folding of the flag and so on. That's really a touching tribute. I was privileged to preach Rudy's funeral; I felt honored to be able to conduct that funeral.

My brother Bill's wife Beulah passed away years before he did. After she died, Katherine and I took Bill home with us and cared for him for a short while. His health condition was too much for us, so we enrolled him in a nursing home. It was near us, so Katherine could visit him often. She took him for doctor or dentist appointments and so on. We picked him up and took him to church every Sunday. After church we took him home for lunch, or we might go out somewhere. He was in that nursing home for several years until his death in 2016. He is buried beside his wife Beulah in Riverside, California. I conducted his small memorial service.

My stepbrother Nurney had a wife and a little girl when he went into the service during World War II. His wife divorced him while he was at Pearl Harbor. He never saw his little girl again. He was on the battle ship Oklahoma when Pearl Harbor was bombed. He was injured and was sent home. After he got back, he went to see his mother, Rosella, and gave her about eighteen hundred dollars to help build that little house Dad and a neighbor built. Nurney met and married a nice Indian girl, and they moved to Tulsa, Oklahoma where he worked as a butcher. He also got a pension because of his injury in the war which caused him to limp all the rest of his life. He died in Tulsa.

My cousin and playmate, Homer married Ruth Freeman sometime after he got out of the service. Aunt Ruth, or Aunt Ruthie as we always called her, was the girl who went to missionary school with Aunt Rene. She and Homer made their home in Manteca, California.

When Homer died I conducted his funeral and told how close he and I were. After he got out of service, he'd come and go fishing with me every summer, sometimes in Mexico and sometimes in Alaska, so I had lots of stories about Homer. I told some of them during the funeral services. He and I were good buddies.

When Aunt Ruthie passed away, I wasn't supposed to officiate at her funeral because she had a pastor. He was clear down in Texas when she passed, and hadn't gotten back when it was time for the funeral. I took over until he got there to deliver the sermon.

My Beloved

Being married to a seaman who was gone so much of the time, Katherine had to run the household, handle the bank account, and help me take care of the business in so many ways. From time to time, she worked outside the home to bring in extra income, and she was always busy in our church and community. But her first priority were our children, seeing to all their needs at home and in school. She was such a good mother.

With all of the responsibilities of a fisherman's wife with eight children, Katherine still found time to send me letters. Even when I had a small boat and could only be gone seven or eight days, maybe ten if the fishing wasn't good and I needed to stay longer, if Katherine knew the cannery or market I was going to be selling to, she had a letter waiting for me every day. She kept me informed about the children and what was happening with them

– the baby getting a new tooth or getting potty trained or whatever.

When I was home, we were always trying to catch up with things that had gone undone while I was gone and getting me ready for the next fishing trip. While she was helping me, Katherine took the time to write little notes and slip them into my duffle bag. One of them might say, "Good fishing! We are praying for you, Dad,". She made me feel I was missed and loved, and even though I was gone so much, an important part of the family. I wrote a poem for her.

Notes in my Duffle Bag

I love you, dear, for who you are
And what you mean to me.
And secondly, dear, I love you
For what I've tried to be.

For you are my encouragement
And each stormy day and night,
Your notes from my duffle bag
Inspire me to carry on the fight.

Your sweet notes, "Good fishing!
We are praying for you, Dad."
Like a gift from Heaven, but from you,
Found in my duffle bag.

I find I need clean socks more often,
For I know your note will be there
With "We love you, Daddy,"
And closing with a prayer.

So I'll see you in the windswept sea,
The moon and even the smallest star.
Wherever the boat may take me,
I find that there you are.

No, not your beautiful eyes,
Nor your loving arms,
But just a praying vision
With the spirit of all your charms.
For when the seas are churning
And salt spray fills the air,
I can feel all the yearning
In your ever-present prayer.

"Hurry home, Daddy. We are praying for you."

We were married before Katherine finished high school, and for a long time she wanted to get her GED, or general equivalency diploma. She was determined to do it, and she made her family very proud when she, at age 51, earned that GED at Arroyo Grande Adult School. She finished high school after most of her children did. That says something for her character right there.

One time Katherine got acquainted with a boy from the Cayman Islands, and I can't remember his name just now, but he was friends with the family we sponsored to come to the states. He was strictly a mess boy working on the oil tanker called Universe Challenger. Katherine often picked him up and brought him home with her to eat and be with our family, and she took him to church with the family. She was like that; if she had a chance to befriend or help someone, she did. I don't know how many, many people she fed.

When Katherine found out there was a need for toys to send to missionary children in Okinawa, she contacted Mattel Toys, and they told her to bring a truck and they'd give her some toys. She went over in a pickup, and they said, "Your instruction was to bring a truck. Can't you go get a bigger truck?"

So, she went looking around and borrowed a big ton and a half stake bed truck. They filled it up with Mattel toys. The good part of it was, she knew that a navy ship was going to some of those islands and that they sometimes delivered donated items for the needy. She went to them and got a promise they would drop off those gifts. She also got new mattresses for people who had never slept on a mattress. She got a truck load of new sewing machines and booklets showing how to use them and hauled them to San Diego, by herself, so they could be loaded on navy ships and sent to missionaries. What a woman – what a woman!

It was eight or nine years ago when the family and I got worried about Katherine being so forgetful. We found some medicine we thought might improve her memory, and I gave her supplements I thought might help. For a while, all that seemed to be working, and life went on as usual. Later, she was diagnosed with Alzheimer's. As time went by, it got to where I had to keep a close eye on her all the time. She wouldn't take her medicine regularly, and she wouldn't eat properly, and she wouldn't even bathe without my reminding her. Another change we noticed was that sometimes she was irritable and had a short temper, and that wasn't like her at all. That's the way that disease works.

Katherine always loved parades. She helped organize many local parades, and made costumes for our kids and other kids in the area. A few years ago, we were in the parade. Someone commented that Katherine was excited to actually <u>be</u> in a parade for once.

She and I were honored to be named as grand marshals for the South County Holiday Parade. There is an area in San Luis Obispo County that is called South County. There are several small towns in that area including Arroyo Grande, Shell Beach, Avila Beach, Pismo Beach, Oceana and Grover Beach. Being chosen for grand marshals was an honor that came because we were longtime residents and had been involved in community activities for so long.

Katherine loved glamour, and she loved celebrity, especially on television. She really liked game shows. Back in 1982, she arranged for our family to be on Family Feud. Katherine and the four girls were supposed to be the contestants, but while they were preparing them to go on, for some reason they decided they wanted me, so Kerry got bumped off the panel. Anyway, we didn't win, but the girls, all but Susie, got a kiss on the lips from the host at that time, Richard Dawson. You know how he loved to kiss the women. Susie's husband, Ken Morton, told Susie not to let that man kiss her. So she turned her head and got only a peck on the cheek.

Grand marshals

Being on that show was quite an experience for all of us. Katherine had set that up, but she didn't do anything to get our family featured on the Bizarre Foods show. It's kind of interesting how that came about. The show was filming an episode about fishing along the Central Coast of California. They interviewed some fisherman who were supposed to take part in the film, but they backed out. The film crew went into Morro Bay to eat and wound up at the Dockside Restaurant. They got to talking with the owner, Mark Tognazzini; I've known him for years and have sold lots of fish to him. He recommended me to fill in because I was the oldest fisherman he knew about, and I'm pretty well known in the area. They suggested the crew get ahold of Danny, my grandson who fishes the Lucy L.

Eileen was at our house for dinner that evening, and she and Katherine and I were just sitting around talking when the phone rang. Danny said, "There's a television crew coming to your house. They'll be there in about twenty minutes."

We were shocked! What in the world were they coming to our house for? Anyway, a crew from Bizarre Foods came and interviewed us and took pictures of us. They stayed two hours. A couple of days later they asked if they could come on the Lucy L and get fishing pictures. That day while we were unloading fish, Andrew Zimmern, host of the program, found me and asked if I knew where we could have a barbeque. A couple of days later, seven Land Rovers for equipment and crew came to our daughter Susie's house to film, plus have a barbeque. There must have been twenty men in that crew. The trucks had to park in the street, and two men guarded them while they filmed me fileting a fish, Susie made her clam chowder and other members of the family milled around during the barbecue. We never expected anything like that to happen; it was something new, but we had a good time and that film has been shown lots of times and in lots of places, even in the UK and Europe.

I want to add one more thing about that evening. First I need to tell you that after five or six years living with Alzheimer's, Katherine had gotten a lot worse, but she had always been upbeat and playful, and she had a good sense of humor. That part of her personality didn't completely go away with the Alzheimer's. That evening when Mr. Zimmern asked how she felt about being married to a fisherman for seventy-five years, she quickly replied, "It made my hair turn white."

Six months after the filming of that show, Katherine was in the hospital with congestive heart failure. Her heart was in such bad condition, nothing could be done. We took her home, and some months later had home health come in to help us. Our girls, Eileen, Susie, Jan and Kerry and Beckie, our granddaughter, were in and out doing everything they could to help, besides spending every moment they could with Katherine. When her condition became critical, the boys came, Fred and Tom from Oklahoma City and Phil from Alabama. Others in the family all had opportunity to come in and say goodbye.

I wrote her a love poem every morning the last few weeks she was with us, and when I read one to her, we would usually cry together.

The whole family was with her when she passed away on July 28, 2017.

The funeral was held in our church with a big, big crowd, some of them coming from great distances to be with us. Kerry prepared a wonderful slide show, she is good at things like that, and it meant a lot to the family and those who loved Katherine. Pastor Vince Llamas gave the sermon using Proverbs 31:10-31 for his text. Those verses describe a woman who loves and honors her Lord, her husband and her children and works tirelessly to provide for them and in all ways lives a virtuous life. Our children and I thought that passage was perfect for our Katherine. It was a beautiful service.

I don't know any other couple that had closer ties than Katherine and I, and I haven't known but one other couple in my life that was married for seventy-five years. We had some great experiences over the years, and I wouldn't trade the memories of them for anything.

A Beautiful Family

Katherine and I had a beautiful family. There were nine children all together. We lost our first little baby, and we lost our Richie to drowning. We were very proud of our large family when they were growing up and very proud of the adults they became. They all grew up in the Nazarene Church and are Christians and practice the principles of our faith. They're good, good people.

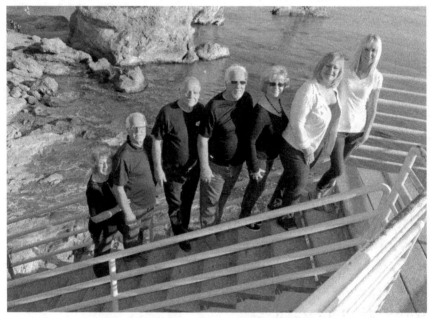

Eileen, Fred, Tom, Phil, Susie, Jan, and Kerry

Now, I need to tell you, when one of our kids married someone who had children, those children became part of our family. Katherine called them "inherited." Eileen keeps up with the figures. I can hardly believe the totals. I have twenty-eight grandchildren, fifty-seven great-grandchildren, and twenty, I think it is, great-great grandchildren.

Now, that's a big family. What makes it so beautiful is, without exception, I think, they loved and respected Katherine and me. How could I ask for a greater blessing than that?

From time to time, the kids got together and conspired to do something special for Katherine and me. They really liked to surprise us. We had been on a trip one time, and after driving all day, we were both worn out when we drove up into our yard. We were in for one of their surprises when we walked in our back door. The kids had gotten together and completely remodeled our kitchen. New flooring, paint and a brand new refrigerator with French doors. Oh, Katherine was so proud of that refrigerator, the rest of it too, but that refrigerator was special. That was a great thing the kids did for us.

They all got together in 2006 and arranged for a surprise sixty-fourth wedding anniversary celebration for us. And what a bunch of fibs they told us to make it a surprise! The Madonna Inn is a big fancy hotel, and it has a really nice restaurant. They were having a celebration for the beginning of a program to honor local senior citizens on a particular evening of every week. We all decided to go out and have a nice dinner. Well, Katherine and I thought that was what we were going to do. Eileen had bought Katherine a really nice dress in Mexico, but she had to talk her into wearing it; she told her they were going to film the party, and everyone would be dressed up. Then, they had to talk me into getting dressed so I would look good enough to accompany my beautiful wife.

Our daughter Susie and husband, Ken Martin, owned a limousine service at the time, so they came to pick us up in their limo. Then Jan's daughter, Hailee, called Ken and supposedly told him she was at the church with her youth group, and wanted Katherine and me to come meet the kids. Of course, when we got to the church, it was all decorated for a party. Come to find out, the party was for us. We were definitely surprised. We didn't have a clue anything like that was going on.

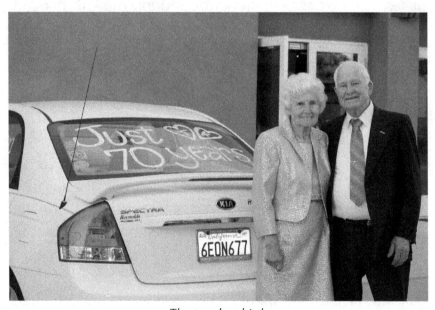

The two lovebirds

Then in 2012, they gave us another party for our seventieth anniversary. It was at the church and a grand affair with a huge four layer cake and a chocolate fountain, and other kinds of goodies. All our children were there, along with grandchildren and great grandchildren, even some great-greats, and that was a pretty good crowd. When you added a bunch of good friends, now, that was a pretty big crowd. We repeated our vows and that was a beautiful thing. Just think, seventy years and still in love.

Friends and family members came from far and near to help us celebrate. There were about a hundred and fifty guests. It was a wonderful evening the kids put together.

On Father's Day this year, 2020, I was up at my usual hour and had had my breakfast and was sitting in the living room watching TV. Out of the corner of my eye I noticed something. My son Fred, from Oklahoma City was just sitting there on the couch. I really have no idea how long he'd been there. Pretty soon, Tom, who also lives in Oklahoma City, came walking in. Finally, Phil, who lives in Alabama, came in. I was really surprised, but oh, so happy to see those guys. None of the girls knew they were coming, so they had a good surprise too. Of course, we all got together and had a good time. But then, it's always a good time when they're all together.

I understand that deal was Fred's idea. He's the spontaneous one of the bunch. He called Phil in Alabama and told him to catch a plane and get to Oklahoma City. "We're all going to drive out and surprise Pops." And they certainly did!

Yes, Katherine and I had a beautiful family. I have been blessed beyond measure. I'm not sure I deserved it, but God has sure blessed me.

Nowadays

One old friend, Pastor Richard Scharn, was my pastor during the sixties. We became friends then, and we're still good friends; he helped at Katherine's funeral. I see him at church all the time, and he comes by the house to visit often. There are a lot of people who go to my church that I call friends. They'll come by just to visit, or they might come to ask for prayer for some problem. Once in a while someone comes bearing a gift of home baked goodies of some kind. I especially like those visits.

All of my girls, Eileen, Susie, Jan and Kerry live nearby, and they were with me when Katherine passed and stayed with me as long as they could. Jan works at the church, but she stayed with me at night for some time. It was very comforting having her here at the house with me. Believe me, they all watch after me and give me advice from time to time on various things I should and shouldn't be doing. The boys don't get to come visit as often as we here in California would like, but when they do, we make every effort to get everyone together, and boy, we enjoy that!

Eileen has a home here in nearby Grover Beach, but she still owns her home at La Paz where she and husband, Fidel, lived until he became critically ill. Since he passed away, she spends a month or two down there every year. Eileen and I spend quite a bit of time together; she helps me out, and I help her out. We have done some traveling together too. Last October we went to Oklahoma City for a visit with Fred and Tom and their families, then on to Amarillo, Texas for a visit and interviews with Louise. Then in February of this year, at age ninety-seven, I got my passport, and Eileen and I flew to La Paz. She needed to take care of some business down there, and I had always wanted to see her home and that country. It is beautiful, and the people are very friendly. Oh, that was a wonderful trip.

I don't go out fishing with my grandson Danny unless he has problems, such as net adjustment, hydraulic or engine problems. Of course, after all those years on the ocean I miss it, but I manage to keep busy here at home, and I help the girls out when I can. Just think, it was 1959 when several doctors told me that my heart was so bad that I should sell my boat and not expect to work again, but God answers prayers, and prayer prevailed. From '59 to '69, '79 to '89, and on and on, and I'm still going in 2020.

Lately, I've been building shrimp pots. A good friend, Kelvin Gould, and I plan to go out a few miles and drop the pots, leave them overnight and go back to pick them up the next day. I'm looking forward to that. It will be good to be out on the ocean again, even for those short trips.

The Way I See It

I've studied the Bible since I was six years old and I still get new insights. It not only searches the heart, it cleans the heart if you allow it. It's amazing.

One Bible story that I think has a message for anybody is in First Samuel. Young David goes to battle dressed in his flimsy little tunic and carrying a slingshot to meet the huge Goliath in full armor carrying a great big sword; he even has a shield bearer. When David confronted Goliath, he shouted, "I don't need the sword and shield that you carry, for the battle belongs to the Lord!"

I have been thinking about the many Goliaths in peoples' lives today, such as unsatisfactory jobs, bad marriages, bitter divorces, stress, handicaps, addictions, financial problems and on and on. There are so many that life becomes one continuous battle unless we are willing to do as David did – that is, put your trust in the Lord.

People wonder about why we are faced with so many Goliaths. I wrote something about the question "why?"

Shortly after the Mount St. Helens' eruption, Katherine and I were driving to Chehalis, Washington to see her relatives. After leaving a cousin's place near Kelso, we decided to take Highway 504 that leads from I-5 along the Toutle River to a viewpoint near St. Helens. Because of the massive eruption, the river was clogged with trees, ash, silt, mud and debris of all sorts. I was dumbfounded that one eruption could so upset the terrain. Now the productive salmon, shad, and other fishes were blocked. And it all happened so suddenly.

How tragic! Why? Where was God? Didn't He care that many fishing families and Native Americans would suffer?

I was upset and pulled off at the first observation point to meditate, look and pray. My heart was heavy. Acres and acres of trees, large and small, lay like matchsticks, all facing the same direction away from the mountain.

Why? Oh, why, O Lord, why?

Sure there had been warnings, and most had fled, leaving behind their earthly possessions. Now their homes and the ones who stayed behind were buried in tons of soil, ash and debris. The entire river valley was a mess! Tragic! Indescribable!

We drove up to the next observation pullout where there were many signs describing the event, before and after. One could hardly believe the change. As we drove on up to Uncle Park's farm near Chehalis, we could see many farm crops destroyed by ash. Uncle Park's wheat crop was lost, and the crop of Christmas trees looked as if snow had already fallen. I must admit that we had some deep thoughts and conversation all that afternoon.

At the last observation point, I scanned that huge mountain with binoculars. Deep scars and creases ran down the face. Looking on up toward the peak, I couldn't see the top for clouds and snow. As I looked closer at the scarred mountain side, I could see streams of water tumbling downward, muddy, ash-laden water. Farther down, the stream's size had increased and begun to clear, almost as if the mountain was weeping with me at the destruction it had caused. Haven't we all felt that way at times, because of the hurt we were responsible for? I know I have.

AT UNCLE PARK's Farm...

In my bunk that night I had some serious, deep talks with the Lord. Sure, the sun shines on the just and unjust, but there are so many people, now and in the future, that this tragedy will affect. Does God really have complete control? Does He care about our hurts? I was upset and let Him know it.

A FEW YEARS LATER...

Katherine's brother, Fred, was visiting from Pennsylvania. We drove up to visit with him at Uncle Park's farm. I was still upset and discussed it with all the relatives. The next day, several of us decided to go see Mount St. Helens again, for I just couldn't adequately describe the destruction to brother Fred. Arriving, we stopped at the higher observation point. The site had been improved with plenty of parking and historical signs. It was late summer and much of the snow had melted and we could almost see the peak. What had been little muddy rivulets before, were now heavy streams of white water filling every crack and crevice of the mighty mount! Clear, beautiful life-giving water!

As we shared the binoculars, we were thrilled with the greenery and change. Down near the valley floor a huge, azure lake of several hundred acres had formed. A blue body of water that had not existed before the eruption was standing before our eyes! And the mighty Toutle River was flowing again!

My heart leaped for joy! Glory! What had seemed such a needless disaster was now bringing forth new life! If anyone ever had doubts about the Biblical Resurrection, this sight would allay them. "O Lord, forgive my doubting."

Just then I was reminded of an old story that many of you will probably remember. There was an old stick of hardwood that was being shaped and whittled into a flute. The stick was complaining. "Stop, you're hurting me! Don't you care? Why are you destroying me? Just look at all that sawdust and shavings! Ouch! Please stop!"

The carver replied, "Oh, silly stick! Be more compliant.

If I do not carve and drill and sand you, you will always be just an old stick lying there, rotting away, fit only for the fireplace. If you will just yield to my tools, after all my labors, you will become a highly polished, stained and varnished instrument, and all will claim you are an object of beauty."

I realized, God knew the end result, just as the carver did. That trip spawned the following poem:

SCARS
Consider the rift in the side of a mountain,
Or the twist of an old gnarled tree.
The deep, deep cut of a winding river,
Or the rocky shoreline along a tumultuous sea.

Each has been scarred with distortion,
Yet each has this message to bring,
"The very presence of what would destroy me
Has made me a beautiful thing."

Now, I must cry out, as did the father with a sick child in Mark 24, "Lord, I do believe: help Thou my unbelief."

P.S. I need to add that the former ash and mud have been used to build a levee on each side of the Toutle River to prevent flooding. Also, I think the huge new lake has been named "Spirit Lake."

You know, I've said "Easy living doesn't build character." It's the hardships that we experience in life that makes us what we are. I believe I'm a better man because of the hardships I had to go through. Now, I don't want to go through anything harder just to get better, but I really believe that it's the tough challenges you have to overcome that makes you who you are.

God has such a unique way of leading our paths. He seems to have placed me in just the right place at just the right time to fulfill His plan for my life which included the opportunity to make a difference in some others' lives. He seems to have placed some of the people in my life too; exactly the right people, just when I needed them and their wisdom.

I was born to poor uneducated parents who separated when I was eight; about the time the dire poverty resulting from the Great Depression and the Dust bowl came along. My mother left the family, and we seldom saw our father after my brothers and I were sent to live with grandparents. Some people might think that suddenly being without our parents would be a severe hardship. And for a while it was, but when I think of the experiences I had in the following year, I consider those circumstances to be to my advantage.

Thanks to my two young aunts, Rene and Alta, and my precious Christian Grandma, I was taught to read and write and think about what I was reading. What a gift that was! Grandpa was a patient and loving teacher, and for a time, I was closer to him than to my own father. By example, he taught me patience and kindness. He also taught me the value of being frugal. Remember how he straightened used nails for future use?

Later, my dad taught me work ethics that aren't so common nowadays. He said, "They're paying us for an hour's worth of work, and we're going to give them an hour's worth, or more." Carrying a file in his pocket when we were chopping cotton taught me the value of getting ready to do a job. Rosella insisted that the collar and cuffs of a shirt I just scrubbed be spotless. From that I learned the satisfaction of doing a good job. At times I watered crops at night and went to school during the day, and at fifteen, I spent a month alone working on a huge ranch. Hardships? Yes, they were. But, I learned how to survive and be self-sufficient.

I have to give credit to the mentors that I've had all through my lifetime, such as wonderful school teachers, some good bosses, Hank being one of them, and those Italians who so patiently helped me learn about fishing.

There were many others who added something to my life and helped me have the drive and courage and confidence to do what I've done. Was it just good luck? I don't think so. I think it was some of God's handiwork.

People may call those events that somehow lead us to a different and better place just good luck, or providence, circumstance, or mere coincidence. But I believe the promise of His plans for me. I think my life has proven the scripture: Jeremiah 29:11. For I know the plans I have for you, plans to prosper you and not harm you, plans to give you hope, and a future.

In other words, I believe that what I was able to achieve as a ship's captain, a fisherman and representative of my fishing fleet, and what I am today, a friend to many, a much loved father, grandfather and great-grandfather, a lay preacher and disciple of Jesus Christ, came about only because of God's hand throughout my life. I believe there were plans for me.

Just one more thing, I look forward to my demise because of God's promises. But now, I'm not looking for an agent selling tickets just yet.

I went out this last week and helped Danny do the yearly maintenance work, sanding and painting and other work on the Lucy L. Then we launched it and, of course, I had to go out on the first run.

August, 2020

One happy old salt

Afterword

Captain Travis Evans and my husband, J.A., were first cousins. I was introduced to Travis at a family gathering at my mother-in-law's home in Pampa, Texas in about 1995. He stayed busy that day getting reacquainted with his Texas cousins, and I stayed busy getting to know his wife, Katherine and daughter, Eileen, and visiting with other relatives. Our communication with each other was little more than hello and goodbye.

A few years later, Travis and his lovely wife were on their way home from a trip and stopped at our house in Dumas, Texas, for an overnight visit. Katherine was tired from the traveling and went to bed early. My husband, who was profoundly hard of hearing, became frustrated with trying to keep up a conversation and left Travis and me to talk it out. And that we did. We sat on the back porch and talked and talked, until almost midnight. By then, I knew I had a friend.

In the letters that followed for the next ten or fifteen years, Travis often invited me out to see wonderful, wonderful California. In 2011, I accepted his invitation and went for a visit. Oh, how I loved that drive up the coast on

Highway I. During my visit, I was shown as many sights as there was time and energy to see, but nothing topped that. (Thank you, Susie.)

In the week I was there, if we weren't on the road to go see another sight, Travis and I were taping interviews. There were no plans for a book when I took my recorder. I had interviewed his aunts, Mae and Rene, and written their life stories. His story was to be added to theirs for family records. Travis is good story teller and was not as reserved as his aunts. He gave me family history they didn't mention. There were so many stories of his youth, we barely got into his life on the ocean.

The seed was planted. I came home wishing for more interview time and thinking about what an interesting book his story would make. In spite of the fact that Travis was in California and I was in Texas, I made the decision to give it my best effort, no matter how impractical it seemed.

Making it happen offered a number of challenges; the greatest, of course, was getting together for the interviews. I made a second trip to California, and he and his daughter Eileen came to Texas twice. Still, details were missing. His bad hearing ruled out telephone interviews, so I mailed questions, he answered and mailed them back after Eileen read and edited and added to them. If I needed only a short response then she served as our go-between on the phone.

One challenge for me was the terminology. I barely knew fore and aft. I never heard of a foc'sle, ballast, wet-fish, or moon pool. Travis never seemed impatient with my "What's that?" And there were many of them. Actually, I think he enjoyed educating me in ocean vernacular.

The man is a walking encyclopedia in everything that has to do with commercial fishing, particularly the technical aspect of it. I learned to get ready if he said, "Well, that's sort of technical." I might learn about the tiniest little screw, where it belongs, and maybe when and where it was made, and the name of the company that made it. I told him once he should write a book about the technical knowledge he's gained over the years. There was a hint of sadness in his voice when he told me it would all be outdated.

There were many challenges, but my good friend and I have a few things in common. We're both pretty old, we're both kind of stubborn, and we've both had plenty of experience with challenges.

Author's Page

Louise Carroll George didn't know she wanted to write until she was nearly sixty years old, and once she started, she's not been able to stop. She believes that everyone has a story, and when she retired, she began to pursue those stories. She interviewed and wrote twenty life stories of men and women, ages eighty-three to one hundred and one, who spent their lives in the Texas Panhandle. Using excerpts from those, she compiled two books about everyday life in a barely settled Panhandle.

It was love at first sight when, at age seventeen, Louise saw and heard the ocean for the first time. Many years later, she became friends with Captain Travis O. Evans, and was captivated by his stories of life on the ocean. They were too good to resist.

Also by Louise Carroll George

No City Limits, The Story of Masterson, Texas

Some of My Heroes Are Ladies
Women Ages 85 to 101 Tell About Life in the Texas Panhandle

Some REAL Good Old Boys
Men Ages 84 to 95 Tell About Life in the Texas Panhandle

Images of America – Dumas, Texas

For additional information:
Louise Carroll George
PO Box 7062
Amarillo, TX 79114

CPSIA information can be obtained
at www.ICGtesting.com
Printed in the USA
LVHW082028161121
703477LV00009B/48/J